In the
Global Classroom 1

GRAHAM PIKE

DAVID SELBY

Pippin Publishing

Designed by John Zehethofer
Typeset by Jay Tee Graphics Ltd.
Photography by Suzy Zehethofer
Printed and bound in Canada by AGMV Marquis Imprimeur Inc.

We acknowledge the support of the Government of
Canada through the Book Publishing Industry
Development Program for our publishing activities.

Canadian Cataloguing in Publication Data

Pike, Graham
  In the global classroom: book 1

Includes bibliographical references and index.
ISBN 0-88751-081-7

1. Global method of teaching. 2. Activity programs in education.
I. Selby, David. II. Title.

LB1029.G55P54 1998   371.3   C98-930477-9

ISBN 0-88751-081-7

10 9 8 7 6 5 4 3 2

We dedicate this book to our friends and colleagues in
global classrooms around the world

Contents

Acknowledgments

The idea for this book arose out of work with teachers involved in the Ontario Green Schools Project (OGSP), undertaken by the International Institute for Global Education, Ontario Institute for Studies in Education of the University of Toronto, from January 1993 until July 1996. Integral to the Green School vision is a democratic, equitable and humane classroom environment in which students deepen their understanding of local and global issues through collaborative and participatory learning processes. Grateful thanks are due to the Project's principal funder, the Richard Ivey Foundation, London, Ontario; also to the Lawson Foundation, London, Ontario, and the Halton and London School Boards for their financial support.

We would like to express our heartfelt appreciation to the teachers, non-teaching staff, parents and community representatives of the schools in Halton and London Boards which participated in the Project. We would also like to thank the officers of the two Boards for their support, and the other members of the OGS team—Janet Munro, Jim Rule and Nancy Syer—for their signal contribution.

Our grateful thanks to Karen Grose and Judy Ross for writing accounts of their classroom experiences. Due acknowledgments are given at appropriate points in the text.

Karen Grose, who is Principal of Sir Samuel B. Steele Junior School, Toronto District School Board, also orchestrated Scarborough Board's involvement in the book's preparation. We would like to express our appreciation to Scarborough Board for their cooperation and participation. Most of the activities were field tested by teachers and students in the following Scarborough schools: Cedar Drive Junior Public School (teacher: Janice Palmer); Charles Gordon Senior Public School (Alka Sahai); Woburn Junior Public School (Lisa Butler, Karen Byromshaw). Many thanks to the children for the wonderful photo opportunities they provided throughout the process. Best of luck for your futures!

Some of the activities were originally developed as part of the Economic Awareness Project and the North East Environmental Education Initiative (NEEDI) between 1989 and 1992, while the authors were attached to the Centre for Global Education, University of York, England. We would like to express our thanks to the then National Curriculm Council for England and Wales and to IBM UK respectively for supporting these projects. Similarly, some of the activities were, in their original form, outcomes of the Perspective Consciousness Project, which the authors directed between 1985 and 1992. Our thanks to the European Community, the then School Curriculum Development Commitee for England and Wales, Christian Aid, the Joseph Rowntree Charitable Trust, the Gulbenkian Foundation and the World Wide Fund for Nature UK for their funding support.

The authors would also like to thank former colleagues and Visiting Fellows at the Centre for Global Education, especially David Dunetz, David Elton and Sandy Parker, for their contribution to the Perspective Consciousness Project and Pam Pointon for her contribution to the Economic Awareness Project and NEEDI.

We are indebted to Connie Russell for the many data collection and research tasks she undertook as we were writing this book.

Heartfelt thanks are due to Pam Ko, former Secretary to the International Institute for Global Education, for word processing the manuscript; also to Sonia Hopwood, her successor, for undertaking final manuscript preparation work.

Our partners, Kate and Bärbel, were a source of constant support and encouragement as we wrote this book.

Graham Pike
David Selby
Toronto, May 1998

Introduction

Weaving threads: learning in the global classroom

Fatima's story

At the end of the decade, Fatima was born. It was the International Year of the Child, according to the United Nations. It was a time when the world's media focused just a little more attention on the circumstances of children around the globe; children who shared in the pangs and pleasures of development and discovery, yet whose different horizons were etched by the distinguishing forces of culture, wealth and geography.

It had been a decade of change. The Brave New World, heralded by the optimism of the previous ten years, had failed to materialize. Indeed, the dramatic moments of this decade had only served to reinvigorate feelings of confusion, of uncertainty and of cynicism. The multiple impacts of decisions by the oil-producing countries of the Middle East to quadruple the price of their precious resource had been felt in every corporation and corner store. Communist advances into Indo-China had instigated the 'boat people's' desperate flight in pursuit of a precarious future in unknown lands. An ignominious retreat from Vietnam, coupled with the dishonorable resignation of their President, had caused much soul-searching among Americans and those who looked up to their version of democracy. And despite a second UN Decade for Development, two-third's of the world's four billion people had, at the end of this decade, fewer chances of fulfilling their potential than at the beginning.

Such omens were not, of course, part of Fatima's consciousness as she took her early tentative steps into the next decade, a decade of unimagined extremes. The Cold War, fuelled in the very first hours by Soviet incursions into Afghanistan, melted in the decade's closing days with the destruction of the Berlin Wall, a symbolic crumbling of the century's most radical political experiment. As the full extent of Communism's economic impoverishment came into view, the fluctuating fortunes of the free market exacerbated the material gulf between rich and poor in the rest of the world. Excessive spending turned once creditworthy nations into the biggest debtors of all time, setting a course of retrenchment that was to dominate the political landscape until the end of the century.

As if in sympathy with the prevailing mood of destabilization, this was also to be a decade of disaster. Bhopal, Chernobyl, Lockerbie, Zeebrugge ... names of ordinary towns and cities were immortalized overnight by the media spotlight on human tragedy. Another name, Ethiopia, was similarly transformed through television images, painful reminders to the prospering minority that among the majority of the now five billion people, many were still unable to realize their smallest dreams.

It was during this decade that Fatima left the security of her home and ventured, with cautious excitement, into the uncertain world of the school. The classroom, she discovered at first, was really an extension of home with more opportunities for playing and learning. It was a comfortable and comforting environment that reinforced, in the main, her nascent understanding of the world around her. Towards the end of the decade, however, Fatima began to perceive — albeit without clarity or comprehension — that the world in which she lived was not as secure or ordered as she had assumed. New children, with different faces and unfamiliar languages, suddenly arrived in the class. She learned about some problems, in her community and far away — garbage disposal, homeless people, endangered animals. She was dimly aware, too, of great changes taking place in the geography and politics of Europe. From time to time, even the shape of her own country seemed to be under discussion.

In the final decade of the century, ethnic conflicts in Africa and Europe descended into chaotic and pointless wars. Almost as startling were the political deals that brought potential resolution to long-established disputes over the control of land and resources in the Middle East and southern Africa. The balance of economic power continued to swing to the East. In the South, those among the six billion people least able to care for themselves suffered disproportionately from the self-serving sentiments prevailing in the North. As the decade drew to its close, the human species realized that, for the first time in its history, its demand for food had outstripped its capacity to produce it.

This decade was much like its predecessors: a time of chaotic change, both good and bad, of instability and uncertainty, an era of increasing connectedness in which personal lives were transformed through decisions hastily taken in another part of the globe. During this decade Fatima began to comprehend some of the global trends that impinged upon her life: fluctuations in the global economy that determined the origin, quality and price of the goods she bought; environmental conditions that affected her present and future health; technological developments that altered the nature and size of the workforce she hoped to enter; political alliances that changed forever her citizenship and identity.

At school, too, the final decade was played out much like its predecessors. The curriculum, neatly organized into subject blocks since the early years of the century, was marginally updated. Fatima and her classmates were still expected, however, to memorize a wealth of data — about their country's past and present, about names of cities and chemical compounds, about decimal fractions and parts of speech — without perceiving the relevance of this information to their lives and their dynamic, changing world. Though their lives were to be pitted, inevitably, by the challenges of making far-reaching decisions around complex problems, they were still trained to think in a linear fashion, to look for single solutions and right answers, to believe that their future was in safe hands.

Despite fundamental changes in patterns of labor that cried out for a flexible mindset, skill diversity and constructive teamwork, Fatima's formal education continued to oil the obsolete cogs of industrialization: individualism, passivity, diligence and specialization.

Belatedly, some educational planners had noticed the widening gulf between school experience and global reality. Prompted by parental and corporate concerns, which merely expressed dissatisfaction with the present rather than offering coherent ideas for the future, changes were introduced. The new model of schooling was fashionably in keeping with prevailing economic thinking. Under the banners of efficiency and accountability, schools had to be seen to produce more with less. Objective and measurable standards, stock-in-trade of the industrial era, were fitted like dental crowns onto the irregular teeth of the curriculum. The outcomes of students' learning were confidently predicted, extracted by teachers and self-referentially validated. Unfortunately, such changes, clothed in the fabric of modernization, failed to heed some age-old wisdom: that students, unlike microchips, cannot be uniformly programmed; that the most profound, most exciting learning is that which is unpredictable; that the clarion call of accountability tends to focus attention on statutory requirements rather than on human potential; and that education for twenty-first century uncertainty is foolishly crafted from reincarnations of nineteenth-century regularity.

As the new millennium dawned, the educational planners congratulated each other, and Fatima set out, ill-prepared, into a tumultuous world with hope, vigor and not a little trepidation....

Global education: relevant learning for the new millennium

Although it is a relatively recent term[1], global education brings together two strands of educational thinking and practice that have had some marginal influence on schooling during the past century. The first of these has been called **worldmindedness** [2], a commitment to the principle of 'one world,' in which the interests of individual nations must be viewed in light of the overall needs of the planet. Education, it is argued, has a role to play in the development of young citizens who demonstrate tolerance of, and respect for, people of other cultures, faiths and worldviews, and who have an understanding of global issues and trends. Such thinking emerged in the United Kingdom during the inter-war years and was influential in the establishment of UNESCO in 1945[3].

The second strand, **child-centerdness,** has an even longer lineage that has drawn inspiration from some notable progressive educators in many countries, including John Dewey, Friedrich Froebel, Maria Montessori, A.S. Neill and Leo Tolstoy. Central to this concept is the idea that children learn best when encouraged to explore and discover for themselves and when addressed as individuals with a unique set of beliefs, experiences and talents. Global educators argue that, in the interdependent world of today, the two strands are vital, interrelated components at the core of relevant education. Worldmindedness is no longer a luxury, but a necessity for survival in the new millennium. Encountering diverse viewpoints and perspectives engenders, too, a richer understanding of self; personal discovery is critical to self-fulfillment and to the generation of constructive change on a global scale.

In constructing our model of global education[4], we have set these two strands within the contemporary framework of systems theory. We have borrowed from the insights of leading-edge scientists and philosophers who argue that relationship is everything: complete understanding is derived not from studying the atom, the person or the nation in isolation, but only in relation to all other phenomena with which they are connected. Our four-dimensional model (Figure 1)

Figure 1

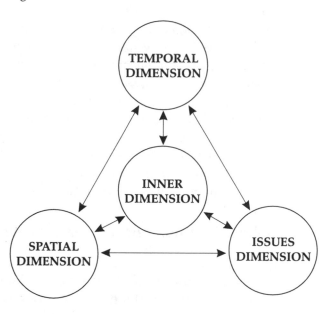

attempts to weave the multifaceted and interlocking threads of global education theory and practice into a rich and seamless tapestry.

The **spatial dimension** addresses the central concept of **interdependence.** At an ecological level, this dimension is concerned with the cycles and systems of nature that regulate all planetary species. In economic, social and political terms, included here are the global connections, propelled by movements of goods, people and information, that link all humanity, albeit not always within relationships that are just and equitable. At a personal level, this dimension focuses on the interconnectedness of an individual's mental, physical and spiritual make-up. Students, it is argued, should have an understanding of the interdependencies that, at so many levels from personal to global, influence their present and future lives. Furthermore, they should be helped to understand the connections that exist between all levels: for example, how their personal well-being is entwined with the economic and political decision-making of governments around the world; how global environmental trends are influenced by human behavior and changes in local ecosystems. **Local** and **global** should be viewed not as opposite ends of a spatial spectrum, but as overlapping spheres of activity in constant and dynamic interplay.

In order to grasp the complexities of interdependent relationships, students need to have an understanding of the properties and functioning of a **system.** Within the spatial dimension is a critique of much traditional educational practice, with its heavy emphasis on the compartmentalization of subjects, on the skills of analytical and sequential thinking, and on the quest for single right answers. Such practice poorly prepares students for a reality that is not neatly divided, in which there are multiple perspectives and alternative solutions that can only be generated through creative and lateral thinking. Thus, the implications of this dimension go far beyond the focus of the curriculum to consider how the organization of teaching and learning can best promote systems' understanding.

Three principal ideas are contained within the **issues dimension.** Firstly, any curriculum relevant to students' needs should address the many **issues,** at all levels from local to global, that are pertinent to their lives. Such issues would certainly include economic and political development, the environment, gender and race equity, health, peace and conflict resolution, rights and responsibilities. With appropriate regard for students' intellectual and emotional development, these issues can be explored at all grade levels and at many points across the curriculum; some examples follow later.

Secondly, the issues themselves should be viewed as **interconnected.** An environmental issue, such as deforestation or water pollution, is likely to contain within it aspects that relate to development, health, equity, conflict and rights. A reinforcement of compartmentalist thinking can be avoided by encouraging students to identify and research these connections.

Thirdly, students should be helped to understand that their **perspective** on any issue is but one among many. Consideration of diverse perspectives, from a variety of cultural, social and ideological vantage points, will provide a broad platform of ideas from which individuals can form far-sighted and fair-minded judgments. Encountering perspectives radically different from one's own can also be a catalyst for stimulating reflection on, and ultimately reforming, personal worldviews — a necessary process in a world of constant and rapid change. Through these three elements, the issues dimension suggests a rethinking of curriculum so that students are better prepared to respond constructively to the challenges of global citizenship.

Integral to the **temporal dimension** is the notion that **phases of time are interactive.** As writers and sages throughout history have suggested, past, present and future are not discrete periods but are deeply embedded, one within another. Our present thoughts and actions are shaped not only by our experience and understanding of the past but also by our future visions and aspirations. In the traditional school curriculum, however, the time continuum has been fragmented into the past (located within History) and the present (predominantly found in Social Studies); the future is noticeable only by its absence. In our view, a temporal dimension — integrating past, present and future — is necessary for a profound understanding of any curriculum topic or subject.

Furthermore, we argue strongly for significantly greater consideration of the **future**: to provide students with opportunities, across the curriculum, to dwell on a range of alternative futures. These include the **probable** future (that which is likely to happen should present trends continue), the **possible** future (the futures that could materialize if certain conditions were to change), and the **preferable** future (the futures that students personally would like to have come about). Through envisioning such alternatives, students can be prepared to make realistic and informed choices with regard to their personal lives and to the future of the planet. They can also determine what **action** is required, at personal to global levels, to create the conditions wherein their preferred futures are rendered more probable. Student-directed action, around issues that are relevant to their lives and their community, provides an important grounding in the practice of responsible citizenship.

At the core of the model lies the **inner dimension.** Global education, we are suggesting, is a voyage along two complementary pathways. While the **journey outwards** leads students to discover the world in which they live, the **journey inwards** heightens their understanding of themselves and of their potential. Both journeys constitute a necessary preparation for personal fulfillment and social responsibility in an interdependent and rapidly changing world. In conducive conditions, both journeys can be undertaken simultaneously. Through encountering multiple perspectives, envisioning the future and understanding global systems, students are faced, inevitably, with challenges to their own beliefs, values and worldviews. Personal development goes hand-in-hand with planetary awareness. In this sense, global education is as much an exploration of the global self as of the global village.

If both journeys are to be successfully undertaken by all students, the **process** of teaching and learning has to be considered as carefully as the content of the curriculum. A rich and varied diet of teaching strategies — to include self-esteem building, cooperative and experiential activities, role-play, multi-sensory and visualization techniques alongside more traditional approaches — is required to accommodate the diverse learning style preferences to be found in most classrooms. In addition, a more democratic, equitable and humane learning environment can be created through the frequent use of inclusive and participatory learning methods. In so doing, **medium and message** in the global classroom are harmonized. Cooperation, empathy, fairness, respect and peacefulness are not only preached, but also practiced.

Some strategies for implementing global education

The four dimensions are not intended to constitute a complete curriculum, nor to provide a total alternative to present practice in schools. The model is offered as a catalyst to stimulate reflection on the appropriateness of schooling in the contemporary world and to suggest directions and emphases that responsible and responsive educational reform might take. Some standard goals of formal education remain critical. High levels of literacy and numeracy are clearly pre-requisites for effective participation in society, as are a range of personal and social skills and competence in the use of technology and telecommunications. Important, too, are the particular insights to be gleaned from a range of disciplines in the arts, languages, science and social studies. What is being suggested, however, is that the basic knowledge and skills that are the cornerstones of a sound education can be acquired and refined in ways that are **more effective, more equitable and more relevant** through the implementation of a global education framework.

In addition, global education offers perspectives and strategies that are not commonly found in schools, yet are critical to the development of students who can prosper in a complex, global system and can contribute to the building of a more just and sustainable world. These elements, too, we would contend, are among the 'basics' of education as we enter the new millennium.

Implementing global education, then, comprises two complementary, overlapping and continual processes. The first is one of **filtration** or **percolation**, whereby existing practice in schools is re-evaluated in terms of our latest understanding of global realities and the consequent needs of students. Some practice, undoubtedly, will continue to be deemed important; some will appear outmoded, unnecessary or of low priority. The second process is one of **enrichment**. Global education ideas and approaches that have been hitherto lacking are incorporated into newly invigorated programs. In some cases, additional perspectives and activities can be infused seamlessly; in others, a reconceptualization of existing practice will be required in order to refocus attention on new priorities. The two processes are dynamic and ongoing. As in the many systems from which it is derived, the cycle of change and renewal in global education is constant.

The following chart is intended to aid the process of implementation. Beside each of the four dimensions are listed some key components of global education in terms of knowledge, skills and attitudes. The lists are not exhaustive, neither are the various compartments of the chart mutually exclusive. There are clearly many overlaps within and between columns and some components could well be listed in more than one place. Hopefully, the chart provides an overview of the essence of global education in a way that can be easily and usefully applied in a variety of educational contexts.

The task of reforming curriculum and learning and teaching methods to incorporate the key components of global education, as identified above, can be carried out in two ways: through **infusion** or by **integration**. Infusion entails impregnating existing curriculum sub-

	INNER DIMENSION	TEMPORAL DIMENSION	ISSUES DIMENSION	SPATIAL DIMENSION
KEY IDEAS	• journey inwards • teaching/learning processes • medium and message	• phases of time as interactive • alternative futures • action	• local/global issues • interconnections between issues • perspectives	• interdependence • local ↔ global • systems
KNOWLEDGE	• of oneself — identity, strengths, weaknesses and potential • of one's perspectives, values and worldview • of incongruities between professed beliefs and personal actions	• of the relationship between past, present and future • of a range of futures, including possible, probable and preferred • of sustainable development • of potential for action, at personal to global levels	• of critical issues, at interpersonal through global levels • of interconnections between issues, events and trends • of a range of perspectives on issues • of how perspectives are shaped	• of local/global connections and dependencies • of global systems • of the nature and function of a system • of connections between areas of knowledge • of the common needs of all humans and other species • of oneself as a whole person
SKILLS	• personal reflection and analysis • personal growth — emotional, intellectual, physical, spiritual • learning flexibility (learning within a variety of contexts and in a variety of ways)	• coping with change and uncertainty • extrapolation and prediction • creative and lateral thinking • problem solving • taking personal action	• research and enquiry • evaluating, organizing and presenting information • analyzing trends • personal judgment and decision making	• relational thinking (seeing patterns and connections) • systems thinking (understanding the impact of change in a system) • interpersonal relationships • cooperation
ATTITUDES	• belief in own abilities and potential • recognizing learning as a life-long process • genuineness — presenting the real person • preparedness to take risks • trust	• tolerance of ambiguity and uncertainty • preparedness to consider long-term consequences • preparedness to utilize imagination and intuition • commitment to personal and social action	• curiosity about issues, trends and the global condition • receptivity to, and critical examination of, other perspectives and points of view • empathy with/respect for other people and cultures	• flexibility in adaptation to change • willingness to learn from and teach others • willingness to work as a team member • consideration of the common good • sense of solidarity with other people and their problems

jects, areas or topics with relevant global education knowledge, skills and attitudes, without intentionally or radically changing the structure or organization of the curriculum. It is a legitimate, if limited, response to the question, 'How can I make the curriculum more relevant to the lives of students?' In the more holistic process of integration, an additional leading question is, 'How can I more closely model the reality of the contemporary world in the classroom?' The answer, oftentimes, will require a reconceptualizing of the ways in which opportunities to gain knowledge and to develop skills and attitudes are presented in the classroom.

There are several possibilities, of course, for combining and adapting the infusion and integration approaches to produce other models, such as the integration of two or three subjects around a chosen topic or theme, or the infusion of global education perspectives into multi-disciplinary courses. Indeed, the introduction of global education, with its emphasis on making connections, tends to create momentum towards a more integrated delivery of curriculum. The models described below should be seen, therefore, as occupying positions at either end of a continuum. Let us briefly examine some advantages and disadvantages — from both theoretical and practical standpoints — of each approach.

Infusion

There are countless possibilities for infusing global education knowledge, skills and attitudes into all the traditional subjects of the curriculum. In its simplest form (Figure 2), infusion does not impact upon curriculum organization as the subjects themselves are taught in isolation. Within each subject, however, connections to other curriculum areas can be emphasized, thereby planting the seeds of integration in students' minds. Some examples of infusion in practice, in four curriculum areas, may be seen below.

Figure 2

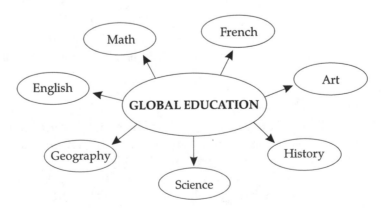

Advantages:
- *there is no need to radically re-write the existing curriculum or throw out current textbooks and resources*
- *there is no need to re-organize the timetable, nor to re-orient students' and parents' expectations of curriculum*
- *implementation can be achieved by individual teachers, to the extent desired; team planning and shared goals are not required*

Disadvantages:
- *presents a compartmentalist view of knowledge that is not congruent with the philosophy of global education*
- *misses opportunities to help students perceive connections between curriculum subjects and topics being studied*
- *could result in a piecemeal implementation of global education (for example, just in the social studies)*

Implementing global education by infusion
Some examples

Language Arts
- using literature to explore universal themes (for example, conflict, justice, love, rights) and global issues
- examining changes in language use over time and in linguistic variations, as they relate to class, culture, ethnicity and gender
- developing awareness of personal attitudes, beliefs, perspectives and values; encountering diverse perspectives and viewpoints
- through role-play and drama, refining the skills of inter-personal communication and empathetic understanding
- reading poems, plays, novels and stories by writers from various cultures around the world
- analyzing library books and text books for examples of stereotyping, bias and distortion
- comparing a range of newspaper and television stories to detect their underlying assumptions, biases and values
- using drama exercises to explore the significance of non-verbal communication in one's own and other cultures
- engaging in group discussion activities to practice communication, negotiation and questioning skills
- developing oral and written presentation skills through engagement with community leaders and politicians around significant local and global issues

Mathematics
- employing statistics from 'real-world' data (for example, from school, community, national or international sources) as the basis for practicing arithmetic skills
- developing competency in extrapolation, projection and prediction using global statistics on birth and death rates, economic growth and the use of natural resources
- assessing the increasing speed of technological change by plotting major developments in human communication on a graph

- practicing basic numerical skills using counting systems and techniques from various cultures
- exploring geometric shape, pattern and symmetry through studying art and design trends in various cultures
- calculating total usage of energy and water in the home or school, then devising, executing and recording conservation measures
- analyzing the costs and nutritional values of items sold in the cafeteria and planning weekly menus that are healthy and affordable
- exploring the concept of exponential growth in relation to interest rates and world population data
- combining data from various statistical sources to devise 'quality of life' indicators for selected countries
- working in teams to devise alternative proposals, including budgets and timelines, for the naturalization of the school grounds

Science
- understanding ecological principles through examining ecosystems, energy flows, cycles and food chains
- studying the chemistry of atmospheric and water pollution, and the costs and benefits of clean-up measures
- examining the impact of mineral mining and quarrying on the health of humans, other species and ecosystems
- weighing up the advantages and disadvantages of alternative means of energy production
- designing and building a model of a wind generator or water pump for use in the developing world
- using guided fantasy techniques to facilitate comprehension of the water cycle or to take a journey into the sub-atomic world
- exploring the contributions of women and visible minority people to science and technology throughout history
- analyzing the role of technology in contemporary lives and envisioning preferred technological futures
- exploring the impact of inadequate nutrition and of substance abuse on human health
- predicting the impact of global warming or ozone depletion on a variety of living species and their habitats

Social Studies
- investigating social change within a neighborhood over time and forecasting trends in family life, work and leisure patterns
- examining the achievements of non-European civilizations and the perspectives of indigenous peoples on colonization
- comparing various world map projections and analyzing their underlying assumptions and values
- predicting economic, environmental and social changes in the light of national demographic trends and immigration policies
- exploring basic concepts in human rights through developing and utilizing classroom codes of rights and responsibilities
- employing peer and group mediation techniques to resolve conflicts in the classroom and schoolyard

- investigating the psychological, social and environmental ramifications of warfare, in the short- and long-term
- developing awareness of personal prejudices and becoming assertive in challenging racism, sexism and homophobia
- undertaking action projects in the community to improve the quality of life of the physically and mentally challenged
- exploring, through simulation games, major global issues such as sustainable development, population and wealth distribution, primary health care and the role of women

Integration

In an integrated approach the guiding premise is the organization of learning in a way that is reflective of, and most easily transferable to, real-world situations. It is based, therefore, on an understanding of the world as a system, in which the full meaning of any topic or subject matter can only be gleaned through exploring its relationships with other connected phenomena. Thus, the curriculum is more appropriately organized around broad themes or issues, through which the knowledge and skills of traditional subjects are taught in interconnected ways.

As suggested in Figure 3, the particular skills and insights of each discipline are still important but, through pooling them around a common theme, the potential for knowledge building and learning is increased. Some examples of this approach, built around themes that are commonly found in school curricula, are to be found on pages 21-23 (the subject areas that would be typically addressed are included in parentheses).

Figure 3

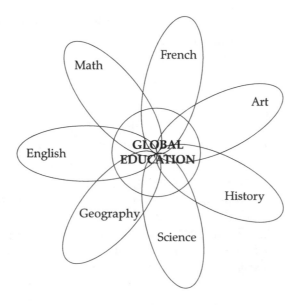

Advantages:
- *encourages students to perceive real connections between issues and phenomena*
- *potential for creating new insights is increased through the interaction of various subject perspectives around a common theme*
- *ensures a cross-curricular, holistic implementation of global education*

Disadvantages:
- *requires time and creative energy to plan new courses or units, and to gather appropriate resources*
- *not available to subject specialists working alone; demands high levels of collegiality and a shared vision*
- *may run counter to, and thereby challenge, existing expectations of curriculum at all levels (ministry, school board, parents, students)*

Implementing global education through integration
Some examples

Population
- tracing and graphing the history of world population growth and some alternative future scenarios (history, mathematics)
- identifying the locations of the most/least populous countries in the world and comparing differences in population growth rates (geography, mathematics)
- exploring the relationship, in both developed and developing worlds, between decline in birth rate and improvement in health and living standards (history, social studies)
- examining birth control methods and comparing their effectiveness (family studies, science)
- considering cultural, religious and other opposition to birth control and its likely impact on world population (social studies)
- exploring arguments surrounding the rights of women to decide their own fertility and have control over their own bodies (family studies, social studies)
- reading literature by women on sexual abuse and sexual freedom (language arts)
- engaging in drama and simulation games on population issues (language arts, social studies)
- examining the relationship between gender and power in the school, family, community and country (social studies)

Racism
- reflecting on personal prejudices and the impact of being unfairly treated (language arts, social studies)
- examining the history of racism through case studies of racial intolerance throughout the world (history)
- using role-plays and experiential activities to develop empathetic understanding of the effects of racism (language arts)
- utilizing national statistical data that is broken down according to ethnic, cultural or religious background (mathematics)

- investigating hate campaigns in the local community and developing assertiveness skills to challenge prejudicial remarks and behavior (language arts, social studies)
- analyzing claims for the genetic or inherent superiority of one race over another (science, social studies)
- exploring the links between racism, sexism, homophobia and cruelty to other species (social studies)
- appreciating the art, music and literature of indigenous peoples and visible minorities in Canada and elsewhere (art, language arts, music)
- examining the history of the Quebec separatist movement and comparing attitudes on the issue from various provinces (French, history, social studies)
- predicting the future impact on Canadian society and identity of the present policy on immigration (social studies)

Technology
- investigating the role of technology in the development of the human species and graphing the rate of increase in technological usage (history, mathematics)
- exploring the use of technology in everyday lives and calculating the benefits in terms of money, time and safety (mathematics, social studies)
- examining some environmental, health and social costs of technological development (for example, automobiles, chemical fertilizers, weapons) and assessing less harmful alternatives (history, science, social studies)
- reviewing case studies of successful appropriate technology initiatives in developing countries (geography, science)
- designing and building simple structures that use renewable energy sources (science)
- understanding the functioning of common machines (for example, automobiles, household appliances, televisions) and effecting simple repairs (science)
- examining the influence of technology on contemporary music (music)
- exploring the relationship between access to/use of technology and class, ethnicity, gender, and people with disabilities (social studies)
- reading about the inventions of Canadians and their contributions to global development (history)
- envisioning preferred technological futures and assessing the personal knowledge and skills required to attain them (social studies)

Water
- investigating the water cycle, the properties of water and the water content of living things (science)
- identifying sources of fresh water on the planet and calculating the amount available for use by humans and other species (geography, mathematics)
- measuring personal and family water consumption; devising and enacting conservation measures (mathematics, science)

- appreciating art, literature and music on water and related themes (art, language arts, music)
- writing poetry and stories on childhood memories associated with water (language arts)
- investigating major causes of water pollution worldwide and studying examples of seriously affected lakes, rivers and seas (geography, science)
- exploring the impact of pollution on the Great Lakes ecosystem and the effectiveness of clean-up strategies (science, social studies)
- examining the link between clean water and health and identifying some examples of water-borne diseases (family studies, science)
- assessing the significance of water scarcity as a catalyst for potential conflict in regions such as the Middle East (geography, social studies)

There are several alternative ways of delivering an infused or integrated curriculum that do not require a single teacher to become widely knowledgeable in areas beyond her teaching speciality. Team planning and cooperative teaching are obvious strategies that have the additional advantage of endorsing collaboration and interdependence, central tenets of global education. Whole-school or whole-grade themes serve as useful curriculum frameworks, allowing related ideas and concepts to be taught separately by different teachers. Re-scheduling the timetable, so that a teacher addresses one component of an integrated theme with all classes on a rotary basis, is another possibility. Whichever strategies are chosen, the goal is one of breaking down — as far as is practicable — the physical walls of the classroom and the epistemological barriers of the subject-driven timetable, thereby helping students to perceive connections between the various elements of their schooling, and between education and the world in which they live.

Learning and teaching processes in the global classroom

The voluminous research on individual learning style preferences suggests that a broad-based and varied program of learning opportunities is necessary, both for meeting the particular needs of all students and for helping each to become a more effective learner in non-preferred styles.[6] It follows that no single style of teaching should enjoy hegemony in the global classroom. The dominant mode of instruction, however, in so many classrooms remains essentially one of **transmission**, whereby selected, pre-packed knowledge is conveyed by the teacher or textbook to passive (though not necessarily receptive) students. The principal skills involved are reading, listening and memorization. The foremost values implied are that knowledge comes from external sources, especially authority figures; learning is a passive and frequently uninteresting chore; personal ideas, emotions and contributions are neither welcome nor important; and the roles of 'teacher' and 'learner' are clearly designated and steadfastly sustained.

At the opposite end of the instructional spectrum is the **transformation** position. Learning is self-motivated and directed; it focuses on the aesthetic, moral, physical and spiritual needs of the student as well as on cognitive attainment; knowledge building entails a dynamic interaction between students and multiple sources of information; and the functions of 'teaching' and 'learning' are willingly undertaken by both teacher and students.[7]

Global education, with its emphasis on student involvement and whole person development, sits much more comfortably at the transformation end of the teaching-learning spectrum. Recognizing the realities and pressures of contemporary schools, however, it is likely that a range of teaching approaches and learning contexts will be found within the day to day life of the global classroom, with students experiencing a blend of teacher-led and self- or group-directed strategies. Such a combination resonates with learning style theories which suggest that, in the average classroom, not all students benefit equally in situations where self-motivation is the key and teacher guidance is minimal.

Whatever the mode of instruction, of central importance is the **climate** or **ethos** of the classroom. The fundamental values espoused by global education — such as respect for rights and freedoms, environmental consciousness, non-violence and social responsibility — will be enshrined within the very fabric of the global classroom, and will imbue the quality and style of relationships between its members. Thus, even within teacher-directed contexts, the negative and limiting aspects of the transmission approach are avoided.

Activity-based learning has a significant role to play in the implementation of global education, for several reasons:

* First, the very nature of the activities, with their emphasis on self-discovery and learning through experience, orients the classroom towards the transformation end of the spectrum. Teacher direction and input has a place, particularly in the critically-important debriefing stage, but here it is essentially built around the students' own reflections on their involvement in the activity.

* Second, the multiple learning styles utilized — often within the same activity, as students move from individual reflection to pair and group discussion, then to collaboratively shaping an outcome — address the needs and preferences of most students within a short time frame.

* Third, global education activities provide relatively secure, yet challenging and motivational vehicles through which students can refine and practice a gamut of skills that are crucial for constructive participation in global society. These skills include communication, cooperation, decision-making, negotiation, and problem-solving.

* Fourth, interaction widens the scope for learning. As with any system, the dynamic interplay of ideas and perspectives creates its own momentum that can lead to hitherto unimagined outcomes from which every participant can benefit.

* Fifth, the principles upon which global education activities are founded help students to both construct and reinforce the democratic, humane and equitable ethos of the global classroom.

* Sixth, activity-based learning affords maximum scope for harmonizing the medium with the message: students actually *practice* cooperation and conflict resolution, empathy and respect, ethical treatment and responsible action.

The activities that follow are offered as significant contributions to the rich panoply of learning experiences in the global classroom. Notwithstanding the enormous potential of such activities, as outlined above, teachers will want to ensure that other learning techniques are utilized in complementary ways. Indeed, as many teachers have discovered, global education activities often serve as a springboard for student research and writing of the highest quality, resulting from the creative energies and motivational forces generated. A critical factor in the successful use of the activities is the maintenance of an appropriate **rhythm** of learning, a cycle of experiences that, typically, would encompass the following phases:

Figure 4

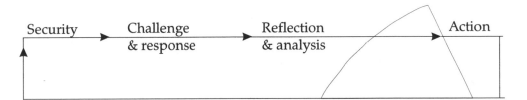

In the '**security**' phase, a student's self-esteem is nurtured through the establishment of a non-threatening, inclusive classroom climate that values the contributions and experiences of all class members and encourages them to freely express their ideas and feelings. There are numerous sources of activities and techniques that, when applied in conjunction with democratic and rights-respectful codes of behavior, can help create such a climate of comfort and conviviality.[8] Many activities in this book begin by reinforcing a sense of personal security, through asking students to contribute ideas or reflections in relatively safe two-person or small group contexts, before mounting a **challenge**. In this second phase, students are asked to respond, as individuals or group members, to a deliberately provocative idea or situation. Skills such as creative and lateral thinking, problem-solving and decision-making are frequently invoked; experimentation and risk-taking are encouraged.

An all-important debriefing and **reflection** phase follows, in which participants are asked to analyze, and draw inferences from, their experiences of the previous phase. At this point, opportunities can usually be found for students to launch out on research, writing or creative arts' projects that build upon and enlarge those experiences. Whatever the outcome of this phase, the goal is for participants to attain something of personal significance: new knowledge or insights, a refinement of skills, a shift in attitude or perspective.

In the **action** phase, students are given a safe forum in which to utilize or apply their recently acquired knowledge and skills. The choice of activity here is potentially enormous, from personal writing and project work to collaborative ventures in the classroom, school or community. What is important, however, is to recognize the need, for some students at least, to return to the comfort of the **security** phase. The experimentation and risk-taking that global education activities encourage can expose the more vulnerable facets of any participant, and sensitive re-inforcement of self-esteem may have to be undertaken before further challenges can be contemplated.

How to use the activities in this book

The activities that follow are organized by **theme**, rather than by subject, in order to facilitate their use across the curriculum and to promote an interdisciplinary approach in the classroom. The six themes selected cover a wide range of contemporary issues and concepts that, we submit, are important for the adequate preparation of students for global citizenship in the new millennium. At the beginning of each chapter, some **key concepts** explored in the activities are introduced. Readers may find these introductions useful aids in planning a thematically based curriculum unit and when conducting the discussion or debriefing stages of the activities.

Following each introduction, a **matrix** of concepts and activities is provided for easy reference. **Connections** to other chapters are given underneath the matrix. Highlighted are activities (appearing elsewhere in this book or in *Book 2*), which explore similar or related concepts, though perhaps from a different perspective. Through exploring such connections in a sequence of activities, students can appreciate the interconnected nature of global issues. They thereby avoid the pitfalls of compartmentalist thinking that even a thematically based curriculum can encounter.

With the exception of some shorter activities in Chapter 1, all activities are presented in a common format, under the following sub-headings.

* **Purpose** briefly states the main intended outcome of the activity.

* **Grade level** gives an indication of the levels at which the activity might be successfully used. Corresponding ages are approximately as follows:

Grade	Age
1	6
2	7
3	8
4	9
5	10
6	11
7	12
8	13
9	14
10	15
11	16
12	17

Teacher discretion is expected. Where a broad range of grades (for example, 6-12) is cited, it is likely that instructions to students and the depth of debriefing will differ from one grade to another. Learning outcomes will vary, as may the place and purpose of the activity within the curriculum. Student materials, where given, may need to be modified to suit age and ability levels. Sensitive adaptation of any activity, in the light of a teacher's knowledge of her students, is the key to its success.

* **Time needed** is a rough guide to the length of time necessary for students to undertake the activity, as described under **Procedure**. Again, teacher discretion is advised, as the actual time required is subject to many variables. In most cases, the length of time stated includes some debriefing (see **Potential** and **Extension**), where this forms part of the activity. It does *not* include extensive debriefing (which may be necessary when students are 'fired up' by an activity) nor, in general, follow-up work suggested under **Extension.** Many activities are designed to fit within a 40-minute lesson; longer activities can often be divided into shorter blocks to suit timetabling constraints. Preparatory and/or follow-up work affords many possibilities for interesting home or fieldwork assignments.

* Under **Resources** are listed materials and other requirements including, where relevant, classroom layout or space. The resources stated assume an average class size of 30 students, though most activities will work successfully with groups ranging from 15-45 (space permitting). Student worksheets and other materials for photocopying and distribution, where provided, often appear after the activity description. They are called Copiable Handouts, to indicate that photocopying permission is granted. The following symbol further identifies them: ❑

* **Procedure** is a step-by-step description of how the activity proceeds, written from the students' perspective. Teachers are expected to give

their own instructions and explanations of the process, based on their interpretation of the activity and their understanding of their students' needs and competencies. Care should be exercised in introducing an activity. While directions need to be clear and comprehensive enough for students to undertake the activity as intended, too much prior explanation may limit its potential to engage students in creative and lateral thinking. Analysis of the activity's purpose should be left, for the most part, until the debriefing stage.

* **Potential** offers a rationale for the activity and often provides further guidelines for teachers as to how students' learning can be maximized. Frequently included are suggested questions for activity **debriefing**, the stage of reflective discussion and analysis that is often the richest source of learning — and the most challenging to facilitate! The questions are merely starters, to gear students' thinking towards issues and perspectives that may not have been considered or articulated. The teacher's role in any debriefing should be that of facilitating the reflective process in ways that ensure the representation of as many ideas and experiences from as many students as possible.

* **Extension(s)** suggest ideas for specific follow-up work, either in class or outside school. Most activities are potential springboards for a rich variety of individual and group follow-up tasks including:
    - report, journal and essay writing
    - library research
    - preparation of oral, dramatic or graphic presentations
    - debating
    - undertaking of action projects

If debriefing suggestions and questions are extensive, they are also included under an **Extension** heading.

* **Variation** provides ideas for alternative ways of undertaking the activity.

Global education activities are designed to be flexible learning tools that can be used in either infusion or integration modes of implementation. The activities in this book (and in *Book 2*) are organized thematically. Within most, however, are opportunities for seating them firmly within the regular slots of the subject-based curriculum. Furthermore, their inherent flexibility offers countless possibilities for modification and adaptation, thereby meeting the particular needs of curricula, students and teachers. Many activity formats can be successfully utilized with a vast array of topics and themes as the foci for discussion.

Indeed, the content and process of virtually all activities can be adjusted in some way to render them applicable to grade levels other than those suggested. In all cases, **outcomes** are neither guaranteed, nor predictable, nor — in one sense — important. It is through the dynamic interactions among students and subject matter, taking place within an open and trusting classroom environment, that profound learning occurs. The final product, be it a tangible construct or a negotiated decision, is merely circumstantial evidence of a learning process. Thus, the inability of students to conclude a particular activity in accordance with the guidelines given, or with teacher expectations, should not be deemed as failure but rather as a diversionary path that merits further exploration. Just as in the design of the activities themselves, flexibility is a key ingredient of productive learning in the global classroom.

Fatima's story, continued

In the third decade of the new century, Fatima began to take stock of her life and the maelstrom that seemed to characterise the world around her. The tragic conflicts in Africa during the previous decade had shaken her, not because they were any more horrific than previous wars but because they were fought over the basic necessities for survival: food and water. She worried, too, about the dangers of the new air-borne viral disease that had appeared from nowhere. She was particularly concerned for — and probably over-protective of — her children, knowing that their tender neurological systems were among the most vulnerable. Fatima recognized, however, the many health advantages that the new energy technologies and waste reduction practices had brought about during the past twenty years. It seemed, at long last, that the ethic of conservation was about to seriously challenge the mania for consumption as the defining principle of a developed society, though not before many countries had followed the industrialized world's path to the brink of environmental catastrophe.

Her professional life, thankfully, was now both exciting and fulfilling; her third career move had made all the difference and she enjoyed the flexibility that telecommunications afforded her, not only in working hours but also in work location. The fact that she could obtain, online, the very latest worldwide information anytime, anywhere, still gave her a thrill, though she missed the comforting feel of her daily newspaper which, like so many others with distinguished histories, had been forced to close due to lack of subscribers. Her parents were still avid journal readers; most of the articles in the print media were targeted at the burgeoning population of retirees, trying to help them find useful and productive roles in a society that was moving rapidly on.

*As her children endured the latest experiments in education, Fatima mused on the relevance of her own schooling. She employed very little of the knowledge that she had so painstakingly memorised, but — to be fair — none of her teachers could have predicted much of what she now needed to know, partly because it was information that had come to light since the beginning of the new millennium. What then, she wondered, had been the purpose of her education? In a world in which the rapid and inventive **use** of information was so critical, some more training in on-the-spot creative thinking would have been beneficial. New ideas now seemed to be obsolete almost as soon as they were hatched. Personal time management had been a*

29

problem, too, since her working life had never been externally regulated by 'office hours' or a daily routine. And, in an era in which she was in touch, electronically, with so many people yet — paradoxically — remained quite physically isolated, Fatima wished that her interpersonal communication skills had been better refined. The opportunities, outside the family, for real human sharing and warmth were few and needed to be eagerly grasped.

But, most of all, she decided, her education had failed in preparing her for decision-making around the many complex moral and ethical choices that punctuated her life. Such was the cybernetic intimacy within the global community that she empathized passionately with the suffering and despair she saw around the world, but felt powerless to intervene. Mind-boggling advances in biotechnology threw impossible dilemmas about life and death, wellness and disease into her lap. And now that ignorance of the harmful impact of her lifestyle on other people and the environment could no longer be claimed with any justification, the choices were clear and stark but certainly not easier to act upon.

Fatima resolved to raise these issues at the next parent-teacher meeting.

References

1. The term 'global education,' of American origin, dates back to the late 1960s. A similar movement in the United Kingdom, called 'world studies,' began in the early 1970s.
2. Richardson, Robin. "The world studies story: projects, people, places." In *PEP Talk* (newsletter of the Peace Education Project, Peace Pledge Union), No. 8, 1985, pp. 4-16.
3. Heater, Derek. *Peace through education: The contribution of the Council for Education in World Citizenship.* London: Falmer Press, 1984, pp. 10-12.
4. For a full exploration of the four-dimensional model, see Pike, Graham & David Selby. *Reconnecting: From national to global curriculum.* Godalming, Surrey, UK: World Wide Fund for Nature, 1995, pp. 4-21.
5. Further discussion of the infusion approach can be found in Pike, Graham & David Selby. *Global teacher, global learner.* London: Hodder & Stoughton, 1988, pp. 235-267. Examples of activities that can be used in specific subject areas (from Grade 7 upwards) are in *Reconnecting: From national to global curriculum,* op. cit., chapters 3-10.
6. For an overview of learning styles research and some implications for teaching, see **Ibid.**, pp. 30-35.
7. Miller, John P. *The holistic curriculum.* Toronto: OISE Press, 1988, pp. 4-7. Pike, Graham & David Selby. *Greenprints for changing schools.* Godalming, Surrey, UK: World Wide Fund for Nature/Kogan Page, 1989, pp. 44-46.
8. See, for example Pike, Graham & David Selby. *Global teacher, global learner,* op. cit., pp. 98-124. Selby, David. *Earthkind: A teachers' handbook on humane education.* Stoke-on-Trent: Trentham Books, 1995, pp. 59-77.

1

A friendly classroom for a small planet[1]

The activities that follow are designed to establish and maintain an ambience appropriate for participatory learning in the global classroom. For both the *journey outwards* and the *journey inwards*, students need a classroom environment which is affirming, secure and challenging. They need this to encourage them to examine their own assumptions and perspectives; to take risks in their learning; to share their opinions and values; and to be receptive to the feelings, ideas and perspectives of others. Exploration of emotive and controversial issues, personal to global, will be more effectively accomplished in a context in which all participants are actively involved in a range of these activities; not only on first meeting, but at appropriate intervals throughout their time together.

The chapter is divided into four sections. The first section, *Icebreakers and Climate Setters*, includes activities encouraging students to exchange personal information in non-threatening ways, loosening-up activities designed to raise energy levels and to reduce personal anxieties and group tensions, and activities designed to change the pace and mood of the learning process. The focus here is on initial **group building** and fostering and maintaining a convivial classroom climate.

The second section, *Knowing Ourselves and Others; Valuing Ourselves and Others*, comprises activities designed to build **self-esteem** and **self-awareness**, to explore **self-perception**, and to realize the concomitant goals of **group affirmation** and **mutual awareness**. The emphasis is upon developing in all members of the learning community a sense of personal worth, a sense of shared responsibility for each other's well being, a shared commitment to the learning task, and a belief in their own potential and ability to contribute to the learning process in a positive and unique way. **Genuineness** in communicating with and relating to others; **appreciation of commonalities and differences**; and the promotion of **mutual respect, trust, empathy** and **sensitivity** are leitmotifs of these activities.

The third section, *Learning to Cooperate; Cooperating to Learn*, offers a range of activities designed to promote **cooperative attitudes** and

skills. Skills specifically addressed include: **discussion, non-verbal communication, listening, negotiation, consensus building, problem solving, conflict avoidance** and **conflict/grievance resolution.**

The fourth section of the chapter, *Skill Builders*, presents activities that in many cases develop the same skills, but that are also intended to give practice in a range of other basic and higher order skills. These include: **memorization, observation, description, notetaking, picture/photograph interpretation, questioning, drawing, extrapolation, prediction, textual analysis** and **lateral/divergent thinking.** Skill building exercises such as these are another important component in building a non-threatening, inclusive classroom climate. As the **Potential** sections of a number of the activities indicate, they can usefully be undertaken prior to attempting activities in later chapters, which utilize the same skills but often in a more demanding and sophisticated way.

As the matrix makes clear, the division of the activities into discrete sections is, in the final analysis, an artificial device. The introductory activities promote cooperation, self-esteem and self/group awareness. The self and group affirmation and cooperative activities also help build basic skills. The skill building activities, in turn, promote cooperation, awareness and respect. In the same way, most of the activities in later chapters have a cooperative and affirmative subtext and also reinforce a range of basic and higher order skills.

SKILLS INVENTORY

Most of the activities in this chapter, but especially those in the
    Learning to Cooperate; Cooperating to Learn section (pp. 43-47),
    enable students to develop *cooperative skills* and *communication
    (including listening) skills.*
Questioning skills are addressed in the following activities: **Tell Me,
    Shapes, Sizes and Spaces, One Big Question, Splitting Images.**
Problem-solving skills can be practiced through **Cooperative Balloons,
    Cooperative Loops** and **Going Dotty.**
Observation skills can be practiced through **Human Jigsaw,
    Photographic Memory, Surrounds** and **Splitting Images. Human
    Jigsaw** and **Photographic Memory** also involve using *memory* skills.
Drawing skills are utilized in **Cooperative Squiggles, Surrounds** and
    Splitting Images.
One Big Question offers practice in *drawing up interview schedules.*
Shapes, Sizes and Spaces and **Divergent Thinking** can help build
    thinking skills.
Photographic Memory involves using *notetaking skills.*
Sharing Circle can be used to practice and refine *conflict resolution skills.*

FRIENDLY CLASSROOM

CONCEPTS

ACTIVITIES

CONCEPTS \ ACTIVITIES	Divergent Thinking	Splitting Images	Surrounds	One Big Question	Shapes, Sizes and Spaces	Photographic Memory	Going Dotty	Cooperative Loops	Cooperative Balloons	Human Jigsaw	Cooperative Squiggles	Likes and Dislikes	Head Tapes	Who Am I?	You're Like...	Tell Me	Meeting Needs	Sharing Circle	Strength Bombardment	Best Qualities	The Pencil	Double Line-Up	Art Gallery
Group Building							*	*	*	*	*	*		*	*	*	*	*	*	*	*	*	*
Self-esteem															*			*	*	*			*
Self-awareness/perception							*					*	*	*	*	*	*	*	*	*			*
Group Affirmation							*	*	*	*		*		*	*		*	*	*	*			*
Mutual Awareness										*		*	*	*	*	*	*	*					*
Genuineness																*	*	*	*				
Commonalities/differences												*					*		*				*
Mutual Respect																*	*	*	*				
Trust							*																
Empathy/sensitivity												*				*	*	*	*				
Cooperative Attitudes/skills	*						*	*	*	*	*							*				*	
Discussion		*	*	*							*	*		*	*	*	*	*				*	
Non-verbal Communication							*						*										
Listening							*			*						*	*	*	*				
Negotiation									*		*												
Consensus Building										*	*							*					
Problem Solving								*	*	*													
Conflict/grievance Resolution																		*					
Memorization						*				*													
Observation		*				*				*													
Description						*																	
Notetaking						*																	
Picture/photo Interpretation		*	*			*																	
Questioning		*		*	*																		
Drawing		*	*		*						*												*

Art Gallery

Purpose	Building a sense of community in a new class and revealing the potential of its members
Grade level	2 and up
Time needed	30 minutes (15 to prepare presentations and 15 to view the art 'gallery')
Resources	1 sheet of newsprint, 2 sheets of paper and at least 1 marker for each student. Masking tape.

Procedure

Students are asked to fold their sheet of paper into quarters, reopen it and draw in lines and a central circle, as in Figure 1.

Figure 1

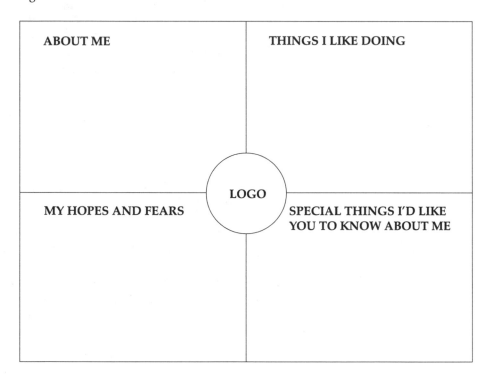

In the upper left quarter, they write in some basic personal details. In the upper right quarter, they describe things they like doing. In the lower right quarter, they list special things about themselves (for example, talents, skills, abilities and interests). In the lower left quarter, they register their hopes and concerns for the future. In the central circle, they draw a logo that tries to capture the essence of themselves and their view of the world.

Their presentation completed, students stick it onto the wall and attach a piece of paper to it.

Students are invited to walk around the 'art gallery' to learn about each other. They are encouraged to browse the 'exhibits' and write notes on the attached paper concerning things they have in common, or sentiments, ideas and experiences they would like to share with the person featured.

The activity can end at this point or, alternatively, students can be invited to stand by their sheets and take turns introducing themselves and briefly speaking to two items they have included on their sheet. The 'art gallery' can usefully be left for further browsing, for a period of time.

Potential

An excellent activity for building a sense of community and collegiality within a new class and for revealing the wealth of interests, talents and experiences among its members. The **Hopes and Fears** quarter can provide a useful springboard for work on futures (Chapter 7).

The topics for each quarter can, of course, be varied, as can their level of sophistication (thus allowing the activity to be used with all grades). Students can be asked to **draw** rather than write in each quarter, thus simulating an art gallery more precisely.

Source
After an idea in *Making a World of Difference: Creative Activities for Global Learning.* New York: Friendship Press, 1990, pp. 39-40.

Double Line-up

A row of chairs, one per student, is set out in an open space. Students are asked to form a line in front of the chairs according to the month and date of their birthday. One end of the row is designated 1 January, the other 31 December. They are to avoid speaking, but can use gestures and mime. When each participant has taken up a position, a verbal check is made by going along the line person by person. Participants in the wrong places are encouraged to change positions.

Students are then asked to remove their shoes and stand on the chairs. Their second task is to re-form the line according to height with the tallest at one end of the row, the shortest at the other. There is to be no speaking, and everybody is to do their best to ensure that others do not have to get down from the chairs unless this is absolutely necessary in order to re-form the line as specified.

Both halves of this activity will generate fun and laughter; the former giving practice in non-verbal communication, the latter requiring physical contact. The second half is especially effective in highlighting the need for cooperation and promoting a sense of group achievement and solidarity.

Source
Milan Caha, EVANS, Czech Republic.

The Pencil

Students form a loose circle. They are asked to imagine that, lying on the floor beside them, is a giant pencil. Using mime, they pick it up and insert the unsharpened end of the pencil into their belt buckle (real or imaginary). The pencil is heavy and cumbersome and must be held at all times. Each time the teacher utters a letter, number or short word, they are to write it with their pencil using exaggerated body movements. As a culmination they are asked to sign their names.

This is a hilarious, often uproarious activity that can be employed as an icebreaker or as a means of allowing students to 'let off steam' after activities that have demanded intense concentration or involved considerable personal challenge.

Source
Jan Selby.

KNOWING OURSELVES AND OTHERS; VALUING OURSELVES AND OTHERS

Best Qualities

The class is divided into equal-sized groups. The students each have a sheet pinned to their backs. At the top of the sheet is written: *Some of my best qualities are....*

Students are asked to write positive statements about each member of their group on small slips of paper, taking the six words at the top of the sheet as the beginning of each statement.

Slips are taped to the appropriate students' sheets. The sheets are then unpinned and read silently. If a student wishes, she can write her name at the bottom of the sheet and display it on the classroom wall.

Source
Stanish, B. *Connecting Rainbows*. Carthage, Illinois: Good Apple, 1982.

Strength Bombardment

Students form groups of five or six.

Focusing on one person at a time, group members bombard that person with all the strengths and good qualities they can see in the person. Members of the group take turns acting as recorder, listing what is said and handing the list to the person when the bombardment is finished. Only positive comments are to be contributed, and 'put-downs' are to be avoided. Nobody's list should be more, or fewer, than 15 items.

After everybody's strengths have been bombarded, groups are asked to identify the different types of strengths that emerged from the activity. They report back on their findings.

Plenary discussion follows.

As a potentially powerful reinforcer of this activity, students can be encouraged to ask their parents to similarly bombard the strengths they see in them.

Source
Canfield, J. & H.C. Wells. *100 Ways to Enhance Self-concept in the Classroom*. Upper Saddle River, New Jersey: Prentice-Hall, 1976.

Sharing Circle

Sharing circles can be a mainstay of the affirmatory classroom. The idea is very simple. Students stand in a circle so that everybody can see everyone else. The facilitator (or a student) introduces the circle theme.

Then everybody has a chance to contribute thoughts or feelings as the right to speak passes from one person to the next.

The class can decide to go around the circle more than once. Circle time can be used to affirm the qualities of each class member or the group as follows.

- I am glad to be me because...
- A success I had recently is...
- I feel proud that...
- I feel happy to be in this group because...
- (Name of person to left), you remind me of a(n) (name of an animal, flower, tree) because...
- (Name of person to left), I've appreciated you lately because...
- (Name of person to left), I'd like to have your (description of positive quality)...

Sharing circles can also be used to share news, or to develop mutual awareness through the expression of feelings ('I feel sad when...' or 'I feel best when people...'). They can be used to brainstorm ideas, to promote empathy with people and animals—perhaps using glove puppets, to build consensus, and to resolve conflicts and/or grievances.

As a conflict/grievance resolution exercise, the students involved can be given two minutes each of uninterrupted time to present their side, then a further minute to clarify any points.

After the group has been given two minutes' quiet time for reflection, the sharing circle begins, with students giving their opinions on the issue on the first round and their suggestions for resolution on the second.

Circle time can also be used after a particularly successful or powerful activity for a sharing of feelings, reflections on what has been

learned, or appreciation for what others contributed to the activity. In every case the right to pass should be respected by the facilitator. The group should, however, discuss in general and without reference to any specific individual the consequences of not contributing when the object of a sharing circle is to affirm others.

Meeting Needs

Groups of five or six are formed. Working individually, students list as many answers as they wish to the question 'What can we do to make you happier in this class?'

Upon completion of the lists, the group members each read their responses to the question, elaborating if necessary, and the others react to the individual's needs.

In the plenary session that follows, groups give a report—not specific to any individual—on the needs expressed, and suggest how the class might meet those needs. The subtext of the activity is that a learning community is at its most effective when the needs of the members are satisfied.

This activity can be attempted now and then throughout the school year as a means of monitoring the health of the classroom climate and relationships, and as a way of confirming or identifying difficulties that individuals may be encountering.

Source
Greenberg, J.S. *Health Education: Learner-centered Instructional Strategies*. Dubuque, Iowa: Wm. C. Brown, 1989.

Tell Me

Working in pairs, students take turns putting to each other one of the 'Tell Me' statements listed on the board (examples are given in Figure 2).

Alternatively, each student in a group of three or four puts the same statement in turn to the other group members (there can be several rounds in which members take turns choosing statements). Students should be urged to react honestly and in some detail.

Later in the activity, students can be encouraged to devise their own statements. Towards the end, each person can be given the opportunity to react to a particular 'Tell Me' statement that has not been put to them.

Figure 2

Tell me:
1. something that you like about yourself
2. something that you dislike about yourself
3. a vivid early school memory
4. about the best thing that ever happened to you
5. what you like doing
6. about your greatest success
7. how you feel about this class
8. something that most people don't know about you

9. about a person who has influenced you a lot
10. what you look for in a friend
11. about your hopes for the future
12. about your worries regarding the future
13. what you fear
14. what you'd most like to change about yourself
15. what you think of yourself

Source
Greenberg, J.S. *Health Education: Learner-centered Instruction Strategies*. Dubuque, Iowa: Wm.C. Brown, 1989.

You're Like...

While the activity *Tell Me* asks group members to reveal things about themselves, this activity calls upon others to reveal their perceptions of the individual they are focusing on.

Each person in a group of four or five is focused on in turn, with the others speaking to one of the *You're Like* statements (Copiable Handout 1 ☐). Several rounds can be attempted.

After each round—or after several rounds—the group can discuss the extent to which group members feel they have been accurately perceived by others. If mismatches have occurred between self-perceptions and group perceptions, how is this to be explained?

Source
Greenberg, J.S. *Health Education: Learner-centered Instruction Strategies*. Dubuque, Iowa: Wm. C. Brown, 1989.

Who Am I?

Each student receives a sheet of plain paper and folds it in half. On the top half of the sheet, they print as many of their personality characteristics as they can think of. The teacher collects the sheets, shuffles them and tapes them on the classroom walls.

Class members then walk around the room, reading the descriptions. As they walk around, they write—in small letters on the bottom half of each sheet—the name of the person they think is being described.

This phase completed, students retrieve their own sheets and form groups of four or five. First, they read the bottom half of their sheet to discover who they were most often judged to be. Themselves? Someone else? If the latter, are they surprised to be perceived as like this person? Groups share reactions and reflections. Before they do so, the teacher should caution against disparaging comments about others in the class. Class discussion follows.

A frequent outcome of this activity is a realization that our personal sense of ourselves can differ markedly from others' perceptions of us.

Head Tapes

Students form discussion groups of six. Strips of masking tape, upon which specific roles are written, are placed on the forehead of each person without the person knowing what her role is. Hence, group members can see the roles of others but not their own.

Avoiding mention of each other's roles, the group engages in discussion of a given topic, group members treating the others as though they

1. You are happy when...

2. You get angry at...

3. You dislike...

4. You enjoy...

5. You care deeply about...

6. You think this class is...

7. The thing you like most about yourself is...

8. The thing you dislike most about yourself is...

9. You like people who...

10. You feel hurt when...

11. You feel a sense of injustice when...

12. You wouldn't miss...

13. The thing you like most about school is...

14. The thing you like least about school is...

15. Right now you feel...

were the type of person identified on their head tapes. Examples of roles are given in Figure 3.

Figure 3

intellectual	aggressive
bossy	a sex object
a know-it-all	full of ideas
hot-tempered	untrustworthy
trustworthy	athletic

As the discussion moves along, participants write down notes as to what they think their role is. When all group members think they have guessed their roles, tapes are removed and individuals determine the degree to which their guesses were accurate.

Group discussion (out of role) follows. What behaviors and signals on the part of others convinced individuals as to what was written on their head tape? As realization dawned, were they happy or uncomfortable with their appointed role? To what extent does the activity mirror everyday life? To what degree are people pigeonholed? How easy/difficult is it to escape labels once we are given them? What could we all do to help each other escape?

Source

Greenberg, J.S. *Health Education: Learner-centered Instructional Strategies*. Dubuque, Iowa: Wm. C. Brown, 1989.

Likes and Dislikes

Purpose	Promoting self- and group awareness
Grade level	7 and up
Time needed	80 minutes
Resources	Paper and a pencil for each student

Procedure, Stage A: Likes

1. Working individually, students are asked to write a list of 'Things I like to do.' They are informed that lists will not be seen by anyone else, and are encouraged to write freely and without inhibition. List items should be written in columns, one under another.

2. Students are asked to go through their lists and put appropriate notations against each item as follows.

F and/or M - Something their fathers and/or mothers would have liked doing at their age.

D and/or S - Something their daughters and/or sons will probably like doing at their age.

T or A	-	Involves being together (**T**) with others or alone (**A**).
5	-	They will still enjoy doing this in 5 years' time.
*****	-	Is probably enjoyed by people their age in (specified country).
> or <>	-	Directly or indirectly affects (**>**) or involves (**<>**) people in other countries.

3. Students reflect on the activity so far by undertaking a sentence-completion exercise. They are given sentence openers such as the following, and are asked to continue them.

- I've learned from this exercise that...
- I'm surprised in this exercise that...
- I'm puzzled by...
- I'm pleased that...
- I'm concerned that...
- I'm intrigued by...

Completed sentences can be read out, pinned to the wall or collected by the teacher and duplicated (anonymity may be preferable).

Once they have been considered by everybody, whole-class discussion follows.

Procedure, Stage B: Dislikes

The same procedure is followed around things students don't like doing or having done to them. Additional or alternative criteria to consider during the second phase of the activity are as follows.

| **G or B** | - | The item is good (**G**) or bad (**B**) for them. |
| **S or O** | - | They can act to change the situation by themselves (**S**) or they need to get organized with others (**O**). |

Potential

An activity that can stand by itself as offering considerable scope for promoting self- and group awareness (and greater realization of how many feelings and impulses are commonly shared), or can be used as a lead-in to specific areas considered in this book.

For example, the **F and/or M**, **D and/or S** or **S or O** questions can be used as a prelude to work on **change** and **futures** (Chapter 7). The ***** questions can serve as a platform for work on **perspectives** (Chapter 5). The **> or <>** question can be a starter for **interconnectedness** (Chapter 2) and the **S or O** question can be related to **citizenship** (*Book 2*).

Variation

The same process can be used for thinking about students' **hopes** and **fears**.

Source
Richardson, R. *Learning for Change in World Society: Reflections, Activities and Resources*. London: World Studies Project, 1976, p. 82.

Cooperative Squiggles

Students form pairs. With their eyes firmly closed or blindfolded, both members of the pair put their pencils in the middle of a large piece of paper and then move the pencils around (never taking them off the paper). They continue until they think all areas of the paper have been covered by squiggles.

Opening their eyes, pairs must agree upon a picture they can make out of the squiggles. The pictures are drawn. Finished products are shared with the class.

This activity promotes cooperation, creativity and problem-solving.

Human Jigsaw

Purpose	Reducing inhibitions and increasing awareness of others
Grade level	Kindergarten to 4
Time needed	15 to 20 minutes
Resources	A clear area, preferably carpeted

Procedure

The rules of the activity are first explained. A chain is to be formed by the students joining one hand to the person in front of them. As students join the chain, they can either sit, stand, kneel or lie down, but must avoid doing the same as the person with whom they are joining hands.

When the chain has been formed, students are urged to take notice of where they are in the chain, or human jigsaw. They are then asked to drop hands, walk around the room and return to make the same formation.

It is probably best to do this activity a few times, since the first time the students may be too concerned with the rules to obtain the full benefit from the activity.

Potential

An activity that will help to reduce the inhibitions students have about physical contact, and that will increase awareness of others. It also emphasizes the need for observation, memory and cooperation.

Variations

1. The activity can be attempted with small groups.

2. As students become more confident and secure, different types of body contact can be encouraged.

3. The activity can be attempted with blindfolds (or closed eyes).

4. The activity can be attempted on a further occasion with the re-forming of the jigsaw not taking place until a few hours have elapsed.

Source
Alan Simpson, West Walker Primary School, Newcastle upon Tyne, England.

Cooperative Balloons

Purpose   Solving a problem through cooperation
Grade level   Kindergarten to Grade 4
Time needed   20 to 30 minutes
Resources   4 large baskets or boxes. 1 inflated balloon for every 2 students. 1 thin card strip 3 cm x 65 cm (1 inch x 26 inches) per student. A large clear area, preferably a hall. An even number of participants (the teacher can make up the difference).

Procedure

A large basket is placed in each corner of the room.

Students sit in circle formation with the inflated balloons placed in the center.

The students are each given a card strip and told they can only hold their strip at one end.

They are then told that the problem is to pick up the balloons using the strips and take them to the boxes. The activity commences.

With younger children, the teacher can ask for suggestions. Each suggestion is tried. If no solution is forthcoming, the teacher can draw attention to the number of balloons, the number of children and the fact that they can hold the end of each other's card strip.

Potential

Allows for the solution of a problem by active cooperation. The activity also gives scope for imagination, listening to others, seeing number relationships and practicing coordination. Suggested lines of questioning in the debriefing might include:
- What did you think when first faced with the problem?
- How did you arrive at a solution?
- Can you think of any similar problems which might have similar solutions?

Source
Alan Simpson, West Walker Primary School, Newcastle upon Tyne, England.

Cooperative Loops

Purpose	Promoting cooperation
Grade level	Kindergarten to 4
Time needed	30 minutes
Resources	Drawing paper, pencils, crayons

Procedure

Each student is given a piece of paper with a pencil and crayon, and the class is split into two groups.

Students in one group start to draw with a pencil from the top left corner of the paper to the bottom right corner, making five loops as they draw.

Students in the second group start at the bottom left corner and end at the top right, again making five loops.

Each loop then has to be colored in with a different color. However, the students can only use two colors each. They must, therefore, get help from each other to complete the coloring.

When all have finished their coloring, the students are asked to join their lines together into one continuous line, perhaps by standing in a circle holding their pieces of paper, if there is an even number in the class. Alternative colors for adjacent squiggles have to be maintained.

Figure 4

Potential

A useful activity for promoting cooperative attitudes and skills. Also good for practicing communication and problem-solving skills.

Source
Alan Simpson, West Walker Primary School, Newcastle upon Tyne, England.

Going Dotty

Purpose	Establishing the need for cooperation to accomplish a group task; heightening the importance of non-verbal communication
Grade level	3-12
Time needed	20 minutes
Resources	Small, self-adhesive colored dots, in at least four colors, one for each participant. An open classroom space so that students can move about freely.

Procedure

Students form a circle, close their eyes and remain silent.

Each participant has a colored dot stuck on their forehead. The different colors should be spread among the class so that neighboring students do not have the same color, but there should be an approximately equal number of each color.

Students then open their eyes and try to form groups of the same-colored dots without speaking, pointing at colors, looking for reflections or peeling off the dot.

Potential

A simple exercise with a variety of possible uses. It establishes very quickly the need for cooperation among individuals in order to solve a group problem. There is a degree of affirmation in bringing individuals together through a short, enjoyable problem-solving exercise; it heightens the importance of non-verbal communication and raises issues surrounding trust.

At a conceptual level, the exercise provides an illustration of the concepts of interdependence and identity. Nobody can accomplish the task save through mutual dependence and trust. Everybody's sense of identity (understanding of their dot color) is dependent upon everybody else. This activity, therefore, can provide an effective springboard into work on interconnectedness (Chapter 2 in this book) and citizenship (*Book 2*). At a practical level, the activity can be used as an enjoyable means of organizing students into random groups for further work.

Variations

The activity model described here has multiple classroom uses:

1. In **science** it has been used to reinforce students' understanding of body parts. A large outline of the human body is chalked on the floor. Students, with eyes closed, have a sticky label—with the name of a body part written on it—stuck to their backs. Avoiding speaking, they help each other take up the appropriate juxtaposition within the body outline. They then have to guess the part they represent.

2. In **geography** the activity has been used similarly to develop locational knowledge of the cities, towns, rivers, mountains and other key features of a country, using a chalked country outline (see the activity **Globetrotting**, p.71, for a global version).

Students can be encouraged to use body sculptures to good effect in both the above suggestions (for example, lying on the floor with body curled to represent intestines or the meandering of a river).

3. In **math** the activity can be employed to practice fractions or decimals. For instance, students have a decimal number placed on their back and, in silence, must form groups of five in which the sum total of the numbers equals, say, 2.5.

4. In **language arts,** students can be asked to form groups in which the word(s) and/or punctuation mark stuck on their back forms part of a grammatically correct sentence.

In all these variations, nobody has completed the task until all class members have been placed. Acquisition or reinforcement of knowledge is, thus, combined with the practice of non-verbal and cooperative skills.

Photographic Memory

Purpose	Practicing basic skills
Grade level	All grades (with appropriate pictures)
Time needed	20 minutes
Resources	1. A copy of the same photograph, and a paper and pencil for each student.
	2. A set of 2 different photographs, and paper and pencils for each pair of students.

Procedure, Part A

Students quietly study their individual photographs for one minute.

Photographs are then removed from sight, and students sketch them from memory.

Procedure, Part B

Working in pairs, partners are given a different photograph and, avoiding discussion, are asked to study it for one minute.

Photographs are then removed from sight and, taking turns, the students describe their photographs to each other, while the listeners take detailed notes about everything they are told. Listeners should not ask questions.

Finally, notes and pictures are compared.

Potential

Two simple but useful exercises for basic skills practice and reinforcement. Both utilize memory and observation skills, while the latter also draws upon listening, notetaking and reviewing skills. Both emphasize the point that photographs can be seriously studied as opposed to being casually glanced at. As such, one or both of the above activities can be attempted prior to activities such as the following: **The Rumor Experiment** (p.171), **Alpha Observers** (p.180), **Two Mules** (*Book 2*).

Shapes, Sizes and Spaces

Purpose	Reinforcing questioning and lateral thinking abilities
Grade level	5 and up
Time needed	25 minutes
Resources	A sheet of paper and a pencil for each student

Procedure

Students form pairs and sit in back-to-back chairs. The shapes chart (*Figure 5*) is displayed.

Individuals, avoiding talking, are to draw three shapes of their choice (triangle, rectangle, square, circle, etc.) on their sheets of paper, deciding the size and location of each shape. Shapes can overlap or be placed within another shape.

The students, in turn, question each other about their shapes, the aim being to replicate as precisely as possible their partners' drawings on the reverse side of their own sheets of paper. The partner can only respond to closed questions (that is, questions requiring a 'yes' or 'no' answer). All temptations to look over the partner's shoulder are to be resisted!

The drawings completed, pairs compare original drawings and replicas and discuss the difficulties they faced and how they were best overcome.

Whole-group debriefing follows.

Potential

At first glance, a relatively simple exercise that will make considerable demands on students' questioning and lateral thinking abilities. The debriefing should focus on questioning strategies employed, as well as the relative strengths and weaknesses of closed and open questioning.

Variation

The activity can be undertaken in simple stages with earlier grade levels by, for example, beginning with one shape, moving on to two identical shapes, two different shapes and so on.

Figure 5

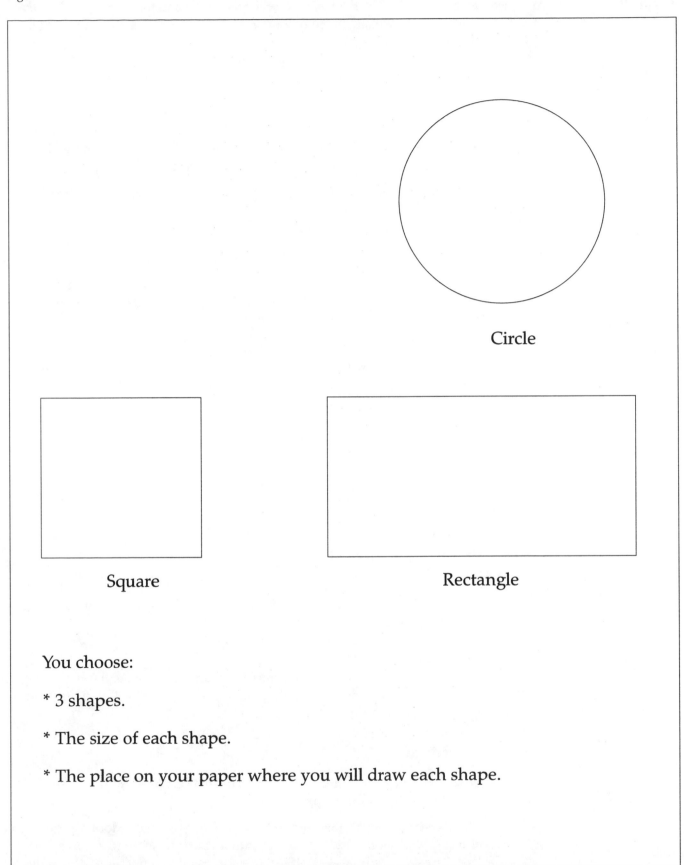

Circle

Square

Rectangle

You choose:

* 3 shapes.

* The size of each shape.

* The place on your paper where you will draw each shape.

One Big Question

Purpose	Constructing interview schedules and formulating open-ended questions
Grade level	5 and up
Time needed	40 minutes
Resources	A pencil and a sheet of paper for each student

Procedure

The class divides into groups of eight. Each group chooses one well known person whom they would like to interview.

Working individually and avoiding discussion, the group members think about and write down the one question they would each most like the well known person to answer.

Groups gather again and are given two further tasks:

a. To draw up an interview schedule from the eight questions and list supplementary questions they would want to be ready with, given the response to each of the eight questions.

b. To think of the one big question most likely to elicit from the well known person—who might be pressed for time—all the information the group wants.

Reporting back in plenary session follows.

Potential

A fun activity giving practice in the construction of interview schedules and in the formulation of effective open-ended questions. Groups should be encouraged to critically evaluate each other's work, and to suggest alternatives and amendments to the proposed interview schedules (order and content of questions) and the one big question.

Surrounds

Purpose	Practicing observational, discussion, negotiation and drawing skills
Grade level	All grades (with appropriate picture)
Time needed	40 minutes
Resources	A photograph (or the center section of a photograph), a sheet of newsprint and 3 pencils for each group of 3 students. Paste or glue.

Procedure

Students, working in groups of three, paste their photograph in the center of a sheet of newsprint.

Their task is to scrutinize the photograph very carefully, looking for clues as to what might be in the picture if the lens were to zoom away from the present image, enabling the surroundings to come into frame.

The surrounding images that they agree upon are drawn in using pencil.

Groups share and discuss their work in plenary session. Should a center section of a photograph be used, the real surroundings (surround) should only be revealed towards the close of the plenary discussion.

Potential

An excellent exercise for practicing observational, discussion, negotiation and drawing skills. The activity can be very usefully attempted twice—first with each group having the same photograph, and second with each group using different photographs.

Groups should be encouraged to critique each other's decisions and assumptions. With appropriate photographs, the exercise lends itself to consideration of racial, gender and other stereotypes. The activity **Splitting Images** (below) offers a further development of this activity.

Splitting Images

Purpose   Practicing detailed observation, photographic interpretation, discussion, questioning, negotiation, consensus building and drawing

Grade level   3 and up

Time needed   30 minutes

Resources   For each group of 3 or 4 students: a photocopy of a photograph, cut into 2 parts (Copiable Handout 2▢); a sheet of newsprint; a pencil; 2 markers of different colors; and paste or glue

Procedure

Students form groups of three or four and are given the small section of the picture. They paste this onto their sheet of newsprint.

Their first task is to brainstorm feelings, responses and questions prompted by the part-picture, writing these around the outside of the newsprint adjacent to the image.

Their second task is to decide what the unseen part of the picture might contain.

Once agreement is reached, the chosen content is drawn in pencil as an extension of the picture-part they have before them.

Copies of the second part are then distributed and laid over the drawing. Groups brainstorm feelings, responses and questions prompted by the complete picture, writing these on the newsprint using a marker of a different color.

Discussion follows around the extent to which the pencil drawings accurately anticipated the contents of the photograph.

Potential

As with the photograph example offered in Copiable Handout 2☐, it is a good idea to choose an image which, when the second part of the photograph is revealed, has shock or surprise value. In this way, the activity can be effectively used to confront stereotypes or unsettle assumptions around a variety of themes and issues. It offers practice in detailed observation, photographic interpretation, discussion, questioning, negotiation, consensus building and drawing.

Divergent Thinking

Purpose	Encouraging wide-ranging thinking and cooperation
Grade level	5-12
Time needed	20 minutes
Resources	Paper and pencil for each group of 3 or 4 students

Procedure

Students work in groups of three or four, one acting as secretary.

Groups are given the name of an object (for example, paperclip, blanket, snowshoe, piece of chalk). They are asked to brainstorm and write down as many uses for the object as they can think of in two minutes.

When time is up, groups are asked to stop and count up the total number of uses brainstormed.

In addition they choose, from the uses they have written down, the *three* uses which they consider it *least likely* other groups will have thought of.

Each group reports back their number of uses listed and their three least likely uses.

Discussion follows.

Potential

A light-hearted activity that will encourage wide-ranging and imaginative thinking, as well as group cooperation. It can be used to practice brainstorming prior to using the technique for a topic-related purpose. As an illustration of the variety of ways in which people perceive everyday objects, it can also be as an introduction to many of the activities on perspectives in Chapter 5.

Source
Sandy Parker, based on an idea from Tony Buzar.

Reference
1. The title of this chapter is borrowed from Prutzman, P. et al. *The Friendly Classroom for a Small Planet*. Garden City Park, New York: Avery, 1978. (A classic handbook for building the cooperative and affirmative classroom.)

2

Interconnections

At the heart of global education lies the concept of **connectedness.** Its centrality is evident at a number of levels. In its most obvious manifestation, connectedness characterizes the complex web of **global connections.** Such connections bind all peoples, cultures and countries into a dynamic, ever-changing system in which an event occurring, an action taken, or a decision made at one point on the globe can have multiple repercussions, both now and in the future, in countless other places.

The conduits of connection are the constant flows of people, money, ideas, goods and services that propel the emergence of increasingly multicultural, multilingual communities. They permit us to enjoy breakfast foods grown in several continents. They afford intimate glimpses — via the television screen — into the drama of everyday lives in distant and unknown places. Such is the pervasiveness of these connections that traditional perceptions of **local** and **global** have become blurred and are now inadequate descriptors of reality. The world can be readily found in neighborhood schools and stores, while locally crafted products and ideas circle the globe.

A significant feature of connectedness in the contemporary world is **interdependence.** In its purest and most equitable form, interdependence signifies a connection between two or more parties that is of mutual benefit. Goods wanted in one country are given by another in exchange for other desired goods or money of equal value. In reality, interdependence in the global system is often less equitable. In practice it is often **asymmetrical.** Through exercising control over the world's markets, wealthier countries maintain a situation in which poorer nations are more dependent upon them than *vice versa.*

Interdependence, of course, operates at all levels of global society. Lasting personal friendships thrive upon a basis of reciprocity. In a **community** that functions well, members provide goods and services for the benefit of each other and for the overall good of the community. Consumers, manufacturers, advertisers and the mass media exemplify an increasingly potent interdependent relationship. We also need to recognize that it is not just lands and peoples that are interdependent. The **global issues** we face are profoundly interlocking in nature —

sub-systems within a global system of issues. Hence, environmental concerns are also issues of development, equity, health, peace, rights and so on. At the planetary level, ecological interdependence is the key to the maintenance of life. The mass extinction of thousands of species each year is tragic evidence of the risks involved in tampering with the delicate balance within and between ecological systems.

Fundamental to our understanding of connectedness — at all levels, personal to planetary — is an awareness of the operation and impact of **systems**. This involves a comprehension of how the multiple, incessant interactions of all components of global systems contrive to create a whole that is more than the sum of its parts, and a whole that is subject to continual **change**. Within all systems, the full significance of component parts is only discernible through their interactions with all other parts.

This **relational holism** — to borrow a term from subatomic physics — is evident, too, in the global system. Such is the intensity of the multi-directional and multi-dimensional flow of ideas, materials and people between countries that each nation's identity is profoundly dependent upon the sum total of exchanges with all other countries. Thus, Canadian or Brazilian or American politics, economics or culture can only be finally understood through exploration of the connections that exist in these spheres with all other nations. As with 'local' and 'global,' distinctions between 'domestic' and 'foreign' affairs are increasingly hard to find.

Connectedness has significant and far-reaching implications for schooling, if education is to prepare students adequately for the real world. **Relational thinking** — the ability to create and detect links, relationships and patterns among ideas and concepts — is profoundly important for understanding systems. It is profoundly important for appreciating the full consequences of personal decisions and actions. In addition to the activities that follow, subject integration and thematic approaches to curriculum can promote students' capacity for relational thinking. (See the discussion of integration and infusion, in the introduction chapter, for ideas and examples.) Profile 1, at the end of this chapter, illustrates how one high school has attempted to harmonize medium and message. This has been done by facilitating students' exploration of global connections in a team-taught, interdisciplinary course that stresses cooperative learning and peer evaluation.

SKILLS INVENTORY

All of the activities in this chapter provide opportunities for students to develop and refine the *skills of relational thinking* — seeking connections, relationships and patterns among diverse ideas, experiences and other phenomena.
Most activities require students to practice *cooperative skills*.
Analytical thinking skills are necessary in many activities, especially in the second half of the chapter.

CONCEPTS

ACTIVITIES	Connectedness	Global Connections	Local/Global	Interdependence	Assymetrical Interdependence	Community	Global Issues	Systems	Change	Relational Holism	Relational Thinking
Only Connect	*										
My View of the World	*	*	*			*			*		*
My Place	*	*	*			*			*		*
The World in the School	*	*	*			*					*
The World in the Shopping Mall	*	*	*	*	*	*	*				*
Dependency Webs	*			*	*	*		*	*		*
Neighborhood Linking	*		*	*	*	*		*			*
Connections Board	*	*		*	*			*		*	*
Globe Trotting	*	*									*
Econobingo	*			*			*				*
Made in Canada	*	*	*				*	*	*	*	*
Global Rose	*								*		*
Declaration of Interdependence	*			*	*		*	*	*	*	*

Connections • Many activities in this series illustrate and explore connectedness; see, especially: **Likes and Dislikes** (p.41), **Key Events in My Life** (bk 2), **Narrowcast or Broadcast?** (bk 2) and, for temporal connectedness, **Inventing the Future (Backwards)** (p.233). • Global interdependence is another common thread—see, especially, **World Food Distribution** (bk 2), **Picture Linking** (bk 2), **Development Cartoons** (bk 2), **The Trading Game** (bk 2); interdependence is actively illustrated in **Nine-Square Cooperative Squares** (bk 2), **The Two Mules** (bk 2) and **Whispers Game** (bk 2). • Other useful activities for exploring systems are **Rainforest Fantasy** (p.107), **Decision Wheel** (p.146), **Catching On** (p.148) and **Futures Wheel** (p.236). **Going Dotty** (p.46) and **Plural Identity Badges** (bk 2) can help students understand relational holism. • **Right Up Your Street** (p.105) provides a framework for exploring attitudes around communities.

Graphic and/or Mapping skills are addressed in **My View of the World, My Place, The World in the Shopping Mall, Connections Board, Globetrotting,** and **Econobingo.**

The skills of historical empathy are developed in **My View of the World** and **My Place.**

Research and information gathering skills are practiced in **My Place, The World in the School, The World in the Shopping Mall** and **Connections Board.**

Decision-making skills are utilized in **Made in Canada.**

Only Connect

Purpose   Developing connections between seemingly unconnected events

Grade level   4-12

Time needed   20 minutes

Resources   5 slips of paper and a pen/pencil for each student

Procedure

Students are asked to write down five words, one on each slip of paper, to represent each of the following categories.

1. a natural object
2. a manufactured object
3. an animal
4. an emotion
5. a hope for the future

Any words can be chosen; they do not have to follow a particular theme or pattern. The above categories are written on the reverse sides of the respective slips, and students place the slips on tables in front of them with the category names uppermost.

The teacher, who also acts as timekeeper, asks two students, chosen at random, to turn over their 'natural object' slips and call out what they have written down. The two students then have ten seconds to think of at least one way in which the two natural objects are connected. Should they fail to do so in the time allotted, other class members can contribute.

Each of the two students then chooses a classmate, whose challenge is to find connections between the two new objects revealed by turning over their slips. Other categories can be chosen at any time, the task always being to find connections between the two items on the slips.

When the activity is progressing well, the categories can be randomly mixed: connections can be sought between, for example, 'a manufactured object' and 'an emotion.' (As well as choosing a classmate, students can also select a category.) At this point, creative thinking will be required in abundance, and any type of connection should be allowed. The goal is to develop and enhance creativity, rather than to discover the 'optimum' connection.

Potential

This is an enjoyable and lively activity, using a 'game' format, that encourages the development of lateral and creative thinking skills and heightens students' sensitivity to potential connections between disparate phenomena.

Such skills and awareness are important if students are to fully understand the mechanics of the global system and how seemingly unconnected events and decisions can have an impact on their lives.

The development of relational thinking (seeing patterns and connections) also helps students to perceive connections between different curriculum areas and between the curriculum and the real world, thereby fostering a more holistic and relevant learning experience.

My View of the World

Purpose	Creating awareness of differences in worldviews and the reasons for them
Grade level	4-8
Time needed	40 minutes
Resources	Paper and a pen/pencil for each student

Procedure

Students read, or listen to, the extract (below), in which Flora Thompson describes childhood in a tiny Oxfordshire village in the 1880s.

> Beyond their garden in summer were fields of wheat and barley and oats which sighed and rustled and filled the air with sleepy pollen and earth scents. These fields were large and flat and stretched away to a distant line of trees set in the hedgerows. To the children at that time these trees marked the boundary of their world. Beyond their world enclosed by the trees there was, they were told, a wider world, with other hamlets and villages and towns and the sea and, beyond that, other countries where people spoke languages different from their own.... But they had no mental picture of these, they were but ideas, unrealised; whereas in their own little world within the tree boundary, everything appeared to them more than life-size and more richly coloured.
>
> *- Lark Rise to Candleford* by Flora Thompson,
> published by Oxford University Press, London.

There follows small group or class discussion about the kind of understanding of the world — or 'worldview' — the children in the reading would have had, compared to children today. What things would they **not** have experienced, seen or known about? Conversely, what things would they have understood or experienced more clearly than children today?

Working individually, students then reflect upon their own worldviews and draw up a map or sketch which represents their understanding of the world. They should think about their own travel and holiday experiences, as well as about knowledge gained from the media, books, parents and teachers. The map should have themselves in the center, with significant places, local to global, drawn around them. It should reflect the ways in which, through the influences of media, transport, telecommunications and travel, global perceptions are part of every student's experience — as compared with the world of Flora Thompson.

A series of overlapping ellipses or flower petals, each having a particular theme, could be used to graphically represent such a worldview:

Figure 1

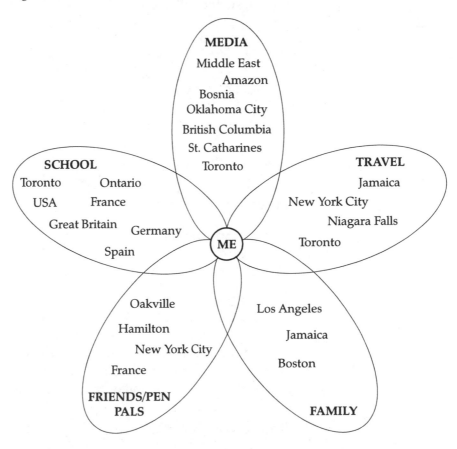

On completing their own maps, students meet in small groups to share and discuss their worldviews.

Potential

This activity encourages students to reflect upon their views of the world, how they have acquired them and how different they are from the worldviews of children living well over a hundred years ago.

Debriefing

Follow-up discussion might explore the impact or implications for individual students of such worldviews. For example, has the family holiday in Jamaica or the TV program on the Amazon led to any changes in personal habits, attitudes or behavior? Is there a corresponding line of influence the other way; for example, the impact of individuals spending their holiday time in the Caribbean or reading about Germany in a history book?

Further discussion could explore student predictions of how worldviews might change over the next hundred years, in the light of ever more sophisticated telecommunications and transport systems. What might be the ramifications for our ideas of 'local' and 'global?' Do we need a new term to describe the interconnection between local and global, such as 'glocal'?

My Place

Purpose — Stimulating thoughts about social changes that take place over time within the same neighborhood

Grade level — 6-9

Time needed — Several hours

Resources — Chart paper. Pens. Archival material from the neighborhood; for example, old machines used in the past, old dishes, old maps, historical documents and photographs.

Procedure, Part A

Working individually and from memory, students sketch maps of their own neighborhoods, marking those places which are significant to their lives (for example, home, school, park, youth club and shops).

In groups of four or five, the information presented on the individual maps is transferred to one large map; for this purpose, an actual street map of the area can be referred to in order to provide some measure of scale and distance. Other important sites in the neighborhood that come to light through discussion can be filled in at this stage, and brief notes written about some of the significant places.

Procedure, Part B

Students are then asked to imagine themselves in a time-machine, going back 25 years. Using any available archival material or anecdotal reports from parents and local residents, each group draws up another map of the same neighborhood, this time from the imagined perspective of a student of similar age 25 years ago. In particular, changes in land use or buildings should be recorded, as well as reported or imagined differences in leisure activities, shopping, transportation and road systems. Explanatory notes can be written, where appropriate.

Groups then meet to share and discuss their maps.

The above process of going back in time and re-drawing the map of *My Place* can be repeated as many times as desired, and at varying intervals of time depending upon the availability of archival material.

Potential

This activity is designed to stimulate thinking about social change within a neighborhood as viewed from a child's perspective. It utilizes and develops the skills of historical empathy in order to 'get into the minds' of children living at different periods but in the same location as the students themselves.

At any point in the process, follow-up work — at a particularly significant period, for example — might be undertaken.

Alternatively, students can put their time machines into forward gear. (See Extension below.)

A superb stimulus for this activity is the Australian children's book *My Place* (see Supporting Resources below), which documents, in ten-year intervals, 200 years of social history in fascinating and graphic detail.

Extension

Students go forward 25 years in time. What do they think their neighborhood will look like to students of similar ages? They should be encouraged to reflect upon the ramifications of possible/probable changes in transportation, employment, leisure and shopping habits, and to draw maps accordingly.

Variation

The same process can be directed towards identifying the degree of globalization of the locality in different time periods. To what extent was the locality caught up in the global web in terms of trade, dependence on imports and exports, population, manifestations of global cultural trends and media links, when the students' parents, grandparents and great-grandparents were children?

Supporting Resource
Wheatley, N. & D. Rawlins. *My Place.* Melbourne: Collins Dove, 1987.

The World in the School

Purpose	Developing connections between the immediate environment and the wider world
Grade level	4-6
Time needed	Several lessons
Resources	Paper and pen/pencil for each student

Procedure

Students divide into small groups, and each group plans to investigate and report on some aspect of the school's connection with the wider world. Some suggested areas of investigation are given in Figure 2.

Figure 2

Focus	What to look for/ask
Cafeteria	* national origins of dishes served * origins of ingredients used * places of manufacture of equipment
Library	* resources about other countries/ cultures/regions/religions * books in other languages * representation of variety of cultures in charts, photographs and illustrations
Caretaker	* origins of raw materials used throughout school (wood, metals, fabrics, etc.) * places of manufacture of technical and other equipment * multinational corporations providing goods and services
Staff	* staff who have lived in, been educated in or taught in other countries * staff who have traveled to other countries * staff who speak other languages
Students	* students who were born in, or whose parents came from, other countries * students who speak other languages * students who have traveled to other countries
Principal	* school links with people or schools in other countries * local residents from other countries/ cultures who support the school * curriculum areas that focus on other countries/cultures/religions

Before beginning their investigations, each group compiles a survey chart documenting their research strategies; for example, what questions to ask and of whom; what to observe and where to look; and what information to record and how to write it down.

Following the data collection, groups prepare an oral presentation based on their findings, using maps, charts, graphs and other visual aids where appropriate, to illustrate the nature and degree of the school's connectedness to other places.

Potential

This activity clearly illustrates the extent to which the school is a microcosm of the global community. It also develops and refines a range of research and data presentation skills.

Follow-up discussion could revolve around the question 'To what extent can we call this a Canadian school?'

Where links with schools in other provinces/countries exist, survey results could be exchanged.

Variation

A similar process could be used for a research project on 'The World in the Home.'

The World in the Shopping Mall

Purpose	Illustrating the immediate community's dependence on the global trading system
Grade level	6-9
Time needed	Several lessons
Resources	A world map. Various colored yarns. Pins. A Survey Chart (Copiable Handout 1▢) for each student.

Procedure, Part A

Students are divided into groups of three or four, and each group is asked to conduct a survey into the origins of goods, other than Canadian, sold in a particular local store. The stores selected should provide a good range, where possible — from food stores to hardware stores and pet shops. Previous contact with the stores is advisable to secure the shopkeepers' cooperation. A particular department could be chosen in a large store.

Working as a team, students complete Handout 1 as appropriate. For some items, all three columns can be easily completed; for others, only one or two will be possible (see examples given in Figure 3). In some cases, the help of a store clerk may be required where packaging is not used or the place of origin is not stated.

Figure 3

ITEM	WHERE GROWN/ MADE/ PROCESSED/ PACKED	MAIN RAW MATERIAL/ INGREDIENT	COUNTRY OF ORIGIN
Can of Corned Beef	Processed in Argentina	Beef	Argentina
Oranges	Grown in USA		
Coffee	Packed in Canada	Coffee beans	Kenya
Shirt	Made in Hong Kong	Cotton	USA
Table	Made in England	Mahogany	Brazil
Television	Made in Japan	Various	

ITEM	WHERE GROWN/ MADE/PROCESSED/ PACKED	MAIN RAW MATERIAL/ INGREDIENT	COUNTRY OF ORIGIN

Procedure, Part B

On returning to the classroom, each group's survey data are recorded on a class chart.

The countries specified are then marked on a large world map by a strand of colored yarn connecting two pins — one stuck on the country of origin, the other in the home village, town or city.

Different colored yarn can be used to indicate various categories of goods (for example, food products, building materials, electronic equipment).

Potential

A simple but effective way of illustrating the concept of a community's dependence on the global trading system. Also a simple but effective way of illustrating the concept of primary and secondary industries.

Debriefing

The activity can be used as a springboard for a variety of further research and discussion. What countries/regions are over-/under-represented on the world map? Why? Do we rely on certain countries for particular categories of goods? What are the reasons for different countries appearing in columns two and four of the chart?

Some important environmental issues can be explored; for example, the impact on the tropical rainforest ecosystem of importing hardwoods such as mahogany, and of using valuable fertile land in developing countries to grow cash crops to satisfy our demand for different foods.

The activity is a good vehicle for developing research and mapping skills.

Extension

The survey could also include local companies and factories, in order to determine the countries to which goods and services are exported, thereby illustrating the concept of the community's interdependence with the wider world.

Dependency Webs

Purpose	Exploring dependence and interdependence within a working community
Grade level	4-6
Time needed	40 minutes
Resources	Paper and a pen/pencil for each student

Procedure

Working individually, students draw up lists of people whom they regularly depend upon in the course of their everyday lives, and briefly explain the nature of that dependence. For example:

I am dependent upon:	for:
my mother/father	clothes/food/love/shelter
my teachers	new ideas and resources
my friends	friendship/fun/support
shopkeepers	goods I want to buy
police officers	a safe community
etc.	etc.

Students should be encouraged to think of people whom they depend upon but who are generally unseen; for example, hydro and telephone workers, bank employees, garbage collectors.

Individual lists are then shared in small groups, before discussion takes place. Questions such as the following should be considered by each group.

a. Do the people you have listed in any way depend upon you? If so, is the degree/scale of dependency equal or weighted towards one partner?

b. Whom do you think the people you list depend upon?

c. Are there different types or categories of dependency?

d. What would happen to your life if people upon whom you are heavily dependent were to suddenly withdraw their support?

Finally, students can draw their own dependency webs reflecting points raised in the discussion.

Potential

This activity encourages students to explore the concepts of dependence and interdependence through examining their own lives and communities.

Opportunities should be sought, too, to illustrate a fundamental property of a system — that the whole is equal to more than the sum of its parts (for example, things can happen in the community, as a result of people working in interconnected ways, that would not happen if they worked in isolation).

Extension

This activity is good preparation for the activity immediately following this one — Neighborhood Linking.

Neighborhood Linking

Purpose	Recognizing interdependence in neighborhoods
Grade level	4-8
Time needed	40 minutes
Resources	10 sheets of chart paper. 30 sticky labels. 10 variously colored balls of yarn. Scrap paper. Masking tape. A large open space in the classroom.

Procedure

Working in groups of three, students make lists of the neighborhood people they or their families have depended upon over the past week, explaining the nature of the dependency in each case (for example, doctor — for my medicine, garage attendant — for gas for the family car).

A class list is then compiled, and ten examples from the list are selected; these could be the ten people most frequently mentioned by groups, or the people whom the students consider the 'most significant' to the neighborhood.

Each group of three students now selects one of the ten chosen people, writes this person's title on three of the sticky labels (which are then affixed to each group member) and at the top of a sheet of chart paper (which is then affixed to the classroom wall).

Each group chooses one member to be a 'static negotiator'; the other two are 'mobile negotiators.' The ten static negotiators form a circle in the center of the room, but near their chart paper sheets (see Figure 4). Each static negotiator ties the end of his ball of yarn around his waist.

Figure 4

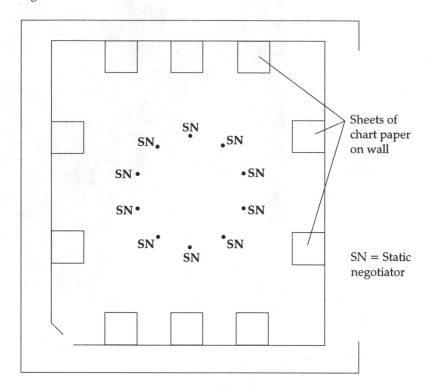

The task is for students to negotiate dependency links or connections between the ten people represented, imagining that they are all living and working in the same neighborhood. Negotiation takes the form of discussing and agreeing upon a likely two-way connection (for example, the doctor depends upon the garage attendant for gas for her car, and the garage attendant seeks the doctor's advice when he is ill). Both static and mobile negotiators can be involved in the discussion process, but static negotiators must remain firmly in position in the circle.

Each time a dependency link between two groups is agreed upon, the two balls of yarn are passed across the circle and looped around the waists of the static negotiators of the two groups concerned. It is important that the yarn is kept taut and that the ball is brought back to the static negotiator from whom it started each time. Mobile negotiators have the responsibility of recording the agreed connection on their respective sheets of chart paper.

As the activity continues, a spider's web of connections between the ten chosen people will be produced. Negotiations continue until all possible links have been made.

Potential

The multi-colored web offers a potent visual symbol of neighborhood interdependence.

Debriefing

Throughout follow-up discussion it is helpful to keep the web intact; this can be done by asking static negotiators to sit down, simultaneously, where they have been standing.

Students can be encouraged to describe some of the connections made — using the chart paper sheets as reminders — and instances where links were not found or agreed upon.

Consideration could be given to different types or degrees of dependency. Are certain people more vital than others to the existence and functioning of a neighborhood?

Links can also be made to global systems of interdependence — how is the web that has been constructed similar to/different from the interconnectedness of countries in the world? In what ways is the local dependency web connected to global economic, environmental and political systems? What might be the impact in the neighborhood of a dramatic national or international event (for example, a sudden embargo on all oil imports, a collapse of major stock markets in the Far East, or a rapid increase in average temperatures worldwide)?

It is important to help students realize that the two dependency webs — the personal and the global — are interconnected in many ways, and that an interdependent relationship is not necessarily of equal benefit or cost to all partners.

Connections Board

Purpose	Understanding Canada's place in the global system
Grade level	6-9
Time needed	Regular slots of time over several weeks or months
Resources	Large world map. Markers of different colors (or different colored yarns and pins).

Procedure

Students are encouraged to regularly monitor news programs on radio, television and the Internet, and to read newspapers and magazines. Their task is to seek out reported connections between Canada/Canadians and other countries, and to write explanatory notes about the nature of the connections. A connection should be defined as an event or trend that involves, or has implications for, both countries/citizens concerned (for example, Canadian peacekeepers in Bosnia, not just a news item about Bosnia on Canadian TV). Regular class time is set aside for student reports on connections they have discerned.

Once a connection has been reported and accepted by the rest of the class, it is entered on the Connections Board — a large world map pinned to a bulletin board — in accordance with a color-coded classification scheme. Some suggested categories of connection are:

Trade — goods	Entertainment
Trade — services	Sport
Aid	Arts/Culture

Emigration/Immigration	Environment
Tourism	Defence/Military
Natural resources	Law
Medicine/Health	Education
Human rights	Technology

A marker of the appropriate color is used to draw a line between Canada and the country or countries specified (or pins stuck in the relevant countries are connected with colored yarn). Where the links occur between particular regions or towns/cities, these can be located on the map and joined by the marker or yarn; otherwise, the seat of government in each country can be the point of connection. Letter and number grid systems can be used to aid location by students.

A further stage would be to consider the advantages brought about by the connection — who benefits most from this link (culturally, economically, politically, etc.)? The principal benefactor can be identified on the map by means of a one-way arrow on the line; two-way arrows signify mutual benefit of similar proportions. (If yarn is used, beads positioned in one or both countries can perform the same function.)

Periodic reviews of the Connections Board should be held, to discuss the nature and degree of Canada's connectedness to the rest of the world.

Potential

As the Connections Board is filled up over time, it will clearly indicate Canada's place in the global system.

Debriefing

Questions can then be asked about some underlying reasons for these connections and about the impact they have on the respective countries and their citizens. Are the connections 'one-off' events, as they often appear in the media, or do they have a history and a probable future? Are the connections principally to the advantage of Canada or of other countries, or are they of mutual and similar benefit? Why is this, and what does this say about Canada's economic and political status in the world?

How do the connections identified have an impact on the personal lives of students? What would happen in their lives if a significant set of connections (for example, trading links with the USA or Japan) were suddenly severed?

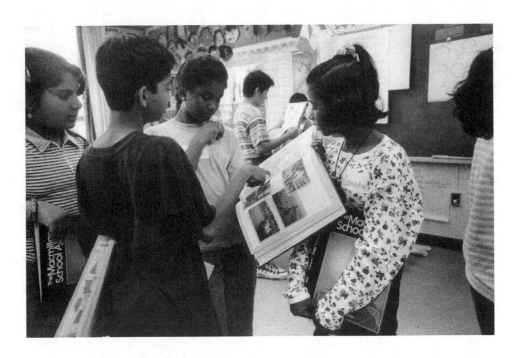

Globetrotting

Purpose   Reinforcing geographical knowledge and Canada's
connections with other countries

Grade level   6-9

Time needed   30 minutes

Resources   2 sets of sticky labels (Copiable Handout 2 ☐). Several atlases.
An open classroom space so that students can move about
freely.

Procedure

Students form a circle and close their eyes. The students each have a
label stuck on their arms; half the labels describe a connection between
Canada and another country, and the other half give the names of the
countries (see Copiable Handout 2 ☐).

When students open their eyes, they should find an appropriate partner, so that all countries and connections are suitably matched.

The teacher then asks the pairs to form groups according to various criteria (see suggestions below). Atlases can be used by students at any
time to help with gaps in their geographical knowledge.

1. Using the **countries** identified in each pair, form groups according to:
    a. northern and southern hemispheres
    b. 'industrialized' and 'developing' countries
    c. continents
    d. coastal and land-locked countries
    e. population (for example, less than 100 million, 100- 999 million
       and over 1 billion)

COUNTRY	CONNECTIONS
AUSTRALIA	A fellow member, with Canada, of the Commonwealth of Nations. Exports meat and dairy products to Canada. Aboriginals lived here for thousands of years before Europeans arrived.
BANGLADESH	An Asian country that exports clothing and yarn to Canada. Receives a large share of Canada's foreign aid. Dacca is the capital city.
BOSNIA	A European country where Canadian soldiers have served as peacekeepers. A civil war took place here in the 1990s.
BRAZIL	A South American country that exports coffee, rubber, footwear and automobile parts to Canada. A recipient of Canada's foreign aid. The soccer team is one of the world's best.
CHINA	An Asian country that exports salt, chemicals, clothing and toys to Canada. A recipient of Canada's foreign aid. This country has the world's largest population.
ENGLAND	The country from which the largest number of immigrants have come in the 20th century. The home of Canada's monarch.
FRANCE	The country from which some of Canada's first European settlers came. Now exports cheeses and perfume to Canada. Their language is one of Canada's official languages.
HONG KONG	An Asian territory from which the largest number of Canadian immigrants came in the years 1980-1995. Became part of China in 1997.
JAPAN	Canada's largest Asian trading partner. Exports photographic goods, rubber, machinery and vehicles to Canada. Tokyo is the capital city.
KENYA	An African country that exports coffee, tea and spices to Canada. A recipient of Canada's foreign aid. Famous for its wildlife parks.
MEXICO	A member of the North American Free Trade Association, and Canada's largest Central American trade partner.
RUSSIA	Modern name of the place from which some of Canada's Native peoples originally came. Now exports iron, steel, precious stones and metals to Canada. Moscow is the capital city.
SAUDI ARABIA	A wealthy country in the Middle East that exports oil to Canada. Mecca, the holy city for Muslims, is here.
SCOTLAND	Country of birth of Alexander Graham Bell, the inventor of the telephone. Many people from his country emigrated to Canada in the first half of the 20th century. Edinburgh is the capital city.
UNITED STATES OF AMERICA	Canada's largest trade partner, accounting for 75% of all exports and imports. The biggest foreign investor in Canada. Provides over 90% of Canada's tourists.

2. Using the **connections** described in each pair, form groups according to:
   a. categories of connection (for example, trade, migration, tourism and foreign aid)
   b. connections that directly impact on students' lives and those that do not

Variation

Students having a sufficient background of knowledge and experience in group work could carry out the activity without speaking. In this case the labels could be stuck on students' backs, rather than their arms.

Potential

This is a lively activity that assesses and reinforces students' knowledge about Canada's global connections and the geographical location of various countries.

   The whole group's success depends upon the degree of cooperation shown — not only in matching countries with connections, but also in helping each other to form appropriate groups.

Extension

As a final challenge to their global sense of place, the pairs can be asked to organize themselves, by country, into a human world map, with the teacher first taking up a position that represents Canada and students then adapting relative positions around her.

Econobingo

Purpose	Developing awareness of Canada's trading and economic connections
Grade level	7-12
Time needed	30 minutes
Resources	An Econobingo handout for each student (Copiable Handout 3 ▢). Open classroom space so that participants can move about freely.

Procedure

Students spread out and are given copies of the Econobingo handout (Copiable Handout 3 ▢). The purpose of the exercise is for each student to fill in as many squares as possible by obtaining information from other students. It should be emphasized that the name of the students and their answers should be written in the appropriate square, and that a particular student's name should only appear once on a sheet, so as to encourage the maximum possible interaction within the group.

ECONOBINGO

Find someone who:

A has an electrical appliance made in another country	**B** can name a country that receives foreign aid from Canada	**C** can name a country to which Canada exports timber	**D** has been a tourist in another country
E can name another country in which a Canadian company operates	**F** enjoys eating foods from another country	**G** has a pet whose species originates in another country	**H** can name a country where Canadian peacekeepers have operated
I has a watch or jewelry made in another country	**J** can name the country that is Canada's biggest trading partner	**K** can name another member of the G7 group of countries	**L** has seen a news item about the economy of another country
M can name a country from which Canada imports coffee	**N** has a friend or relative who works in another country	**O** has communicated with someone living in another country	**P** can name a country where clothes are made for sale in Canadian stores

A name _____ country _____	**B** name _____ country _____	**C** name _____ country _____	**D** name _____ country _____
E name _____ country _____	**F** name _____ country _____	**G** name _____ country _____	**H** name _____ country _____
I name _____ country _____	**J** name _____ country _____	**K** name _____ country _____	**L** name _____ country _____
M name _____ country _____	**N** name _____ country _____	**O** name _____ country _____	**P** name _____ country _____

Each time a row of four squares — horizontally, vertically or diagonally — has been completed, the students should call out 'Econobingo!' They should go on to attempt more rows (ten are possible).

It is important to encourage students to actively ask questions of each other, rather than passively swapping sheets.

Potential

This is a useful starter activity for work on Canada's trading and economic connections; it can also be used as a summary activity to assess students' knowledge. Students will probably make some surprising discoveries about their classmates, too. One way into follow-up discussion is to first ask about those surprises.

Debriefing

After exploratory discussion, the class can be encouraged to analyze and categorize the types of connections found during the activity (for example, links created through the movement of goods and people, by telecommunications and by the transfer of money) and also to examine and explain the frequency with which certain countries or regions appear on students' sheets.

Extension

Follow-up work could include plotting the countries mentioned on a large world map — to show the extent of Canada's economic connectedness — and exploring any one connection in more depth. Why, for example, are some Canadian clothes made in other countries? What is the rationale for Canada's foreign aid program, or for her peacekeeping services?

Source
Derived from an idea in: Johnson, J. & J. Benegar. *Global Issues in the Intermediate Classroom*. Boulder: Social Science Education Consortium, 1981.

Made in Canada

Purpose	Recognizing the potential global impact of individual decisions
Grade level	6-12
Time needed	40 minutes
Resources	A Decision Wheel chart (Copiable Handout 4 ☐). An information sheet on Canada's automobile industry (Copiable Handout 5☐). A pen/pencil for each student.

Procedure

Working in small groups, students read through and discuss the information sheet on the Canadian automobile industry. They are then given the task of reaching a decision on whether, as Canadian residents

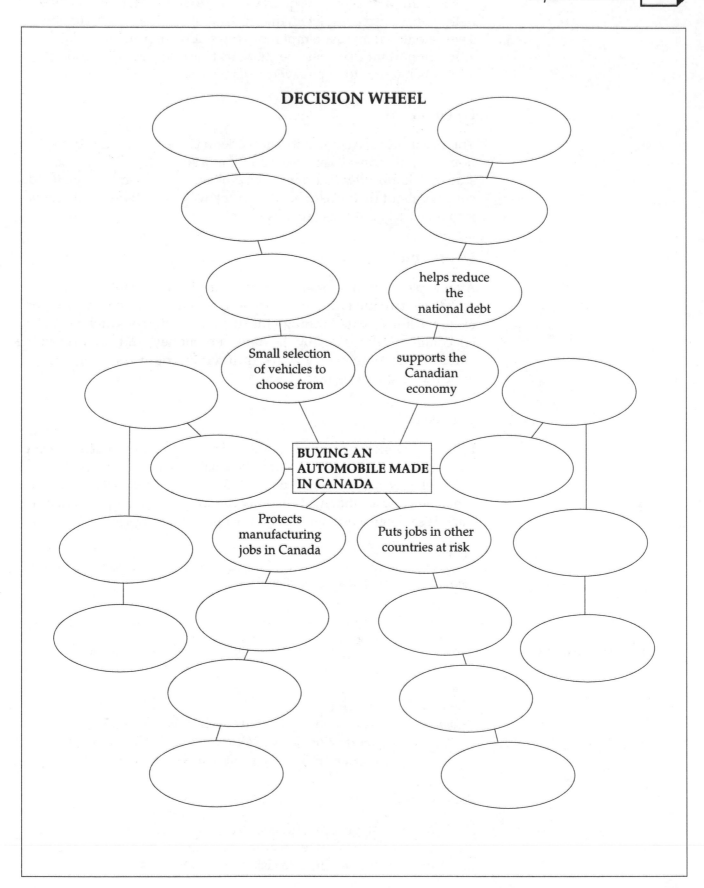

DECISION WHEEL

helps reduce the national debt

Small selection of vehicles to choose from

supports the Canadian economy

BUYING AN AUTOMOBILE MADE IN CANADA

Protects manufacturing jobs in Canada

Puts jobs in other countries at risk

CANADA'S AUTOMOBILE INDUSTRY

- Since the beginning of the automobile industry in Canada in 1904, vehicle manufacturing has grown into one of the largest industries in the country, worth over $40 billion a year. Canada's industry is the seventh-largest in the world.

- The industry is especially important in Ontario, where 80% of vehicle production takes place. Two cities, Windsor and Oshawa, are heavily dependent on this one industry.

- 75% of Canadians use cars to get to work, and for nine out of every ten trips they make. To make this possible, Canada has 850 000 km (528 179 miles) of roads requiring regular maintenance.

- About 150 000 people are employed in manufacturing vehicles and automobile parts, accounting for 7% of all manufacturing jobs. A further 80 000 people are employed in the sales and distribution of automobiles.

- North America accounts for two-thirds of total world production of automobiles, and has the two largest companies — General Motors and Ford.

- There are approximately 900 companies in Canada involved in making automobiles and parts. Many are owned and controlled by US companies. All vehicles built in Canada are designed elsewhere.

- Automobile companies are major consumers of steel, rubber, aluminum, glass, carpeting and fabrics. The production and processing of these materials accounts for about 300 000 jobs. The raw materials are imported from many countries around the world.

Sources of Information
Junior Encyclopedia of Canada.. Edmonton: Hurtig Publishers, 1990.
Statistical Review of the Canadian Automotive Industry. Ottawa: Statistics Canada, 1992.
DesRosier Automotive Consultants, 1996.

and consumers, their families should purchase a Canadian-made automobile (as opposed to one made in another country).

The decision-making process is to be undertaken by completing the Decision Wheel chart, based upon their interpretations of, and feelings about, the information they have read. Completing the chart involves filling in some or all of the remaining consequence wheels immediately around the central box (further wheels can be added if other potential consequences occur to students). Both positive and negative consequences should be included.

Groups then consider the second-order consequence wheels (in effect, the potential consequences of the first-order consequences) and complete the remaining wheels. Third-, fourth- and even fifth-order consequences are similarly written on the chart.

Finally, students examine all the recorded consequences, weighing the relative merits of any contradictory or inconsistent points that may have emerged, before coming to a final decision on whether to buy a Canadian-made automobile.

Group decisions, and their underlying reasons, are shared with the whole class.

Potential

This activity is designed to help students examine, in a structured fashion, the multiple consequences of any personal decision — not only for themselves, but also for other people at various points in the global system. Group members are to be encouraged to record a variety of potential consequences, without everyone necessarily agreeing upon their validity.

In reaching a decision, students might also briefly consider the reverse scenario — what are the potential consequences, in Canada and elsewhere, of purchasing a foreign-made car?

An understanding of the multiplicity of consequences of any personal choice can then be applied in many aspects of the students' own lives.

Variation

Older students can be asked to do their own research into the Canadian automobile industry before constructing their Decision Wheels on sheets of chart paper.

Source
Adapted from an idea in: Fitch, R.M. & C.M. Svengalis. *Futures Unlimited*. Washington, D.C.: National Council for the Social Studies, 1979.

The Global Rose

Purpose	Exploring global issues through themes/topics across the curriculum
Grade level	9-12
Time needed	60 minutes
Resources	A pen/pencil and a copy of the Global Rose sheet (Copiable Handout 6 ▢) for each student. Newsprint. Markers. An overhead projection transparency of the Global Rose (if Variation is followed).

Procedure

Following a class unit, a viewing of a film or a presentation by a visiting speaker, copies of the Global Rose sheet are distributed (Copiable Handout 6 ▢). Groups of four or five are formed, and students discuss the issues and questions raised by the unit/film/presentation through the lens of each of the petal headings.

Notes are written in each petal space. In the central 'Me' space, groups note implications that the content of the unit/film/presentation has for their own attitudes, behaviors and lifestyles. It is important that each heading is also addressed with an eye to future, as well as present, implications.

Heading by heading, groups present the issues and questions they have listed, with class discussion following.

Potential

A simple but effective way of raising students' consciousness regarding the presence of global issues and themes within any topic that features human beings interacting with each other and/or nature. As such, it will also consolidate understanding of how the several issues/themes interweave.

The Global Rose is best used on a recurring basis, across the curriculum. For instance, it can be applied to a Shakespearean play, a film on urbanization in developing countries used in a geography program, a unit on World War I, the score of an opera, or to the study of the social impact of scientific and technological breakthroughs. It can also be employed for analyzing photographs, cartoons or current news items.

Variation

A transparency of the Global Rose sheet is reflected on the wall. Each group traces the outline onto a sheet of newsprint. Issues and questions are written in, using markers.

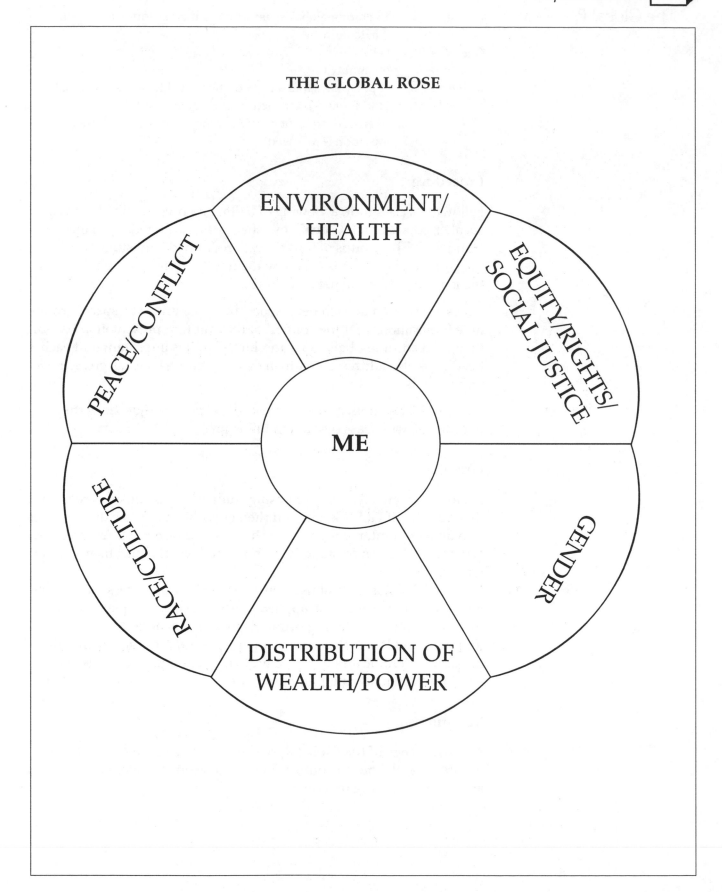

THE GLOBAL ROSE

Declaration of Interdependence

Purpose	Reinforcing understanding of interconnections
Grade level	9-12
Time needed	Several class periods
Resources	Masking tape. Newsprint and markers for each of the 4 groups. A copy of Copiable Handout 7 ☐ for each student.

Procedure, Part A

Towards the close of a course or program of study that has explored interdependencies within ecosystems, human-animal relationships, the interrelationship between human societies and the natural world, and/or the interdependence of lands and peoples globally, students are given the challenge of devising a Declaration of Interdependence.

Historical examples of national and international declarations are introduced (Copiable Handout 7 ☐), and their style, format, nature and purposes are discussed.

It is important to point out that most declarations are, in effect, three documents in one: a catalog of problems or grievances to be confronted, a general statement of values or first principles, and a listing of particular rights, obligations and/or resolutions that follow from the values/first principles enunciated.

Procedure, Part B

Dividing into four equal groups of seven or eight members, students brainstorm:
   a. the **various forms of interdependency** which they think should be addressed in the Declaration (for example, interdependencies at various levels of human society — local to global — between species and between the organic and inorganic)
   b. the **problems, distortions, inequities and threats to societal and planetary health** that currently mark the workings of the interdependencies identified (for example, the inequalities between the developed and developing worlds and between different groups within societies, the exploitation of animals and the destruction of species and ecosystems).
   c. the **values** that should be embraced if interdependent relationships are to be played out in the future in ways that promote the interests and well-being of all people, all species and the planet
   d. the **rights** that all people and all species should enjoy and, consequently, the **obligations** upon human beings within an interdependent global system

Four brief rounds of reporting back follow, the teacher collating ideas presented by groups under each of the four headings.
The class then discusses differences of opinion and emphasis that have emerged prior to determining a framework and structure for the Declaration.

Procedure, Part C

The four groups are then assigned the task of drafting one or more sections of the Declaration, drawing upon the lists of ideas and taking into account the issues raised in the plenary session.

In the agreed order, draft sections are presented, discussed and amended. (Should an impasse occur, students can be asked to return to their groups to draft alternative versions of the disputed text before reconvening to consider each others' drafts.)

The resulting Declaration is scrutinized for ambiguities and inconsistencies — first in groups and then in a plenary session — before its final approval by the class.

Potential

A demanding but rewarding cooperative process that will help students identify the shifts in values, priorities and behaviors necessary if relationships which are more just and equitable are to be achieved within and between human societies, and if human beings are to live more lightly on the Earth.

Extension

Copies of the Declaration can be sent to community, environmental and humane organizations; political and religious groups; and politicians, for feedback and comment. Alternatively, the Declaration can be transmitted by e-mail to groups in different parts of the world with an invitation to enter a dialogue.

Profile 1

Connections

by Judy Ross

Iroquois Ridge High School, located in Oakville, Ontario, is a new Halton Board school which has developed a school-wide philosophy to educate for a global perspective. In Grade 9, global issues are the framework for all programs. In Grade 10 through to graduation, the global perspective is infused into courses where possible. Such a focus has provided a structure for shared beliefs, interconnected practices and creative, activity-oriented learning. Central to this philosophy is the development of the characteristics of global learners. Global learners:

- recognize the interconnectedness of the world around them and develop the ability to think in terms of systems

- understand different perspectives, value the commonality of the human experience and recognize that there are diverse cultural views and beliefs

We hold these truths to be self-evident: That all men are created equal; that they are endowed by their Creator with certain unalienable rights; that among these are life, liberty and the pursuit of happiness; that, to secure these rights, governments are instituted among men, deriving their just powers from the consent of the governed; that whenever any form of government becomes destructive of these ends, it is the right of the people to alter or to abolish it, and to institute new government, laying the foundation on such principles, and organizing the powers in such form, as to them shall seem most likely to effect their safety and happiness.

          - **Declaration of Independence** of the American people, July 4, 1776

The representatives of the French people, organized in National Assembly, considering that ignorance, forgetfulness, or contempt of the rights of man are the sole causes of public misfortunes and of the corruption of governments, have resolved to set forth in a solemn declaration the natural, inalienable and sacred rights of man, in order that such declaration, continually before all members of the social body, may be a perpetual reminder of their rights and duties.... Accordingly, the National Assembly recognizes and proclaims the following rights of man and citizen.

1. Men are born and remain free and equal in rights; social distinctions may be based only upon general usefulness.
4. Liberty consists of the power to do whatever is not injurious to others (etc.).

          - **Declaration of the Rights of Man and of the Citizen**, France, August 27, 1789

Whereas recognition of the inherent dignity and of the equal and inalienable rights of all members of the human family is the foundation of freedom, justice and peace in the world,

Whereas disregard and contempt for human rights have resulted in barbarous acts which have outraged the conscience of mankind, and the advent of a world in which human beings shall enjoy freedom of speech and belief and freedom from fear and want has been proclaimed as the highest aspiration of the common people,

Now, therefore, the General Assembly **proclaims** this Universal Declaration of Human Rights as a common standard of achievement for all peoples and all nations, to the end that every individual and every organ of society, keeping this Declaration constantly in mind, shall strive by teaching and education to promote respect for these rights and freedoms and by progressive measures, national and international, to secure their universal and effective recognition and observance, both among the peoples of Member States themselves and among the peoples of territories under their jurisdiction.

Article 1
All human beings are born free and equal in dignity and rights. They are endowed with reason and conscience and should act towards one another in a spirit of brotherhood.
Article 2
Everyone is entitled to all the rights and freedoms set forth in this Declaration, without distinction of any kind, such as race, color, sex, language, religion, political or other opinion, national or social origin, property, birth or other status.
Article 3
Everyone has the right to life, liberty and security of person.
Article 4
No one shall be held in slavery or servitude; slavery and the slave trade shall be prohibited in all their forms.
Article 5
No one shall be subjected to torture or to cruel, inhuman or degrading treatment or punishment.

          - **United Nations Declaration of Human Rights**, December 10, 1948

DECLARATION OF INTERDEPENDENCE

THIS WE KNOW

We are the earth, through the plants and animals that nourish us.
We are the rains and the oceans that flow through our veins.
We are the breath of the forests of the land, and the plants of the sea.
We are human animals, related to all other life as descendants of the firstborn cell.
We share with these kin a common history, written in our genes.
We share a common present, filled with uncertainty.
And we share a common future, as yet untold.

We humans are but one of thirty million species
weaving the thin layer of life enveloping the world.
The stability of communities of living things depends upon this diversity.
Linked in that web, we are interconnected —
using, cleansing, sharing and replenishing the fundamental elements of life.
Our home, planet Earth, is finite; all life shares its resources and the energy from the sun,
and therefore has limits to growth.
For the first time, we have touched those limits.
When we compromise the air, the water, the soil and the variety of life,
we steal from the endless future to serve the fleeting present.
We may deny these things, but we cannot change them.

THIS WE BELIEVE

Humans have become so numerous and our tools so powerful
that we have driven fellow creatures to extinction, dammed the great rivers,
torn down ancient forests, poisoned the earth, rain and wind, and ripped holes in the sky.
Our science has brought pain as well as joy; our comfort is paid for by the suffering of millions.
We are learning from our mistakes, we are mourning our vanished kin,
and we now build a new politics of hope.
We respect and uphold the absolute need for clean air, water and soil.
We see that economic activities that benefit the few while shrinking the inheritance of many are
wrong.
And since environmental degradation erodes biological capital forever,
full ecological and social cost must enter all equations of development.
We are one brief generation in the long march of time; the future is not ours to erase.
So where knowledge is limited, we will remember all those who will walk after us,
and err on the side of caution.

THIS WE RESOLVE

All this that we know and believe must now become the foundation of the way we live.
At this turning point in our relationship with Earth,
we work for an evolution: from dominance to partnership;
from fragmentation to connection; from insecurity,
to interdependence.

The David Suzuki Foundation

- adopt healthy lifestyles in order to participate effectively as citizens of the world and to demonstrate commitment to personal and planetary well-being
- have communication, numerical and technological skills required for active participation in a global society
- take meaningful and responsible action to be life-long learners and to shape sustainable and satisfying futures

With support from the International Institute for Global Education at the University of Toronto and from consultants in the Halton Board, the staff, students and community work together to develop these characteristics.

Integration of a global perspective is a key focus of the Grade 9 program of study. **Connectedness** is the overriding theme of the transition program. It is a thread that runs through all courses, but with particular emphasis in the Humanities: a team-taught, integrated English and Social Science program taken by all Grade 9 students. As students work through the four core units, **Rights and Responsibilities, Peace and Conflict,** the **Environment** and **World Development**, their learning concentrates on the development of the broadest perspective possible through making connections at personal, local, national and global levels.

In the introductory unit, students read **A Parable**[1] to help them appreciate the importance of developing a global perspective. From there, students discuss and analyze the poem **The Thread**[2] as an illustration of global interdependence. To demonstrate the point, students, in small groups, take everyday objects (for example, chocolate, tissue, paper, coffee, baby food and t-shirts) and list all the stages, locations and personnel involved in their production. Students consider wages and profit margins, and discuss the moral issues of child labor and exploitation. Both introductory activities give students a flavor of the course as a whole while illustrating the theme of connections.

In the first core unit, **Rights and Responsibilities**, students are challenged to think in a broader context about human rights and citizenship, culminating in the production of an individual passport to demonstrate the rights and responsibilities of global citizenship. *The Chrysalids* (by John Wyndham) is the selected novel, as it effectively provides social commentary on human rights, community and citizenship.

In the **Peace and Conflict** unit, the skills focus is on cooperative group work and team building. Strong emphasis is placed on personal responsibility to enable the group to successfully meet its goals. Grade 12 peer mediators work with the class at the start of the unit to develop skills of collaboration and conflict management. To meet the English learning outcomes, students study *Anne Frank: The Diary of A Young Girl;* working in groups, they research and present topics relating to World War II to satisfy Social Science learning outcomes. Opportunities are taken to connect learning to other programs. For instance, students use skills developed in communications technology to produce hand-outs or even videos of their presentations.

For the **Environment** unit, the skill emphasis shifts to independent and integrated learning, as students select environmental problems to research and report on. Under the series title **Global Stresses, Strains and Solutions,** students produce a small book on the selected topic, appropriate for the Grade 6 level. As a result of the independent study, students are exposed to conflicting views about environmental rights and responsibilities, and are challenged to consider — and to present for discussion — both probable and preferred futures. The culminating activity of the unit occurs when the Grade 6 students from the local feeder school are invited to Iroquois Ridge to read and review the environmental books. This type of authentic task provides an opportunity for the Grade 9 students to 'put their books to the test!'

In the final unit, **World Development**, the concept of interdependence is selected; with the agreement of the whole team of teachers, one key focus statement is used to capture the essence of both interdependence and integrated learning — **the whole is greater than the sum of its parts**. Individual teachers then identify subject-specific skills and concepts to be covered, and work in subject teams to chart the points of connection that can be developed as they plan the unit in more depth from a subject point of view. In Humanities, students research and write a thesis essay with a focus on overpopulation as a global issue. Grade 12 students are invited into class: this time, as peer editors for the essay. Students appreciate the one-on-one attention and advice from the senior students. The culminating performance task of this unit is to create a portfolio of best pieces. The final reflective piece of writing challenges students to connect the unit to the key focus statement. As one student, Rob Edmonds, comments:

> Over the past three weeks, I have learned an incredible amount about world develop-ment. I have found this unit to be the most interesting and informative of the course. It has opened my eyes more fully to the problems our world faces. Learning about the connection between overpopultion and development, I now understand more fully the need for sustainable development and global interdependence. The key focus statement, 'The whole is greater than the sum of its parts,' suggests to me that the world cannot try to mend the problem of overpopulation and development by fixing up each country (the sum of its parts). A global approach is needed to solve the prob-lems that we now face. In fact, we need to make changes to the way our entire world operates (the whole) if we are to overcome these serious problems....

In the concluding unit, students are asked to reflect on the entire pro-gram to show how they have begun to develop the characteristics of global learners and to demonstrate the connections between units.

The program of study at Iroquois Ridge is continuously evolving as staff, students and the community provide input to maintain relevance and practicality. The keys to its success are teachers who are open-minded, diligent and committed to finding what works best, as well as students who are willing to take risks and provide constructive feedback. The result is a vibrant learning environment for all at Iroquois Ridge.

Judy Ross is a Grade 9 teacher and team leader, with responsibility for global education, at Iroquois Ridge High School. She has taught at schools in East Sussex, England, as well as in Ontario, Canada.

References
1. Pike, G. & D. Selby. *Global Teacher, Global Learner.* London: Hodder & Stoughton, 1988.
2. Bryan, S., ed. *The Issues Collection: Global Issues.* Whitby, Ontario: McGraw-Hill Ryerson, 1993.

3

Environment and sustainability

The environment is a broad concept that can be more easily understood when viewed as four interconnected elements, each with a particular focus:

1. **Natural environment.** The ecosystems, local to global, that maintain order and balance in the living world. The regulatory mechanisms of the biosphere that provide the right conditions for living organisms. The diverse flora and fauna — and their habitats — that can be found on the planet.

2. **Built environment.** Human settlements, from village to metropolis. The infrastructure of settlements, including buildings, public services, transportation and waste disposal systems. Individual homes, schools and community facilities.

3. **Social environment.** Interrelationships of people within and between communities and countries. Relationships between different cultures, faiths and other social groups. The interdependence of humans and other species.

4. **Inner environment.** The interconnectedness of views of self and views of environments, as well as of personal and planetary health. Personal awareness of, and attitudes towards, environments. Harmony between the physical, mental, emotional and spiritual aspects of self.

In reality, the environment is not neatly sub-divided. Through exploring the interactions of the four elements above, activities and programs can effectively demonstrate the crucial **interdependence** of all species. They can demonstrate the importance of **biodiversity** to the future of the planet. Thus they can rekindle our perception of humans as *part of* the natural environment.

Alternative **cultural perspectives** — particularly those of Aboriginal peoples — on a harmonious relationship with the environment can be especially enlightening. They can offer a thought-provoking challenge to dominant Western notions of environmental control and stewardship.

Analysis of **natural resource use,** particularly from non-renewable sources in the 20th century, heightens our awareness of the need for

conservation if the goal of **sustainable development** is to be achieved. The World Commission on Environment and Development defined sustainable development as 'development which meets the needs of the present generation without compromising the needs of future generations.'[1]

Intrinsic to the concept of sustainability is an acceptance of the need to consider long-term **futures** in any decision-making about the path of global development. Also intrinsic to sustainability is a commitment to moving swiftly from environmental awareness to action, if the present trends in **environmental degradation** are to be halted in time. Sustainability is predicated on the view that environments, economies and societies are deeply intertwined. Effective solutions to environmental problems will only be found through exploring the economic, political and social factors that have led to humans' abuse of their environments. Critical to sustainability, too, is **equity**. Development that perpetuates inequalities between rich and poor, or favors particular social groups, is neither just nor, in the long term, sustainable.

Effective environmental education is both local and global in its orientation. Awareness of global environmental problems, and the roles that individuals and societies play in their causation, is vital to an adequate understanding of interdependence and global systems. The local environment provides many opportunities for students to explore first-hand some manifestations of global problems. It provides opportunities to refine the skills of **environmental action** through involvement in community projects and campaigns.

Viewed holistically, environmental education has three interlocking strands:

1. Education *about* the environment. Studying environments and environmental issues, local to global, to develop knowledge and understanding of natural and human systems and their interaction. Learning about different opinions, perspectives and values in relation to the environment. Learning about possible solutions to environmental problems.

2. Education *for* the environment. Giving students opportunities to explore personal responses to their environments and to environmental issues. Nurturing appropriate attitudes and values for social and environmental responsibility. Helping students determine a framework of attitudes and practices that will allow human societies to function in ways that are both equitable and sustainable.

3. Education *in* or *through* the environment. Using local environments as resources for hands-on learning experiences and the development of a broad range of inquiry, communication and participation skills.

SKILLS INVENTORY

Many activities in this chapter develop, or can lead to the practice of, *environmental action skills*, especially **Water Watch**, **Carrying the Can**, **The Man Who Planted Trees** and **Our Ecological Footprint**.

ACTIVITIES	CONCEPTS													
	Natural Environment	Built Environment	Social Environment	Inner Environment	Interdependence	Biodiversity	Cultural Perspectives	Natural Resource Use	Conservation	Sustainable Development	Futures	Environmental Degradation	Equity	Environmental Action
Sensory Walks	*	*		*	*	*						*		*
Habitats Picture Match	*	*	*	*	*	*		*	*			*		*
Recycle Run		*						*	*					
Wastewatchers		*						*	*					*
Managing Packaging		*						*	*					*
Water Watch		*						*	*	*			*	*
Carrying the Can	*	*	*					*	*	*		*	*	*
Right Up Your Street			*	*							*			
Rainforest Fantasy	*			*	*	*								
The Man Who Planted Trees	*		*	*	*	*					*	*		*
Fruits of the Forest	*	*		*	*	*		*	*	*		*	*	
Selling Mother	*		*				*	*		*			*	*
Frightening Forecasts	*	*			*						*	*		
Our Ecological Footprint	*	*			*		*	*	*	*	*	*		*

Connections • Many activities in this series discuss the future in terms of environment and sustainability; see, especially, **Our Inheritance, Their Inheritance** (p.230), **Futurescapes** (p.237) and **New Year's Resolutions** (p.242). See, also, **Techno-Future Timeline** (p.206). Sustainable use of natural resources is explored in **The World in the Shopping Mall** (p.63), **World Food Distribution** (bk.2) and **Canadian Capsule** (bk.2). • The social environment is obviously linked to environmental aspects of health in Chapter 4 of this book, especially in **Healthy Classroom Charter** (p.139) and **Health Rights Continuum** (p.141). • **Inner Life** (bk.2) focuses on the inner environment. • Cultural perspectives on the environment are featured in Chapter 5; see **Moon Calendar** (p.158), **Sounds and Colors** (p.161), **Alpha Observers** (p.180) and **Bafa Bafa** (p.189). • A range of environmental issues can be pursued in **Environment Posters** (bk.2). • **Declaration of Interdependence** (p.81) reviews the values, rights and responsibilities associated with living in harmony with the planet.

Most activities incorporate group work at some stage, thereby providing opportunities for students to refine their *cooperation, communication and negotiation skills.*

Some activities require the *use of multiple senses,* notably **Sensory Walks**.

Imaging skills are employed in **Rainforest Fantasy** and **The Man Who Planted Trees**.

Research and information gathering skills are practiced in **Sensory Walks**, **Managing Packaging**, **Water Watch** and **Carrying the Can**.

Decision-making and/or values clarification skills are necessary for undertaking **Right Up Your Street**, **Fruits of the Forest**, **Selling Mother** and **Our Ecological Footprint**.

Selling Mother utilizes *role playing skills.*

Frightening Forecasts and **Our Ecological Footprint** offer practice in *prediction and forecasting skills.*

Sensory Walks

Purpose	Enhancing students' habitat observation skills
Grade level	1-6
Time needed	60 minutes
Resources	Camera. Crayons. String. Magnifying glass. Egg cartons. Hoops. Prisms. Paint sample charts. Paper and a pen/pencil for each student.

Procedure

With sufficient supervision suitable for the ages of the students, groups are taken out to explore a particular habitat; for example, a woodland, beach, field or park. Groups can be given the same or different tasks, depending on requirements. Some suggested tasks:

a. Take photographs of unusual or interesting shapes, or of ordinary objects from unusual angles.

b. Find items to match a rainbow color. (Take a crayon of the same color to draw items, rather than removing them from their settings.)

c. Lie flat and use a magnifying glass to follow the line of a string, for an 'insect's-eye view.'

d. Use mirrors (flat, convex and concave) held under your nose to get different perspectives on the world.

e. Listen carefully to every sound, with your eyes closed. What mental pictures are conveyed by each sound?

f. Place hoops on the grass, then examine and draw varieties of leaves, flowers and grasses within the hoops.

g. Look at plants and flowers through a prism, to simulate an insect's perspective.

h. Find different shades of one color (using a paint sample chart).

i. Using all the senses, discover what you can smell, hear, feel, see and (carefully) taste in any single spot.

j. Collect contrasting objects (for example, rough/smooth, dull/shiny, hard/soft, dry/wet and old/new). Each item must fit into an egg carton compartment.

Where appropriate, students record their observations and discoveries in note and pictorial form. Class sharing and follow-up work takes place back in the classroom.

Potential

Observation skills are essential in this activity, but other senses are also brought into play. Back in the classroom, students' experiences can be used as a stimulus for writing, art and craftwork.

Extensions

1. The same sensory walk can be undertaken in a different season, and the results compared.

2. To develop heightened sensory awareness, students combine their sensory experiences in unusual ways. For example:

   a. draw the color of a dog barking
   b. describe the sound of grass
   c. act out the taste of a hillside
   d. draw the texture of thunder
   e. describe the smell of clouds

Variation

In an urban environment, students can be given cards indicating various items that they need to find and record, such as something:

   a. necessary for life
   b. you think shouldn't be there
   c. that has a strong smell

d. you think is beautiful
e. you think is ugly
f. that sounds unusual
g. that feels interesting
h. that looks like two different things
i. that has two contrasting elements (for example, rough and smooth)
j. you've never seen before

Habitats Picture Match

Purpose	Exploring examples of human interference in natural ecosystems
Grade level	3-6
Time needed	20 minutes
Resources	10 sets of cards (3 pictures in each set) showing a species, its habitat and an example of human interference (Copiable Handout 1 ☐).

Procedure

The cards are given out randomly, so that each student has one card.

First, students are asked to form pairs to match up the species with the habitat. Then each pair is asked to find an example of human interference which destroys that habitat.

The activity is complete when all students are in appropriate groups of three.

Potential

An activity which requires cooperation and negotiation skills — it may be that some students form perfectly acceptable groups of three, but these particular groups prevent other groups from forming. Students then have to decide how they can re-form so that all are included. Discussion can focus on the effects on individual species of damage to their habitats. The words *rare, endangered* and *extinct* can be explained and the consequences explored.

Students might be asked to explore ways of reducing human interference in local ecosystems. What can they do?

Extension

Students get involved in action projects to repair damage to local ecosystems through, for example, replanting, clearing a stream or lake, picking up garbage, or campaigning against the use of chemical fertilizers and pesticides.

Variations

1. Students can be asked to form appropriate groups of three from the start, without first matching the species with the habitat.

2. With older students, the pictures are put out of sight. In order to find their partners, participants describe what is on their card.

Recycle Run

Purpose	Recognizing recyclable waste
Grade level	3-6
Time needed	20 minutes
Resources	6 sheets of paper (each with one of the following words written on it in large letters: *compost, fabric, glass, metal, paper, plastic*).

Procedure

For this warmup exercise, the classroom needs to be cleared and each sheet of paper stuck to walls at various points around the room.

Students gather in the center of the room. The teacher reads through the following story, but first explains to the students that each time they think something is thrown away, they are to rush to the appropriate 'waste collection point.' Then they should return to the center of the room so that the story can continue. As the story proceeds, students will have to listen carefully and interpret what is happening.

> I woke up this morning and went to the bathroom. After squeezing out the last bit of toothpaste, I threw away the tube. I took a new bar of soap out of the cupboard and threw away the carton. In the shower, I finished up the last drop of shampoo and threw away the bottle. After washing, I got dressed and noticed that my socks had holes, so I threw them into the trash can. I went downstairs to prepare some breakfast, but had to feed the cats first. I threw away the empty can. I poured the remaining cornflakes out of the box and ate them along with a banana. When I'd poured my glass of orange juice, the bottle was empty. I looked at the mail and saw that it was all advertising circulars that I didn't want. As I went towards the garbage, I knocked over my orange juice; fortunately, there was a roll of paper towels near by. However, the glass containing the juice was cracked. I wanted some toast, but the bread was stale. I finished off a box of doughnuts instead. I looked into my backpack and pulled out yesterday's sandwich bag, containing an apple core. I discarded some gloves that had become too small for me, and left for school.

The story can be changed, shortened or lengthened as appropriate.

Potential

This short exercise can be used as an active introduction to work on waste and recycling. It is designed to make students think about the number of re-usable or recyclable items that are thrown away during a normal day.

Debriefing

Follow-up discussion might focus on the difficulties of separating waste into different categories. What would be the advantages of having separate bins for different types of waste? What other categories could be included in the exercise?

Students could write their own story for a typical day — what types of waste do they throw away? Can they estimate the weight of the waste they throw away each day?

What are some of the environmental results of so much waste? What costs are involved in disposing of waste? What costs are involved in recycling?

Extension

To introduce the concept of *re-use,* students can be asked to raise their hands (when they reach the appropriate waste collection point) if they can think of a way of re-using the item in question.

Wastewatchers

Purpose	Identifying recycling opportunities and methods
Grade level	4-8
Time needed	20 minutes
Resources	A copy of Copiable Handout 2 ☐ and a pen/pencil for each student.

Procedure

Students are each given a handout with which to move around the classroom asking questions (Copiable Handout 2☐).

The task is to find twenty different people who will enable them to complete the form. A brief note of the response should be made where appropriate. Only one response is allowed from each person.

The activity is drawn to a close when most students appear to have found as many responses as possible.

Potential

This activity provides an introduction to consideration of waste problems, and highlights recycling and re-use opportunities and methods. It encourages individuals to reflect upon their own practices and knowledge, as well as to find out about those of their classmates.

Follow-up discussion could focus on the questions that were more problematic and what these tell us about our conservation awareness and behavior. What are the likely longterm consequences of continuing such behavior?

WASTEWATCHERS

Find someone who:	Name/Response
1. regularly turns off lights when leaving a room	
2. disposes of vegetable waste in a composter	
3. knows where the household garbage ends up	
4. uses recycled paper at home	
5. has given unwanted clothes to charity	
6. can tell a story about how the local environment has been damaged	
7. can tell you where the nearest sewage treatment plant is	
8. knows where the litter bins are in the school yard	
9. turns off the tap when brushing his teeth	
10. can tell you what resources she has conserved this week	
11. wears extra clothes rather than turning up the heating at home	
12. takes a re-usable bag when shopping	
13. can tell you the day of the neighborhood 'blue box' collection	
14. can describe three different ways of re-using a large cardboard box	
15. can tell you ways to re-use plastic containers	
16. has mended something recently	
17. has been wasteful this week, and can tell you how	
18. has taught somebody else about a conservation issue	
19. has disposed of something responsibly this week	
20. uses a watering can, not a hose, on the garden	

Extension

The students each devise a Wastewatchers action sheet containing up to ten different actions that they plan to take over the next week, two weeks or month. Each time the actions are successfully carried out, the sheets are marked accordingly. At the end of the allotted time period, students bring their sheets back to school.

Source
Developed from an idea by: Ann Harbron, Sugar Hill Primary School, County Durham, UK.

Managing Packaging

Purpose   Recognizing the impact of packaging on the environment

Grade level   4-8

Time needed   40 minutes

Resources   A set of 'Packaged Items' slips (Copiable Handout 3 ▢), which should be cut up and stored in an envelope. A marker and a sheet of newsprint for each group of 4 students.

Procedure

Students work in groups of four. On the newsprint should be drawn the two lines of axis (Figure 1).

Figure 1

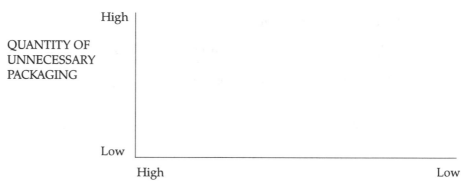

Each of the Packaged Items slips should be discussed in turn and placed approximately on the matrix in the position agreed to by the group. This may take time, since there could be differences of opinion within each group. It is important for groups to consider fully the purpose of the packaging.

A plenary discussion follows with the groups reporting on their decisions:

    a. Which items were easily placed and which were more difficult?
    b. Which items provoked the most disagreement; why?

PACKAGED ITEMS

package of breakfast cereal	canned drink
bottled drink	toothpaste
carton of milk	take-out hamburger
can of beans	sachet of ketchup
small bag of peanuts	prepacked sandwiches
video game	box of fruit
prepacked cheese	batteries
500 g (a pound) of butter	carton of eggs
packet of coffee	box of tea bags
container of yogurt	take-out pizza

c. What criteria did the groups use to assess whether an item ranked high in 'quantity of unnecessary packaging?'
d. How much of the potential for re-use/recycling do we actually realize in our everyday lives?
e. What else could we easily do?
f. Which packaging appears to be the most 'environmentally friendly' and which is the least?
g. What other factors would need to be taken into account before making any final assessment?

Potential

An activity which raises issues about the purpose and wastefulness of packaging. Discussion might lead to what action individuals could take to be less wasteful. How could students bring pressure to bear on a local supermarket or fast food restaurant to introduce a more environmentally friendly policy on packaging?

Extensions

1. Students investigate the percentage cost of packaging for individual items (for example, a package of individually wrapped cheese slices) by requesting information from manufacturers.

2. Students interview parents, grandparents and other older community members to find out about packaging practices in the past. (For example, North American 'newsprint' is called 'sugar paper' in the UK and 'butcher paper' in Australia. Why?)

Water Watch

Purpose	Developing an awareness of personal water consumption
Grade level	4-8
Time needed	2-3 hours over 2 weeks
Resources	A Water Use chart for each student (Copiable Handout 4▢).

Procedure

Using the Water Use chart (Copiable Handout 4▢) as a guideline, students monitor their personal use of water over seven days, in order to find out their average daily consumption. Household water use (for example, for the washing machine, dish washing, watering the garden and waste distribution) should be divided equally between the number of household members.

At the end of the allotted period, individual students' water use statistics are recorded on a class chart, which has been divided into categories such as *personal hygiene, household use* and *food and drink.*

There follows a discussion about the many aspects of domestic water usage, including health, hygiene, habit, comfort and time-saving.

Students are then told to imagine they are living sometime in the future when, due to prolonged periods of drought, the local water company has asked all residents to cut their water consumption by twenty-five per cent. Using their personal water use statistics as a basis, students work out where cuts might be made and then try to put their plans into practice during the next week.

Feedback should be gathered on how well their plans worked and on the resulting impact on their lives.

Potential

An action-oriented exercise which aims to develop students' awareness of their personal consumption of water and ways in which this could be reduced, if necessary.

Debriefing

It should be pointed out in discussion that although the renewable supply of fresh water could sustain many times the present world population, its uneven distribution means that some parts of the world have more than they can use, while others have barely enough for human survival. Climatic changes could seriously diminish the availability of water in parts of North America, while the demand for water from industry and domestic users is rising.

At the end of the activity period, students should review their water conservation strategies to assess which measures they might resolve to practice on a permanent basis.

Extension

The next activity in this chapter, Carrying the Can, is a useful follow-up, to place the issue of water scarcity into a global context.

Variation

A similar process could be used to monitor water use in school, with the help of janitorial and cafeteria staff. A water conservation action plan could then be collaboratively drawn up and undertaken, with resulting conservation figures being regularly broadcast to the school community.

Sources
Water statistics compiled from data from: Environment Canada, *New Internationalist*, Pollution Probe and Water Aid (UK).

WATER USE

(American gallons are referred to in this chart.)

| Personal washing | large basin | 8 | liters (2.1 gallons) |
| | small basin | 4 | liters (1 gallon) |

| Cleaning teeth | with tap running | 4 | liters (1 gallon) |
| | without tap running | 1 | liter (.26 gallon) |

| Flushing toilet | | 20 | liters (5.28 gallons) |

Showering		20	liters per minute (5.28 gallons)
Bathing	half-full	40	liters (10.5 gallons)
	full	80	liters (21 gallons)

| Dish washing | by hand | 25 | liters per day (6.6 gallons) |
| | by machine | 55 | liters per wash (14.5 gallons) |

| Clothes washing | by machine | 200 | liters per wash (52.8 gallons) |

| Drinking and cooking | | 15 | liters/person/day (4 gallons) |
| Garden watering | with hose/sprinkler | 35 | liters per minute (9.2 gallons) |

| Wasted in distribution through leaking pipes and taps | 50 | liters per person, per day (13 gallons) |

Average household use per person in:

Canada	350 liters per day (92 gallons)
UK	175 liters per day (46 gallons)
Nigeria	120 liters per day (32 gallons)
Bangladesh	45 liters per day (from a well) (12 gallons)

Minimum necessary per person for survival: 5 liters per day (1.3 gallons)

World use of water:

household, 7%
industry and agriculture, 93%

Canadian use of water:

household, 51%
industry and agriculture, 49%

Household water use in Canada:

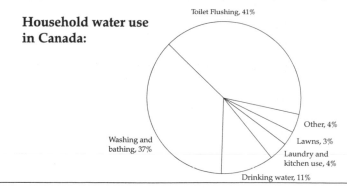

Carrying the Can

Purpose Understanding the world's water distribution and collection methods

Grade level 5-8

Time needed 2-3 hours, spread over a day

Resources A collection of water containers (for example, buckets and cans). Scales that will weigh up to approximately 20 kg (45 pounds). Access to a water tap. Water vouchers in various denominations. A Water Use chart for each student (Copiable Handout 4 ☐ from previous activity).

Procedure, Part A

On arriving at school one morning, the class is told that any water required by class members during the day will have to be fetched, using water containers, from a tap. (This tap is preferably at a distance from the classroom; alternatively, a circuitous route around the building or playground can be devised.) Only the girls are to do the fetching.

Students then assess their probable water needs up to and including recess, using the Water Use chart (Copiable Handout 4☐) as a guide. Every use of water — including washing hands, cleaning up and toilet-flushing — should be included. Drinks other than water, to be consumed at recess, should count as three times their actual quantity, to take into account water used in their manufacturing.

Once a class total has been reached, a group of girls is dispatched to fetch the required amount of water.

On returning to the classroom, each water container is weighed and a record is kept of the amount of water contained. (A liter of water weighs approximately 1 kg. A U.S. gallon of water weighs nearly 9 pounds. An imperial gallon of water weighs about 10 pounds.)

Vouchers, equal in value to the total amount collected, are then held by the teacher. From then on, any student who wishes to use water must first collect a voucher of appropriate value which is deemed 'spent' once that water has been used. The actual water collected can be used if appropriate; for example, for toilet flushing, cleaning, or watering plants in the school garden.

Procedure, Part B

After recess, a review of water used is carried out, and a further assessment is made of probable use up to and including lunch break. This should include a per person estimate of water used in cooking hot lunches and/or producing bagged lunches. Again, the girls are sent to collect the required amount.

The above process can be continued for most of the day, if appropriate, but at some point a full discussion of the issues it raises should take place. All or part of the information below can be shared with students.

Two-thirds of the world's households use a water source outside the home—and the water-haulers are invariably women. A person needs 5 liters (1.3 gallons) a day for drinking and cooking; 25 liters (6.6 gallons) more to stay clean. The most a woman can carry in comfort is 15 liters (4 gallons). Water is heavy—many pots and buckets carried on the head weigh 12 kilograms (26 pounds) when full; 18-liter (4.7-gallon) jerry cans (buckets) now commonly in use weigh (when full) 20 kilograms (44 pounds). It is not uncommon for women in some parts of Africa to spend five hours a day hauling water.

80% of disease in developing countries is related to poor drinking water and sanitation. Water quantity is even more important than quality when it comes to health—because a lot of water is needed to keep the body and household clean. The key to increasing the water consumption of the poor is giving them easier access to a supply. Until their distance from a source is reduced to less than 5 minutes' walk, water consumption does not rise significantly.

- **New Internationalist**, May 1990

Potential

This powerful activity attempts to simulate the reality of water distribution and collection for a majority of the world's people.

Debriefing

A debriefing might start with a sharing of feelings, in separate boys' and girls' groups, about the experience. Comparisons could be drawn with household chores in our own society which the students consider are more appropriate for members of one sex to carry out, and thoughts shared on the reasons why such attitudes persist. Further research and study could be carried out on the work done by women in developing countries.

The discussion should focus at some point on the importance of easy access to water in order to prevent disease; students can probably think of many examples of this in the industrialized world.

Did class members try to cut down on their water consumption during the day? Why? How? Was this potentially harmful to health? Are there ways we can reduce water consumption without prejudicing our health?

Right Up Your Street

Purpose	Understanding the effects of the 'not-in-my-backyard' syndrome
Grade level	6-12
Time needed	40 minutes
Resources	A Right Up Your Street chart (Copiable Handout 5 ▢) for each student

Procedure

Students are asked to imagine that the local government is proposing to locate each of the facilities listed on the streets where they live. It is important that students clearly understand what is meant by each facility — discussion might be needed for clarification. They then fill in the first column of their charts (Copiable Handout 5▢), indicating personal reactions according to the rating scale given at the bottom of the chart.

In completing the column, students should bear in mind any change in land use which may result from each facility; for example, changes:

a. in visual appearance
b. in the way people travel
c. in traffic volume
d. to air, water, soil and noise level
e. in the kinds of people in the neighborhood

When students have considered reactions to the proposed facilities on their own streets, they form pairs to compare and discuss the responses. Each pair then continues by completing the remaining columns on the chart. Class discussion follows, focusing principally on facilities that have been given a 4 or 5 rating.

RIGHT UP YOUR STREET

	FACILITY	On Your Street	In Your Neighborhood	In Another Neighborhood	In Another Town/City
1.	a small park				
2.	a 24-hour doughnut shop				
3.	a landfill site				
4.	a video game arcade				
5.	a funeral home				
6.	a halfway house for the mentally challenged				
7.	a pub with live music				
8.	a doctor's clinic				
9.	a hostel for home-less people				
10.	a self-service laundry				
11.	a place of worship				
12.	a gas station				

Rating: 1 = Highly desirable
2 = Desirable
3 = Don't mind
4 = Undesirable
5 = Highly undesirable

Potential

An activity which is designed to heighten student awareness of the 'not-in-my-backyard' syndrome.

Does feedback from the class highlight similarities in the services which generate most controversy? Do the reasons given only focus on environmental effects or are moral issues involved? What courses of action are open to residents if they wish to protest? Could anyone suggest an alternative to the proposed facility? What issues are raised by scores of 5 right across the grid?

Extension

Students discuss one or two of the facilities that have scored 4 or 5, and decide what course of action they would follow in order to contest the proposal. A list of possible actions should be researched and the potential consequences of each action fully explored.

Variation

This activity could be set within a national or global context, with facilities such as:

a. a toxic waste dump
b. a nuclear power station
c. a deforested area for ranching
d. a safari park
e. an oil terminal
f. a chemical plant
g. a dam
h. a research laboratory for tropical diseases
i. a munitions factory

Rainforest Fantasy

Purpose	Understanding the rainforest ecosystem
Grade level	6-12
Time needed	40 minutes
Resources	Paints, brushes, water and a sheet of paper for each student. A *Do Not Disturb* sign on the door. A clear space in a quiet room, preferably carpeted.

Procedure

Students are asked to take up relaxed positions, seated or lying on the floor, and to close their eyes. The facilitator further promotes a relaxed state by slowly reading the following text in a gentle voice, allowing for pauses at regular intervals.

> Try to make yourself as relaxed and as comfortable as possible.... Listen for a moment to the sounds you can hear outside the room...to sounds inside the room.... Be aware of how you're sitting or lying.... Just let yourself relax....

Let the feeling of relaxation spread through your body.... Be aware of your toes.... Squeeze them tightly...relax them...squeeze them...relax them.... Let the relaxation spread up through your ankles, your calves, your knees and your thighs.... Let the relaxation flood through your stomach, your chest, your neck and your shoulders...and down your arms.... Squeeze your hands tightly...let them relax...squeeze them...relax them.... Let the muscles of your face relax.

After a somewhat longer pause, the facilitator continues by reading *In the Rainforest* (page 109), allowing sufficient time after each new image for students to really grasp and 'live' the experience. Relaxing background music can be useful to help set the appropriate tone. (See Supporting Resources.)

At the end of the reading, the facilitator should allow students a few moments, with prompts if necessary, to return in their minds to the classroom before opening their eyes. (The first paragraph of the script can be used in reverse order.) Without any discussion, students use the painting materials to portray an aspect or image of the fantasy journey which is significant to them. An 'art gallery' of these pictures can be set up as a way into general discussion about the rainforests.

Potential

This fantasy journey is designed to give students a general understanding of, and feel for, a 'typical' rainforest ecosystem, as a precursor to work on the complex issues surrounding rainforest destruction. It conveys a lot of factual information about the rainforest and its inhabitants, presented through a medium which is a powerful aid to learning for many students.

Students who are not used to fantasy or visualization activities may need to practice the necessary skills through some introductory techniques. (See Supporting Resources.)

Debriefing

Follow-up work could take any number of directions, from providing a more scientific and explicit account of the forest ecosystem, to researching, discussing and writing about deforestation and its potential ramifications for the planet.

Supporting Resources
Guidelines for using fantasy and visualization techniques can be found in: Pike, G. & D. Selby. *Global Teacher, Global Learner.* London: Hodder & Stroughton, 1988, pp. 184-193. Good sources of introductory activities are:
Hendricks, G., P. Hendricks, & R. Wills. *The Centering Book.* Upper Saddle River, New Jersey: Prentice-Hall, 1975. Hendricks, G. & T. Roberts. *The Second Centering Book..* Upper Saddle River, New Jersey: Prentice-Hall, 1977.
Other fantasy journeys on environmental themes can be found in: Seed, J. et al. *Towards a Council of All Beings.* Toronto: Heretic Books, 1988.
Spirit of the Rainforest, by Terry Oldfield (New World Cassettes, 1991), provides suitable background music.
Extracts from *Earthrise: The Rainforest Album* (the official 1992 UN Earth Summit album) can be used to stimulate further work on rainforests.

Yanomamo, by Peter Rose and Anne Conlon, is a 90-minute musical on the fate of the Amazon rainforest. Audio cassette, video, full score and words are published by World Wide Fund for Nature, UK, and are available from Green Brick Road, c/o 8 Dumas Court, Don Mills, Ontario, M3A 2N2, Canada; tel. (416) 421-9816 or 1-800-473-3638.

IN THE RAINFOREST

You are to imagine yourself leaving the classroom, floating up into the clear blue sky. You look down and see your school far beneath you, getting smaller. You can now see the outlines of towns and cities, hills and forests, lakes...and you begin to see the outline shape of the continent of North America, with a great ocean on each side as it slides beneath you...(longer pause)...You feel yourself starting to descend....You can just pick out the shape of a country that you don't recognize....You can now make out details of rivers, hills, a city, a town....You seem to be heading towards a mass of trees....You're floating gently down through a tiny space between huge branches... down and down until your feet touch the soft and springy ground.

You find yourself in the middle of a rainforest. You look cautiously around you in the gloomy light. Your eyes follow the slender trunk of a tree straight upwards to a dense, green canopy through which thin shafts of light emerge. Twisted around the trunk, all the way to the top, is a rope-like vine appearing to strangle the tree. You then notice other vines, thick and thin, straight and curly, clinging to every tree and plant, forming a tangled mass in every direction. Following a woody vine down to the ground, you notice that the forest floor is surprisingly bare. Few plants or flowers grow out of the thick, spongy mat of roots beneath your feet, though many large tree roots stick up out of the ground like giant wooden snakes. Some trees seem to be propped up by thick buttresses growing out of their trunks, as though they are very old buildings in danger of collapse. Mosses and lichens cover everything in a cloak of soft green velvet from which curious plants with bulbous stems and thick, waxy leaves emerge. Around your feet, weird and wonderful fungi sprout up like mushrooms in a variety of shapes and colors.

As you stand there, feeling very small beneath the towering trees, you become aware of the stillness of the forest. It's a bit eerie: like being in a deserted place. Then, gradually, you pick out some sounds: the snuffling of a wild pig rummaging around among the roots near by; the squawking of a pair of blue and yellow macaws flying overhead; the scampering of a troupe of spider monkeys high up in the branches of a fig tree; and, in the far distance, the drawn out groan of a giant tree toppling over and finally crashing onto the forest floor.

You become aware, too, of the ceaseless activity of insects, many of which you've never seen before. You recognize some of them—butterflies, beetles, spiders and snails — but their size is astonishing. You feel as though you've shrunk in size, a bit like Alice in *Alice in Wonderland,* when she falls down the rabbit hole. A bright blue butterfly on a nearby fern opens its wings, each as big as the palm of your hand. The millipede inching its way along a twisting vine must be nearly the length of your foot, and the giant snail stuck to the bark of the tree above your head seems in danger of being crushed by the weight of its own enormous shell. Your attention is caught by a thin, never-ending line of leaf-cutting ants, each carrying a piece of green leaf or stalk several times larger than its own body size.

Feeling a little bolder, you move forward gingerly, ducking underneath the trailing vines and stepping over ankle-twisting roots. As you move, your clothes stick to your back and legs and your head throbs, in the hot, humid air. There is a damp, earthy smell everywhere, occasionally overpowered by the sweet scent of an unknown plant. Suddenly, huge drops of water fall on your head. Looking upwards, you realize that you are caught in a tropical storm; however, the green canopy formed by the tree branches high above you is like a giant umbrella, with just a few holes in it. As you watch the raindrops trickling down the tree trunks, the whole forest seems to burst into life. Insects that you've never seen before scurry out of their tree homes; anteaters scuffle around searching for food with their long, sticky tongues. A wonderful array of moths, butterflies and birds display their full colors above your head. Higher still, howler monkeys roar and parakeets cry out.

Then a strange thing happens. You feel yourself being lifted off the ground. You are floating upwards towards the green canopy. You pass skillfully through a tangled knot of vines and, looking down, you catch a fleeting glimpse of a jaguar as it glides through the undergrowth. In a small clearing down to your right, a spotted deer and her young are feeding. As you gently rise, more light filters through and you find yourself among the lower branches of the trees. Here, a long way from the ground, is a wholly different world. You watch the amazing acrobatics of squirrels, mice and monkeys swinging and leaping from tree to tree; snakes, lizards and frogs slide and slither along the branches, while the curious three-toed sloth hangs serenely upside down, camouflaged by the green algae growing on its fur.

Now you are in the thick of the green canopy itself. Huge spreading branches end in sprays of pink and purple flowers; still clinging to the trees the longest vines fight for available space and sunlight with giant ferns and bright yellow orchids. Brilliant splashes of color are provided by birds of paradise and the great orange beaks of the toucans. Monkeys chatter away but with an ever watchful eye on the monkey-eating eagle which hovers above the canopy. You feel the heat of the sun on your head as the rain clouds drift away and you are thrust out into the deep blue of the sky. As you drift higher the vast green ocean of rainforest spreads out beneath you. You can spot the glinting lines of rivers winding through the trees; here and there, in a clearing, thin plumes of smoke show where families of nomadic people are living. On the distant horizon, the menacing clouds of dark smoke tell a different side of the rainforest story.

The Man Who Planted Trees

Purpose   Recognizing the importance of tree-planting programs
Grade level 6-12
Time needed 60 minutes
Resources   A copy of **The Man Who Grew Happiness** article for each student (Copiable Handout 6 ☐) — optional

Procedure

Students read, or have read to them, **The Man Who Grew Happiness** (Copiable Handout 6☐). It should be explained that Jean Giono's

THE MAN WHO GREW HAPPINESS

There is a road that runs from Vergons to Banon, in that ancient region of France where the Alps thrust down into Provence. It has known many travelers and many changes. If you go there today, you will pass through a beautiful forest — verdant, lush and hospitable. It was not always so....

To travel that road at the beginning of this century was almost a sign of madness. It was an unholy area, then. The land was arid and empty; nothing grew there, and no birds sang. The only inhabitants were remote one from the other, and a living could be scratched from the dusty soil only with such great difficulty that life was cheap — travelers and even natives walked alone there with a knife in their belts. Gray shadows cast by the red crags offered shade, but weren't to be trusted. There were no trees against which to rest one's back.

Jean Giono first traveled that road as a student in the summer of 1913. His journey was an attempt to 'find himself,' but at the end of one particular day, he was regretting his simple foolhardiness in setting out to cross the badlands on foot. There were no trees, no windbreaks and no vegetation to fix the soil. His face was stung continually by glassy grains of sand flung at him by the hot wind. The western horizon melted into the burning sky. And like a grumbling jackal, the wind seemed to circle the ruined village Jean had reached, with its roofless houses and the chapel with its crumbing steeple. The cluster of dwellings looked like an old wasps' nest, and the spring was dry. If only there were some water; if only there were some greenery — some sign of life and growth....

All at once, against the sun and stinging wind, an old man appeared, in a beret and woolen waistcoat. 'You look worn out,' the old man said. 'Come with me, and I will give you water, food and shelter for the night. Then tomorrow, you will be able to complete your journey.' There was a look of calm reassurance in the old man's eyes that lifted Jean's spirits; the offer of a roof for the night was more than he could have wished for.

The old man was a shepherd, and his cottage was the only fully roofed dwelling in the ruined village. Jean couldn't see how thirty sheep and one shepherd could sustain themselves in that barren valley without trees, without vegetation, without water. But the old man assured him it was possible. 'Besides,' he said, 'I don't intend to be a shepherd all my life. I am planting a forest, you see.'

Jean accepted this and other strange utterances without probing. After supper, he watched in silence as the old man fetched a sack and poured out a heap of acorns onto the table. He started to inspect them one by one, separating the good from the bad. 'Can I help?' Jean asked.

'Thank you, but no. The task is mine.'

Eventually, the old man seemed satisfied with his heap of good acorns, and he started to count them out in tens, inspecting them even more rigorously than before and discarding those that were small or slightly cracked. Jean watched in silence as the shepherd's fingers thus selected one hundred perfect acorns.

As they slept that night, the wind on the cottage's old tiles sounded like waves lapping on a Mediterranean shore, and Jean dreamed of beautiful green forests with the breeze lightly rustling the leaves; of smiling, healthy people beckoning him to a pool in a glade where others were already swimming and diving.

Next morning, despite having a destination to reach, Jean followed the old shepherd, whose pasture was down in the valley. At first, Jean could not work out why the old man was carrying an iron rod as thick as a man's thumb and about four feet (just over a meter) long. As he watched, it gradually became clear. In addition to his iron staff, the shepherd was carrying his sack of one hundred perfect acorns, and every ten yards (just over nine meters) or so he would thrust his rod into the earth, insert an acorn and refill the hole. He was planting the entire hillside with baby oaks.

'Does this land belong to you?' Jean asked.

'No.'

'Do you know whose it is?'

'No,...I suppose it's common land. Maybe it belongs to someone who doesn't care about it. Anyway, it's not important.'

'How long have you been doing this?'

'About three years.'

'One hundred acorns a day for three years?'

'That's right. I must have planted one hundred thousand. I reckon twenty thousand have sprouted. We'll probably lose half of them to rodents and frost, but there should still be ten thousand oaks soon, where there was nothing before.'

The old man was also studying the reproduction of beech trees, and tending a nursery of seedlings grown from beechnuts near his cottage. He was sure there was water just below the surface of the soil in the valley. 'That valley was just made for beeches.'

Jean left with a curious mixture of memories: of the barrenness of the landscape and the sensuous dream of his cool forest-glade. He completed his journey that day, and put the encounter out of his mind.

Returning to his old life, he was thrust into the Great War (World War I), which he survived. Then, with his...pay in his pocket and memories of mud and fields of white crosses in his brain, he found himself going South — drawn towards the sun as unwittingly as a crocus in Spring. He traveled again down that road between Vergons and Banon, scarcely recognizing it. He assumed that memories of the war had affected all his other memories. But the lack of recognition was a result of the total transformation of the place over the previous six years. Instead of a treeless, barren, erosion-scarred landscape, Jean could see a kind of silver-grey mist that covered the hills like a carpet. Young trees were everywhere.

That night, Jean slept peacefully amongst the lavender bushes and sapling birches growing near a deserted village. Towards dawn, he dreamed he was walking in a beautiful, shady forest and was being beckoned towards a pool in the middle of a glade where young bodies gleamed and flashed in the sunlight reflected off the water. The man beckoning him wore a beret and a woollen waistcoat. He had a look of calm assurance on his face that Jean remembered but couldn't place. He was on the verge of placing the dream when he woke up. The early morning light was gleaming silver on the delicate birch limbs, and there was a rustling breeze in the Spring-green leaves. The man with the beret was looking at him.

'I know you,' he said. 'You were here before.'

Through images of men's faces frozen in death, came the face of the shepherd. Yet surely this was not sheep country? Six years ago, this land had been barren — worse than barren; it had been dead, life-threatening. Yet here vegetation was burgeoning — the air was tranquil and trees stretched as far as Jean could see.

The old man nodded. He wasn't quite smiling, but there was a contented set to his mouth, and his look of silent assurance finally jogged Jean's memory. Oh, yes; he had been there. But he could scarcely believe the transformation. As if he understood Jean's disbelief, the old man nodded and gestured at the trees growing all around them, with the pride of a father presenting his first-born. Later, still with his fatherly pride, the old man led Jean 'round his forest. (He was no longer a shepherd — he had only four sheep, now, and instead looked after one hundred beehives.) The fruits of his labor — ten thousand oaks and one thousand beeches — were as evident as the accuracy of his prediction about the water beneath the sand in the valley.

A vast forest of saplings — oaks, beeches, birches — stretched around them in three sections for a length of eleven kilometers (nearly seven miles) and up to a width of three kilometers (nearly three miles). Jean was struck dumb as the former shepherd led him all day, like a convalescent, around his shoulder-high forest. It was as if Jean had been blinded by staring into the center of an exploding shell, and now the old man was giving him his sight back. The sensual delight of seeing silenced Jean and stilled all memories of war. It was incredible to imagine that in 1915, when Jean had been fighting in Verdun, the old man had been planting birches that now stood slender and delicate as young dancers. It was incredible that a forest should have sprung from one man's efforts; from one man's vision and patient toil.

It wasn't just a forest that had grown. Over the years, the road that runs between Vergons and Banon became busier and busier, as more and more travellers headed for the now beautiful area away from their treeless workplaces. The numbers of picnickers and day-trippers began to pose a threat to the wood, and in the 1930s it was put under the protection of the national forestry department as part of the region's natural heritage. The old man was given a lecture by one of the rangers: 'We can't have anyone lighting fires, now; can we, sir? We wouldn't like to endanger this beautiful forest, now; would we? Especially since it's grown so miraculously of its own accord.' The old man probably smiled and nodded, as he had done to Jean, with the quiet assurance of one who knows that tomorrow he will be out again, planting beechnuts.

As the forest grew, so the little village, derelict and deserted since 1900, started to revive. The ruins were cleared away, and in 1946, when Jean Giono visited the old man for the last time (he was eighty-seven years old and two years from his death), five houses had been restored. By now, twenty-eight people lived there, including two young married couples. Their new houses, freshly plastered, were surrounded by gardens where vegetables and flowers grew in orderly confusion — cabbages and roses, leeks and snapdragons, celery and anemones. Even the air felt full of life; instead of the harsh, hot winds that had stung his face in 1913, a gentle breeze was blowing, laden with scents. A sound like water — the wind in the trees — came from the hillside, and Jean heard the actual sound of water falling into a pool. A fountain had been built.

It was flowing freely, and beside it a linden, probably four years old, was already in full leaf. The old man showed Jean that particular tree with especial pride.

'Someone else is planting, now,' he said.

There is a road that runs between Vergons and Banon, in that same ancient region of France where the Alps thrust down into Provence. Travel it today, and you will discover a countryside aglow with health and prosperity. Neat farms testify to a happy and comfortable life. The old streams, fed by the rains and snows that the forest conserves, are flowing again. Their waters have been channeled. On each farm, in groves of maples, fountain pools overflow onto carpets of fresh mint. Along the roads, you meet hearty men and women, boys and girls, who understand laughter and the delights of shady clearings. All in all, more than ten thousand people owe their happiness to the unfailing greatness of spirit and tenacity of purpose of a single old man — an old man who planted trees and grew happiness.

New Internationalist, June 1988. Adapted by Simon Lewis from Jean Giono's **The Man Who Planted Hope and Grew Happiness**, published by Friends of Nature Inc., Brooksville, Maine.

original story (from which the article is adapted) is an imaginary tale written in 1953 'to make people love the tree or, more precisely, to make them love planting trees.' Since then it has been translated into more than a dozen languages and has inspired reforestation efforts worldwide.

Following discussion about the story, students are asked to imagine that they are returning in forty years' time to an area which they know well but which is, at that time, lacking in tree cover and other natural vegetation. In the meantime, a tree-planting program has gradually changed the landscape of this area.

On their return, what differences do they notice? Students should be encouraged to think about not only the physical changes brought about by tree planting, but also imagined changes in transport, leisure and work patterns, and those resulting from other environmental trends. Their senses of smell, touch, hearing and sight should be used in their imagining.

The outcomes of this future visualization can be recorded as a story or poem, as an individual or group oral presentation, as artwork, or using a combination of media.

Potential

An activity in which students' imaginations are employed in order to help them understand the likely impact and longterm benefits of a comprehensive tree-planting and naturalization program.

The activity also provides a framework for making predictions about the future impact on the environment of present social and economic trends.

Extension

Follow-up discussion could explore what action students might take to improve, in a small way, their local environment. This activity would provide an excellent springboard for schoolground naturalization projects. (See Supporting Resources.)

Supporting Resources
Jean Giono's original story, *The Man Who Planted Hope and Grew Happiness*, is published by Friends of Nature Inc. of Brooksville, Maine.
Useful publications on schoolground naturalization include:
Using School Grounds as an Education Resource, by Kirsty Young and *The Outdoor Classroom: Educational Use, Landscape Design & Management of School Grounds*, by B. Billimore, J. Brooke, R. Booth and K. Funnell. Both books are available from Green Brick Road (see p. 109 for address and telephone number).

FRUITS OF THE FOREST CARDS

Firewood

One-third of the world's people rely on firewood for heating and cooking. In the poorest countries of the world, most wood collected is used for fuel.

Cattle

Large areas of rainforest are cleared so that cattle can be grazed. Much of the resulting beef is used for making hamburgers in wealthy countries.

Medicines

Extracts of many forest plants are used as the basis of modern drugs. Quinine (from the bark of the *cinchona* tree) is widely used to treat malaria, and extracts from the *rosy periwinkle* are effective cancer treatments.

Paper

The world uses an enormous quantity of wood pulp to make paper — an estimated four billion trees are cut each year for paper. One large issue of the *New York Times* is the end product of 400 hectares (988 acres) of forest.

Medical Research

Drug companies are studying thousands of rainforest plant species used in medicines by Native peoples. Some of these may contain cures for diseases like cancer.

Pets

Rainforest birds, such as parrots and macaws, are sold and kept in cages in Western countries. Iguanas are popular house pets, too.

Food

Many common foods — including coffee, bananas, cocoa and rice — originated in the rainforest. Genes from these wild plants are still required to make new strains which are resistant to disease.

Skins

The skins of wild cats from the rainforest — such as the jaguar and the ocelot — are used to make expensive fur coats. An ocelot coat is made from ten skins.

Hardwood

Prized hardwoods — like mahogany, teak and cedar — are used to make quality furniture, window frames, boats and musical instruments.

Mining

Many important minerals — such as gold, iron ore, tin and aluminum — have been found in rainforest areas. Mining causes extensive damage to the land.

Electricity

Over 30 hydroelectric dams are planned in the Amazon basin, with the result that huge areas of rainforest will be flooded. Much of the electricity produced will be used by local industry.

Transport

Mining, logging and other forest industries require the construction of road and rail networks through thousands of kilometers, or miles, of rainforest.

Fruits of the Forest

Purpose	Recognizing forest product uses and their impact on the ecosystem
Grade level	7-12
Time needed	40 minutes
Resources	Glue or paste. Set of Fruits of the Forest cards (Copiable Handout 7 ▢) and a strip of paper (made by cutting newsprint lengthwise into 3) for each pair of students. An extra set of cards and another strip of paper for each group of 6 students.

Procedure

Working initially in pairs, students read through and discuss the twelve Fruits of the Forest cards (Copiable Handout 7▢), which describe some common uses of the world's forests and forest products.

Pairs then try to agree upon where each card should be placed on the paper strip which represents a continuum from 'totally acceptable use' at one end to 'totally unacceptable use' at the other. When agreement is reached on the nature of acceptability and the positioning of cards, the cards are glued or pasted down in position.

Individually, students decide at what point they would 'draw the line' (in effect, between 'acceptable' and 'not acceptable'), and mark that point with an initialed pencil line.

Three pairs then join together to explain and justify their card placements before trying to negotiate a consensus placement for the group of six, using a fresh set of cards and paper strip.

Finally, the students can again mark where they would each 'draw the line,' having listened to the arguments of others.

Potential

An activity which promotes awareness of some major uses of forest products and encourages reflection upon the complex issues that their use generates. Although this is a consensus-seeking activity — to stimulate maximum discussion and sharing of perspective — individuals are still encouraged to state their own value positions in terms of where they would 'draw the line' between acceptable and non-acceptable uses.

Debriefing

In follow-up discussion, it should be pointed out that all of these activities are, to varying degrees, depleting the world's forests or interfering with their complex ecosystems. The concept of 'sustainable use' might be introduced here, along with discussion about practical steps students can take to help safeguard the remaining forests (for example, recycling paper and not buying tropical hardwoods or rare animal and bird species).

Extension

Further discussion and follow-up work could focus on the question of who benefits from the extraction of forest products. Drug companies and food manufacturers have made millions of dollars from such products; many developing nations are now demanding a realistic return for their valuable resources.

Selling Mother

Purpose   Recognizing different cultures' relationships with land
Grade level   9-12
Time needed   20 minutes
Resources   None

Procedure

Students form pairs ready for simultaneous role plays. Without stating the purpose, the facilitator explains the two roles.

Participant A acts as herself — but the exercise assumes that her mother is alive and well. Participant B has an unlimited supply of currency and desperately wants to buy A's mother.

Students role play the attempted purchase for two minutes. The facilitator 'freezes' the action and puts the 'spotlight' on selected pairs, who continue for a minute longer to highlight the frustration and absurdity of the interaction. A and B then swap roles and repeat the process.

The debriefing might begin by considering how it felt to play role A. Students will probably use words like *ridiculous, offensive* and *didn't make sense.* From B students, accounts of frustration and attempts to deceive or perhaps become aggressive may be elicited. Were any transactions completed? How close did the negotiations come to conclusion? The facilitator might then try to elicit from students the purpose of the activity (in effect, to suggest that 'mother' might be a metaphor for land) before reading either or both of the quotations below.

> The land is my mother. Like a human mother, the land gives us protection and enjoyment and provides for our needs — economic, social, religious. We have a human relationship with the land: Mother/daughter/son. When the land is taken from us or destroyed, we feel hurt because we belong to the land and we are part of it.
>
>   - Djiniyini Gondarra, Australian Aboriginal

If there are people you love, you can close your eyes and you can see them. I can close my eyes and see this beautiful Mother any time, and so if I became blind today I would see all and every part of her. The grass and trees are her hair. The rocks are her bones, the soft warm soil her flesh, the rivers her blood. The gentle rains of spring are her tears. And I listen to her in the gentle mountain breeze that bends the bough of the spruce and the cedar. I hear the song. So great is our beautiful Mother that the mountains are the only wrinkles on her face. From the beginning of time she gave of herself to all of life. And when I think of these two, when I think of our Father and our Mother, then I think of how it is with human families, because it's the father and mother of all things.

-Tsonakwa, Native American

Potential

The activity could be used in a variety of curriculum areas to help students understand different relationships that cultures can have to the land and the potential for conflict over land, as has occurred, for example, in North America and Australia, and as is occurring in Brazil.

Extension: Economics

Economics students might compare terms used to classify *land* in contemporary Western societies — for example, *asset, investment, factor of production* and *resource,* and compare these with the kinship metaphors used in many hunter-gatherer and horticulturalist societies.

Extension: History

Historians might reflect on how the prevailing metaphors for *land* evolved, and whether negotiation without conflict was possible in specific conflict situations.

Extension: Language

Language not only reflects people's perceptions, but also channels those perceptions. Lakoff and Johnson (see Supporting Resources) provide a range of examples of the way metaphors affect our everyday behavior. Language teachers might encourage students to suggest and evaluate other influential metaphors in their lives.

To heighten environmental awareness, students might reflect upon what sort of metaphors for land society needs if the environment is to remain capable of sustaining life.

Source
Bob Hill, Charles Sturt University, Australia.

Supporting Resources
Lakoff, G. & M. Johnson. *Metaphors We Live By.* Chicago: University of Chicago Press, 1980.

Forecast Made	Accurate	Partly Accurate	Not Accurate	Reasons
1.				
2.				
3.				
4.				
5.				
6.				
7.				
8.				
9.				
10.				

BOB HUNTER ON THE ENVIRONMENT, 1968

The *Globe Magazine* carried an article in June under the headline *Warning: Our Planet Is Dying.*

'Good Mother Nature,' the article said, 'spurned and ignored by Man as Polluter, may be turning on us like a mad bitch.'

This struck me as being a bit far-fetched. But since then, I have waded through the bulk of a dozen books and as many articles on the subject. I have stopped thinking it is far-fetched.

The problem is not simple to describe. Ecologists and biologists have stopped talking about it merely in terms of pollution. The word is not all-embracing enough. This is why the phrase 'environmental collapse' is now being used.

Environmental collapse applies to land, sea and air. Pollution of the land affects the waterways which, in turn, affect the seas and finally the air. In reverse, pollution of the air affects everything else. Related to all this is the problem of vanishing resources and the deteriorating quality of what resources we have.

Consider first the problem of how our atmosphere is being changed by pollution.

For the last four hundred million years, the level of oxygen in the atmosphere has remained constant at just a little over twenty per cent. Green plants absorb carbon dioxide and give off oxygen during the day, thus maintaining the balance. This process, known as *photosynthesis,* is based squarely on the balanced relationship between carbon and oxygen.

'Should this relationship be altered,' says Dr. Lamont C. Cole of Cornell University, 'life as we know it would be impossible. Man's actions today are bringing this imbalance upon us.'

We are adding fantastic quantities of carbon to the atmosphere much more rapidly than it can be absorbed by the oceans, which are the main reservoirs of carbon.

At the same time, we are tearing up green plants (three million acres — over a million hectares — in the US alone every year), and thereby interfering with the essential process of photosynthesis.

Dr. Cole claims that the carbon/oxygen balance has already begun to collapse. When we reach the point where our rate of combustion exceeds nature's rate of photosynthesis, 'we shall start running out of oxygen.'

It could happen, he adds, in the next couple of decades, or it could suddenly happen next year. We have no guarantee against it.

Austin N. Heller, pollution control commissioner for New York, has predicted that, unless air pollution in North America can be brought under control in two decades, city dwellers will have to walk around wearing gas masks.

And Dr. Cole has said that the existing balance is much more precarious than we think. He said that if a ship the size of the *Torrey Canyon,* loaded with concentrated herbicides instead of crude oil, had sunk off the North American coast, it would have erased the photoplankton of the sea, which produces seventy per cent of the world's oxygen. Those of us in the Northern Hemisphere would soon have found ourselves gasping for breath.

Already, the effects of atmospheric pollution are being felt on a global basis.

Last year, a scientist in search of a sample of uncontaminated air was forced to go all the way to Antarctica. Even there, he could not find it.

The earth's temperature has already been lowered, according to R.A. Bryon, director of the Center for Climatic Research at the University of Wisconsin. He reported in February that the average worldwide temperature has dropped about seven-tenths of a degree.

This was caused by an increase of only two percent in the amount of chemicals in the air. In North America alone, the automobile — only one source of atmospheric pollution — alone adds ten billion invisible particles to the air every second.

Within about thirty years, we will have at least doubled — quite possibly, tripled — the amount of pollution in the atmosphere.

One further danger is the possibility that this much pollution will create a 'greenhouse effect,' meaning that there will be so many compounds like carbon dioxide in the atmosphere they will act like glass in a greenhouse — trapping the sun's heat and causing a rise, instead of a drop, in temperature.

Many scientists have warned that this would lead to a rapid melting of the ice caps. Totally melted, they would raise the sea level by three hundred feet (over ninety meters), drowning cities like Vancouver.

Some estimates say it would take four hundred years for this to happen. But if the process were to start soon — and some scientists argue it could begin to happen very soon — the sea level could well have risen three hundred feet (over ninety meters) by the year 2000.

The Vancouver Sun, September 12, 1968

Frightening Forecasts

Purpose	Recognizing difficulties in predicting the future of the environment
Grade level	9-12
Time needed	40 minutes
Resources	A copy of Bob Hunter's article (Copiable Handout 9 ☐) for each student. Chart (Copiable Handout 8 ☐) for each small group of students.

Procedure

Working in small groups, students read the article by Bob Hunter (Copiable Handout 9☐). The groups' task is to extract the various forecasts contained in the article and discuss whether, and to what extent, they think these predictions have come true.

The groups then each complete a chart (Copiable Handout 8☐) by ticking the appropriate Accurate/Partly Accurate/Not Accurate box and giving their reasons.

Class discussion follows on the accuracy of these forecasts and the problems of predicting global environmental trends.

At some point, students are asked to think of some forecasts about the environment they have come across recently. These can be written up on a class chart. The chart is then left on the classroom wall so that any other forecasts which students come across in their work or from the media, or any further evidence to support or contradict forecasts, can be written in.

Potential

This activity encourages students to take an interest in a long-term, future perspective but, at the same time, to recognize the difficulties of accurately predicting environmental trends. It is likely that they will discover conflicting predictions and contradictory evidence surrounding some issues.

One interesting question to pose is: If 'environmental collapse' was predicted as long ago as 1968, why does so little appear to have been done to remedy the problems over the intervening years? Political inertia is the 'seventh enemy' as described by Ronald Higgins (***The Seventh Enemy: The Human Factor in the Global Crisis***. London: Pan, 1980.) Is this still the most critical problem of all?

Source
Bob Hunter's article appeared in *The Vancouver Sun* on September 12, 1968.

Our Ecological Footprint

Purpose	Exploring the concept of the ecological footprint as a means of gaining new insights into sustainablity
Grade level	10-12
Time needed	60 minutes
Resources	Copiable Handouts 10☐ and 11☐ for each student. Copiable Handout 12☐ for each pair of students.

Procedure

Students read Copiable Handouts 10☐ and 11☐.

Class discussion follows to ensure that the concept of ecological footprints, and the data presented, have been understood.

Students then form pairs to discuss and assess the 'Opinions' statements. Each statement is rated, on a 1-5 scale, according to how acceptable and how implementable students think it is. Any statement may have two different ratings. For example, 5 for acceptable and 1 for implementable would indicate that the students think the statement is very acceptable in theory, but very difficult to implement in practice.

Having assessed each statement, three pairs join together to form a group of six. The three sets of ratings are reviewed and discussion takes place around any significant differences of opinion that emerge. Students may change their ratings, if desired, following discussion and reflection.

Finally each group writes a single statement of a few sentences in length that summarizes their collective opinions on the arguments put forward in the statements. Summary statements should reflect any disagreements that persist among group members.

Class discussion follows the sharing of summary statements.

Potential

This activity is designed to introduce the intriguing concept of the ecological footprint as a way into consideration of the complex issues surrounding sustainability. It should be emphasized that an ecological footprint, though calculated using a wealth of statistical data from United Nations sources, is simply a tool for measuring our use of nature. 'If we cannot measure, we cannot manage,' suggest Mathis Wackernagel and William Rees, authors of the book *Our Ecological Footprint*. What should be done as a result of this information is up to human beings, individually and collectively, to decide. Any decisions — or their lack — will, of course, have an impact not only on human populations but also on other life forms.

Thus, the activity is not intended to show 'how bad things are.' Its aim is to provide students with an assessment of the current situation, so that they can make more informed decisions — based on their own values, assumptions and beliefs — about the best strategies for personal

OUR ECOLOGICAL FOOTPRINT

Obvious but profound: we depend on nature

Many of us live in cities where we easily forget that nature works in closed loops. We go to the store to buy food with money from the bank machine and, later, get rid of the waste either by depositing it in the back alley or flushing it down the toilet. Big city life breaks natural material cycles and provides little sense of our intimate connection with nature.

Despite the estrangement, we are not just connected to nature—we are nature. As we eat, drink and breathe, we constantly exchange energy and matter with our environment. The human body is continuously wearing out and rebuilding itself—in fact, we replace almost all the molecules in our bodies about once a year. The atoms of which we are made have already been part of many other living beings. Particles of us once roamed about in a dinosaur, and some of us may well carry an atom of Caesar or Cleopatra.

Nature provides us with a steady supply of the basic requirements for life. We need energy for heat and mobility, wood for housing and paper products, and nutritious food and clean water for healthy living. Through photosynthesis green plants convert sunlight, carbon dioxide (CO_2), nutrients and water into chemical energy (such as fruit and vegetables), and all the food chains that support animal life—including our own—are based on this plant material. Nature also absorbs our wastes and provides life-support services such as climate stability and protection from ultraviolet radiation. Finally, the sheer exuberance and beauty of nature is a source of joy and spiritual inspiration.

If we are to live sustainably, we must ensure that we use the essential products and processes of nature no more quickly than they can be renewed, and that we discharge wastes no more quickly than they can be absorbed. Even today, however, accelerating deforestation and soil erosion, fisheries collapse and species extinction, the accumulation of greenhouse gases and ozone depletion all tell us our current demands on nature are compromising humanity's future well-being. In spite of these trends, society operates as if nature were an expendable part of our economy.

What Is an Ecological Footprint?

Ecological Footprint analysis is an accounting tool that enables us to estimate the resource consumption and waste assimilation requirements of a defined human population or economy in terms of a corresponding productive land area. Imagine what would happen to any modern city or urban region—Vancouver, Philadelphia or London—if it were enclosed in a glass or plastic hemisphere that let in light but prevented material things of any kind from entering or leaving—like the "Biosphere II" project in Arizona. The health and integrity of the entire human system so contained would depend entirely on whatever was initially trapped within the hemisphere. It is obvious to most people that such a city would cease to function and its inhabitants would perish within a few days. The population and the economy contained by the capsule would have been cut off from vital resources and essential waste sinks, leaving it both to starve and to suffocate at the same time! In other words, the ecosystems contained within our imaginary human terrarium would have insufficient "carrying capacity" to support the ecological load imposed by the contained human population.

The important question to ask now is: how large would the hemisphere have to become before the city at its center could sustain itself indefinitely and exclusively on the land and water ecosystems and the energy resources contained within the capsule? In other words, what is the total area of terrestrial ecosystem types needed continuously to support all the social and economic activities carried out by the people of our city as they go about their daily activities? Keep in mind that land with its ecosystems is needed to produce resources, to assimilate wastes, and to perform various invisible life-support functions.

For any set of specified circumstances—the present example assumes current population, prevailing material standards, existing technologies, etc.—it should be possible to produce a reasonable estimate of the land/water area required by the city concerned to sustain itself. By definition, the total ecosystem area that is essential to the continued existence of the city is its de facto Ecological Footprint on the Earth. It should be obvious that the Ecological Footprint of a city will be proportional to both population and per capita material consumption. Clearly, too, the Ecological Footprint includes all land required by the defined population wherever on Earth that land is located. Modern cities and whole countries survive on ecological goods and services appropriated from natural flows or acquired through commercial trade from all over the world. The Ecological Footprint therefore also represents the corresponding population's total "appropriated carrying capacity."

So What?—The global context

THE ECOLOGICAL FOOTPRINT of any population can be used to measure its current consumption and projected requirements against available ecological supply and point out likely shortfalls. In this way, it can assist society in assessing the choices we need to make about our demands on nature. To put this into perspective, the ecologically productive land "available" to each person on Earth has decreased steadily over the last century. Today, there are only 1.5 hectares of such land for each person, including wilderness areas that probably shouldn't be used for any other purpose. In contrast, the land area "appropriated" by residents of richer countries has steadily increased. The present Ecological Footprint of a typical North American (7.8 hectares) represents four times his/her fair share of the Earth's bounty. Indeed, if everyone on Earth lived like the average Canadian or American, we would need at least three such planets to live sustainably. Of course, if the world population continues to grow as anticipated, there will be 10 billion people by 2040, for each of whom there will be less than 0.9 hectares of ecologically productive land, assuming there is no further soil degradation.

Source
Extracted from Wackernagel, Mathis & William Rees. "Our Ecological Footprint." In **Green Teacher** 45, December 1995-January 1996.

ECOLOGICAL FOOTPRINTS OF NATIONS

The Ecological Footprint measures our dependence on nature. Every nation depends on ecological capacity to sustain itself. A nation's Ecological Footprint corresponds to the total area of land and water that is required by that nation to continuously produce all the resources it consumes, and to absorb all the waste it generates, using existing technology.

   The table below shows the Ecological Footprints of 12 nations, expressed in terms of the amount of 'biologically productive space' (land and water that is suitable for sustaining plants and animals) used on average by each citizen. Remember that only 1.7 hectares (4.2 acres) of biologically productive space is available for each person in the world (at 1997 world population levels), if everyone was to have the same Ecological Footprint.

   The 'available ecological capacity' refers to the total of the biologically productive space available in that country for each citizen (some countries with large land areas and small populations, such as Canada, have a relatively large ecological capacity, even though each Canadian citizen's Ecological Footprint is large, too). The 'ecological credit or deficit' refers to the remaining ecological capacity per person (credit) or the overuse of capacity per person (deficit) in that country. The world deficit of 0.6 (2.3 hectares [5.7 acres] per person used, when only 1.7 is available) indicates that the average Ecological Footprint is 35 per cent larger than the available space. In other words, humanity's consumption exceeds what nature can regenerate on a continuous basis.

	Population in 1997	ECOLOGICAL FOOTPRINT (in hectares per person)	AVAILABLE ECOLOGICAL CAPACITY (in hectares per person)	ECOLOGICAL CREDIT OR DEFICIT (in hectares per person)
CANADA	30 101 000	7.0	8.5	1.5
CHILE	14 691 000	3.5	4.9	1.4
CHINA	247 315 000	1.2	1.3	0.1
ETHIOPIA	58 414 000	1.0	0.9	–0.1
INDIA	970 230 000	0.8	0.8	0.0
ITALY	57 247 000	4.5	1.4	–3.1
JAPAN	125 672 000	6.3	1.7	–4.6
MEXICO	97 245 000	2.3	1.4	–0.9
PAKISTAN	148 686 000	0.8	0.9	0.1
SINGAPORE	2 899 000	5.3	0.5	–4.8
SWEDEN	8 862 000	5.8	7.8	2.0
USA	268 189 000	8.4	6.2	–2.2
WORLD	5 892 480 000	2.3	1.7	–0.6

Source: Extracted from Wackernagel et al. *Ecological Footprints of Nations. How Much Nature Do They Use? How Much Nature Do They Have?* Xalapa, Mexico: *Centro de Estudios para la Sustentabilidad,* 1997.

and global futures. In plenary discussion, the anticipated implications of different courses of action could be explored, perhaps in the form of decision wheel charts (see **Made in Canada,** p. 75 and **Decision Wheel,** p. 146).

Discussion might also focus on those statements where the differential between the 'acceptable' and 'implementable' ratings is the highest. Why is this, and what (if anything) can or should be done to close the gap?

At a more sophisticated level, discussion could include consideration of the implicit assumptions underlying the concepts of 'measurement' and 'management' of nature. If intuition and experience tell us that there are global environmental problems, why do we need measurement tools for verification, and how accurate are they anyway? Why should the human species assume the role of managers of nature? If, as some scientists believe, the planet is a self-regulating system, would it not be better to try to reduce human interference?

Extension

Students are given an approximate breakdown of their ecological footprint according to the following estimated proportion of biologically productive space used to support their daily lives in Canada:

FOOD:	30% (of which animal products account for more than two-thirds of the total)
HOUSING:	20% (includes building, operation and maintenance)
TRANSPORTATION:	20% (of which private transportation accounts for about two-thirds of the total)
CONSUMER GOODS:	20% (includes clothing, furnishings, appliances, books, recreational and personal goods, and packaging — the latter accounting for more than one-tenth of the total)
SERVICES:	10% (includes government, education, health, social services, tourism, entertainment)

Figures based on 1991 Canadian data. Source: **Green Teacher 45,** December 1995 - January 1996.

In the light of statistics showing that Canadians, on average, use about four times the amount of biologically productive space than that required to support the world's present population sustainably and equitably, students decide what, if anything, they would like to change in their own lifestyles. Weekly or monthly action plans are drawn up and progress towards goals set is frequently monitored.

Supporting Resources
Wackernagel, Mathis & William Rees. **Our Ecological Footprint.** New Society Publishers, 1997.

Reference
1. World Commission on Environment and Development. *Our Common Future.* London: Oxford University Press, 1987.

OPINIONS

Ratings:

5 = highly acceptable/highly implementable
4 = acceptable/implementable
3 = borderline between acceptable/not acceptable, implementable/not implementable
2 = not acceptable/not implementable
1 = very unacceptable/not at all implementable

	ACCEPTABLE	IMPLEMENTABLE
1. The population explosion is the biggest problem. The Earth cannot sustain a world population of 8-10 billion people. Countries with rapidly increasing populations should be forced to control their population growth		
2. Wealthy people in all countries use up too many natural resources. They should be required to consume less so that the world's poor can raise their standard of living.		
3. No generation before ours has had to seriously think about the fate of generations to come. Why should we? Each generation should only have to look after its own members.		
4. Present and future calculations about an 'ecological deficit' are based on the current potential of technology. We should put more effort and money into finding technological solutions that will reduce the deficit.		
5. All human beings bear a moral responsibility towards each other and all other life forms. The more nature we use, the greater is our personal responsibility. Individual citizens — particularly in high-consuming societies — have to take the initiative to reduce the size of their own Ecological Footprint.		

	ACCEPTABLE	IMPLEMENTABLE
6. According to the statistics, Canadians have an 'ecological credit' — we use less nature than is available in our country. Therefore, our lifestyle is sustainable — we don't need to do anything more.		
7. Increasing consumption is to be expected — as people get wealthier, they want more things. Governments will have to provide real incentives if they want levels of consumption to decrease.		
8. Developing countries with very large populations (for example, China and India) should not expect their citizens to achieve the same standards of living as those in developed countries. This could result in ecological catastrophe. The United Nations should impose limits on levels of consumption.		
9. Increased consumption is good for the economy — more goods wanted means more jobs. Consumerism should be encouraged worldwide, not restricted.		
10. The planet is not in crisis; only human beings are. Whatever happens, the Earth will regenerate itself in some form, with or without a human population. We should just let nature take its course.		

4

Health

The concept of health can be viewed as being comprised of the following seven dimensions. The first five dimensions are predominantly related to the *health of the individual*:

1. **Physical health.** The functioning of the body and all its component parts. The ability to perform physical tasks without undue stress or fatigue.

2. **Mental health.** The functioning of the mind. The ability to think coherently and to learn effectively, using a variety of mental processes.

3. **Emotional health.** The ability to cope with, control and express emotions in ways that satisfy personal needs and are appropriate to the demands of various situations.

4. **Spiritual health.** The ability to make ethical and moral judgments in accordance with personal belief and value systems. The ability to find 'inner peace.'

5. **Social health.** The ability to form and maintain fulfilling and positive relationships with others.

The final two dimensions are primarily concerned with the *health of societies and environments*:

6. **Societal health.** The functioning of communities and societies. The existence of security, freedom, justice and opportunities for self-fulfillment for all citizens, in accordance with international human rights legislation.

7. **Environmental health.** The quality of natural and built environments. The ability of environments to sustain, on a long-term basis, a diversity of life-forms.

In reality, the seven dimensions of health are profoundly interconnected. Individuals' mental health, for example, is affected by physical, emotional, spiritual and social dimensions. It is also affected by individuals' interactions with society and the environment. The health of a society, likewise, is determined by the health of its individual members and by the quality of its environment. In a similar way, the health of the planet is deeply intertwined with the health of individual humans and other life forms.

This *holistic* view of health is to be found within the traditional belief systems of many societies around the world. It has been challenged since the industrial revolution by the more mechanistic practices of Western medicine. In contrast to *naturopathic* approaches that assist the self-healing potential of the mind and body, the *allopathic* techniques of modern medicine attempt to counteract disease through external agents such as drugs and surgery. A counter-challenge, in the form of alternative therapies — many of which utilize traditional knowledge and skills — is now gaining ground in the West. Common to most alternative therapies is a belief in the efficacy of *self-help* in combatting disease through paying attention to such factors as diet, exercise, sleep patterns, relaxation and personal relationships. While good health is not available to all, *wellness* is within everyone's reach. By taking appropriate self-help measures, all people can strive towards the optimal state of well-being that their physical, mental and environmental conditions allow.

In the developing world *infectious diseases* — such as malaria, measles and tuberculosis — are still the major causes of death. There, *primary health care* is the key strategy for fighting disease. The basis of this approach is the empowerment of ordinary people in the maintenance of their own health. This is accomplished through education and by training selected people from the community to administer essential drugs and treat common ailments. An essential prerequisite in the fight against infectious diseases is the provision of *basic services*, such as clean water and sanitation, adequate food and shelter, and immunization for children. *Education*, particularly of women, is important for the present and future health of the whole family.

A rise in *degenerative diseases* — including heart disease and cancer — has followed increases in prosperity and longevity in all societies. The causes of these diseases are related to *lifestyle choices* — such as lack of exercise, overeating, stress, smoking and alcohol abuse. Causes are also related to environmental factors, including air and water pollution. Environmental abuse, as well, is thought to play a crucial part in the emergence of new and deadly viruses, including HIV and Ebola.

The vast majority of the world's expenditure on health research and treatment is devoted to degenerative diseases which principally affect older people in wealthier societies. Yet about half of all deaths are the result of preventable infectious diseases suffered mainly by children in poorer countries. Health is a matter of *rights and responsibilities*. Everyone's right to enjoy the highest standards of health and medical care attainable is enshrined within human rights legislation. At the same time the importance of individual responsibility for the well-being of others has been heightened by the spread of AIDS and evidence of the harmful effects of second-hand smoke inhalation. Rapid advances in medical technology, enabling people to live longer healthier lives, give rise to complex issues of *medical ethics*. Critical choices between life and death can now be made on a variety of grounds. These include per-

HEALTH

CONCEPTS

ACTIVITIES	Individual Health	Societal/Environmental Health	Holistic Health	Self-help	Wellness	Infectious Diseases	Primary Health Care	Basic Services	Education	Degenerative Diseases	Lifestyle Choices	Rights and Responsibilities	Medical Ethics
Poorly Polly	*			*									
Healthy People Search			*						*				
Wellness Wheels	*		*	*							*		
Graffiti Wall	*	*	*	*	*						*		
Healthy Classroom Charter	*	*	*	*	*							*	
Health Rights Continuum	*	*				*				*	*	*	*
World Health Diamond Ranking	*	*	*	*	*	*	*	*	*		*		*
Decision Wheel	*		*	*						*	*	*	
Catching On	*		*	*		*			*		*	*	

Connections • Many of the self-esteem building activities in Chapter 1 are useful for enhancing personal health; see, especially, pp.31-53. See also **Disable Label** (bk2). • Environmental health issues are addressed in **Carrying the Can** (p.103) and **Right Up Your Street** (p.105). • Ethical issues relating to medical research and links between health and wealth are explored in **Fruits of the Forest** (p.116), **World Food Distribution** (bk2) and **Development Cartoons** (bk2). • **Rights Bingo** (bk2), **Rights and Responsibilities** (bk2) and **Burden of Responsibility** (bk2) all touch on the rights and responsibilities of personal and environmental health. • Contributions of technology to improving health care can be highlighted in **Technology Scrapbook** (p.202) and **Technology Timeline** (p.203).

sonal conscience, government policy, and the availability of funding and resources.

The activities in this chapter (perhaps more than in other chapters) deal with issues that are complex and that may be regarded, in some communities, as being too controversial or an unnecessary invasion of personal privacy. The justification for their inclusion in the book lies in the view that interrelated issues of personal, societal and environmental health are integral to the functioning of global systems. It is, therefore, important for students to have an understanding of a range of arguments around health issues, so that they can make more informed choices in their own lives. However, in using these activities, teachers should be sensitive to the needs and rights of individual students, and the expectations of parents and other community members.

SKILLS INVENTORY

Most activities in this chapter offer potential for the development of *cooperation and communication skills.*
Poorly Polly demands good *listening skills..*
The *skills of self-assessment* are utilized in **Healthy People Search**, **Wellness Wheels** and **Healthy Classroom Charter**.
Values clarification and *perspective taking skills* are addressed in **Health Rights Continuum**, **World Health Diamond Ranking** and **Decision Wheel**.
Healthy Classroom Charter and **World Health Diamond Ranking** promote the *skills of consensus seeking*.
Relational thinking is developed through **Healthy Classroom Charter**, **Decision Wheel** and **Catching On**.
Decision Wheel affords practice in *decision-making skills.*

Poorly Polly

Purpose	Thinking through consequences of health-related actions
Grade level	1-4
Time needed	30 minutes
Resources	A copy of **Poorly Polly**. A clear space in which students can perform appropriate actions.

Procedure

Students are asked to stand in pairs in a clear space, and to listen carefully to the story of Poorly Polly. Each time they think Polly is doing something that is potentially dangerous or a risk to her health, they signal this by making an appropriate action and/or noise. (For example, Polly sliding down the stairs could be followed by students rubbing their backsides, and Polly eating a bitter wild berry might induce some students to groan and clutch their stomachs!) Teachers of younger students may need to give additional prompts where the health risk is not immediately obvious.

Whenever students make such actions and/or noises, the teacher stops reading and asks the pairs to tell each other what the dangers might be (different interpretations should be allowed), before inviting suggestions as to how Polly might reduce risks to her health.

Finally, the class rewrites the story, putting in all the safety features that have been discussed.

Potential

A simple yet engaging way of drawing students' attention to some common hazards to physical health while encouraging them to think through the consequences of their actions. The story can be altered in myriad ways to incorporate other health concerns.

Variation

Rather than making actions and sounds, students have an outline representation of 'Poorly Polly' on a sheet of paper. At appropriate points in the story, they draw Xs at relevant places on Polly's body, to indicate the sites of the pain.

Poorly Polly

Polly woke up one day, feeling very bright and cheerful. She jumped out of bed and slid down the stairs to see what her dad was cooking for breakfast. There was a big pot on the stove that she couldn't quite see inside, so she reached up and dipped her finger in. Porridge — disgusting!

Polly fancied cinnamon toast, so she took out a fresh loaf of white bread and cut off a very thick slice with the very sharp bread knife. As the cinnamon was kept on a high shelf, Polly had to fetch the rickety stool and clamber up to get it. By this time, the toast had jammed in the toaster, but she was able to free it with her fingers. The butter was already out on the table...and so was the cat, looking very pleased with himself. Polly shooed him off the table, scraped what was left of the butter onto the toast, and sprinkled on the cinnamon. Delicious!

As it was a beautiful, warm day, Polly put on her roller blades — which were now two sizes too small — and went outside. Polly was at the top of the hill before she remembered that she had forgotten to put on her elbow and knee pads. Oh, well — too late! Down the hill she went, feeling the wind blowing in her face. On the way back up the hill, she stopped to pick a few of the bright red berries that grew by the roadside. Ugh! They were so bitter!

Back at home, Polly took off her roller blades and went in search of her old bike. It was in the garage, with all the garden furniture piled on top. She pulled and pulled, and at last the bike came free, although she noticed it didn't have any rear brakes. She was at the top of the hill again before she thought about her helmet. Oh, well — too late again! Down the hill she went, with the wind whipping wildly through her long hair.

Polly rode on to her favorite stretch of river, where the water rushes over the rocks but — if it hadn't rained too much — you could just about get across. Leaving her bike on the river bank, Polly took off her shoes and jumped from rock to rock. Good! The old rope was still hanging from the dead tree by the water's edge. She grabbed the rope, pulled it back up the bank, and then launched herself out over the river.

It was such fun by the river that Polly spent all morning there, with the sun burning down on her. It was later, when she began to feel rather poorly and very thirsty, she realized she had forgotten to put on any sunscreen. She scooped up some water from the river in an old yogurt container, drank the water and started to make her way home.

Healthy People Search

Purpose   Thinking about some of the many dimensions of health
Grade level   5-12
Time needed   20 minutes
Resources   A **Healthy People Search** handout (Copiable Handout 1⬜) for each student. An open classroom space.

Procedure

Students move around the open area searching for people who can respond in the affirmative to one of the items in the handout. Each person's name is written in the space next to the corresponding item, and may appear on the sheet only once. Participants are encouraged to volunteer additional information during each exchange, such as giving specific examples to support their answers or sharing feelings at some length.

The activity can continue until everybody's handout is as complete as possible, or it can be halted after a suitable period. Students then gather to discuss how much they found they had in common, and to reflect on what was shared.

The handout can be simplified, and the number of questions reduced, for younger students.

Potential

A lively activity enabling students to discover a great deal about each other very quickly. It also provides a good introduction to some facets of the many dimensions of health (see p. 135) and allows students to explore these in a non-threatening manner.

Questions to trigger discussion might include: What did you learn about someone in the class that surprised you? Did you find that you had much in common with other members of the class? Which questions were the most difficult to answer or find answers to? Was it difficult to be really honest about yourself? If so, why? Have you learned something about yourself through participating in this activity?

HEALTHY PEOPLE SEARCH

FIND someone who:

1.   Takes regular physical exercise.   _____

2.   Feels relaxed in social situations.   _____

3.   Is able to concentrate on their work.   _____

4.   Can cope well with stress.   _____

5.   Eats a balanced, nutritious diet.   _____

6.   Has good personal friendships.   _____

7.   Is in good physical condition.   _____

8.   Expresses emotions when appropriate.   _____

9.   Has not been sick in the last six months.   _____

10.   Enjoys meeting other people.   _____

11.   Follows leisure interests with enthusiasm.   _____

12.   Is a good listener.   _____

13.   Can think creatively.   _____

14.   Has felt really happy recently.   _____

15.   Does not consume harmful substances.   _____

16.   Is making good use of their brain power.   _____

17.   Has helped someone out recently.   _____

18.   Gets enough sleep.   _____

19.   Feels confident and self-assured.   _____

20.   Takes good care of his physical appearance.   _____

Extension

Students write diary entries telling what they learned about themselves and others through the activity.

Wellness Wheels

Purpose   Broadening understanding of health and wellness
Grade level   9-12
Time needed   40 minutes
Resources   A **Wellness Wheel** (Copiable Handout 2❑) for each student. Pencils or crayons.

Procedure

Through class discussion, students explore the many interrelated dimensions of health. In this activity, five dimensions of personal health are featured (see p. 137 for an explanation of these dimensions):

1. Physical health.
2. Mental health.
3. Emotional health.
4. Spiritual health.
5. Social health.

Having clarified these dimensions, students reflect on their own states of wellness, which can be defined as *an individual's achievement of the maximum potential in any dimension, given her present state of health.* (A physically challenged person can still attain physical wellness if he is as active as his physical limitations permit.)

Looking at each dimension in turn, students complete their Wellness Wheels (Copiable Handout 2❑) by shading in (starting from the center) the proportion of each segment that accords with their degree of wellness. The remaining part of the segment (representing their lack of wellness in that dimension) is left blank.

Around the outside of the circle, adjacent to the relevant segments, students write personal notes about the 'unhealthy' portions, to remind them of areas needing improvement.

The Wheels can then be updated by shading in more of each segment as and when improvements are made.

Wellness Wheels are very personal documents that students may not wish to share with each other. In a supportive environment, however, sharing and subsequent discussion can be valuable esteem building and motivational forces.

Potential

This activity helps to broaden students' understanding of health and wellness while encouraging them to assess their levels of wellness in its many dimensions. Through such an assessment, imbalances will

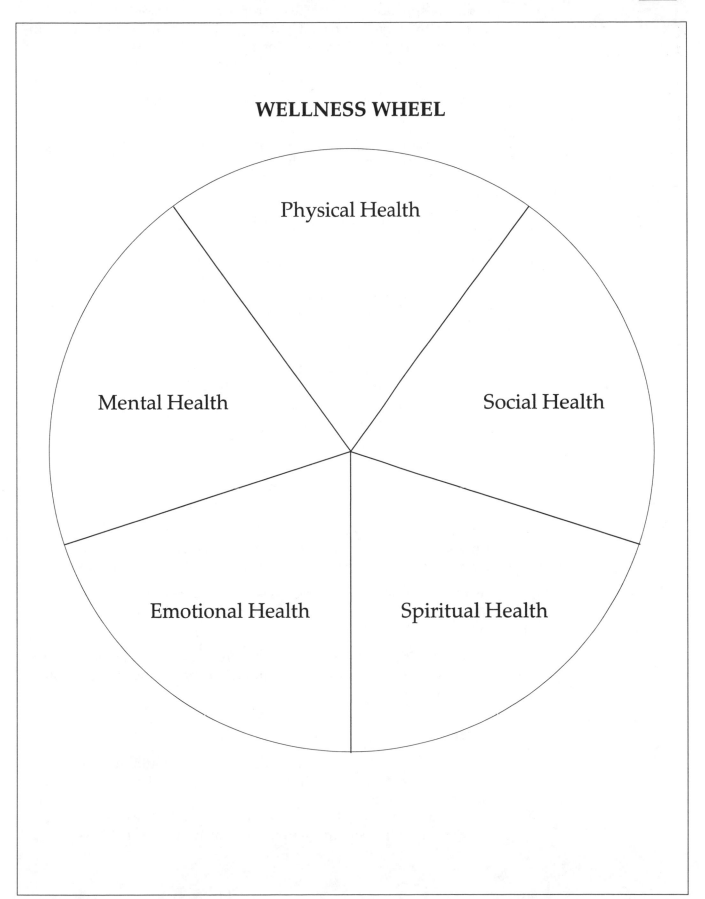

WELLNESS WHEEL

Physical Health

Mental Health

Social Health

Emotional Health

Spiritual Health

become more obvious (the Wellness Wheel only turns smoothly if it is perfectly spherical) and can be appropriately addressed.

The activity can be of great benefit in a personal or small group counseling situation. Students' attention might also be focused on the role of the school in facilitating wellness. To what extent are all dimensions satisfactorily addressed, and what improvements could schools undertake to encourage more balanced wellness among students?

Source

Based on ideas in Greenberg, Jerrold S. *Health Education: Learner-centered Instructional Strategies*, ©1989. Dubuque, Iowa: Wm. C. Brown, reproduced with the permission of The McGraw-Hill Companies.

Graffiti Wall

Purpose	Introducing the multi-dimensional concept of health
Grade level	4-8
Time needed	40 minutes initially; occasional short blocks of time thereafter
Resources	A large sheet or card, marked out as a brick wall. 6 slips of paper for each student. Pens or markers. Glue sticks.

Procedure

At the beginning of a unit or topic on health, students are asked to write, individually, up to three statements beginning with 'Health is....' Each statement should represent a different idea and be written on a separate slip of paper. (A prior brainstorming by the class could be beneficial to stimulate students' thinking about the nature of health.)

Working in groups of five or six, students sift through the slips, discarding (or blending together) any statements that are duplications, as well as grouping statements that express related ideas.

Groups then write new statements (or choose representative statements from those already written) to cover the principal ideas that have been generated. These statements are stuck on the class **Graffiti Wall**.

As work on health issues progresses, any student can propose statements that express additional ideas. These are added to the Graffiti Wall.

Periodically during the unit and at its conclusion, further class time can be allotted for students to review the statements on the wall and make any additions.

Potential

This activity provides both an introduction to the multi-dimensional concept of health and an indication of the extent and nature of students' understanding.

As additions are made to the Graffiti Wall, students can witness the expansion of ideas and the development of awareness that have taken

place through their work on the unit. The initial contributions could be written in one color, with additional statements in another, to clearly indicate the progress that has been made.

Healthy Classroom Charter

Purpose Encouraging personal and collective rsponsibility with regard to health.

Grade level 3-6

Time needed 40 minutes initially; periodic reviews thereafter

Resources Chart paper and markers. A set of **Expectation Cards** (Copiable Handout 3 ❑), paper and pens for each small group.

Procedure

A brief introductory discussion is held around the concept of a 'healthy classroom' — a classroom in which the many interrelated dimensions of health (emotional, environmental, mental, physical, social and spiritual) can be enjoyed by all members.

Each small group of students is given a set of Expectation Cards (Copiable Handout 3❑) and asked to confirm, through discussion, that these represent reasonable personal expectations of a healthy classroom. Cards can be altered or rejected. New cards can be added by the group.

Students are then asked to consider their individual and collective *obligations* — the things they must do if the agreed upon expectations are to be enjoyed by all class members. Each Expectation Card is considered in turn, and agreed obligations are written on a sheet of paper, beginning 'I must....' It is likely that some obligations (such as 'I must get sufficient sleep' and 'I must eat a balanced diet') will be considered relevant to more than one expectation, but need not be written down more than once.

EXPECTATION CARDS

I expect to feel physically fit.

I expect to feel bright and alert.

I expect to feel relaxed and at ease.

I expect to have good friendships.

I expect to be able to work hard.

I expect to be able to enjoy myself.

I expect to be able to communicate my thoughts and feelings.

I expect to work and play in a safe environment.

I expect to feel good about myself and my abilities.

I expect to understand the difference between right and wrong.

I expect to feel 'at home' in the classroom.

I expect other people to feel good about me.

When groups have considered all the cards, a plenary discussion takes place to establish an agreed upon set of expectations and obligations for the class. These are then written out on chart paper, in two columns, and displayed prominently on the classroom wall.

Reviews of the **Healthy Classroom Charter** should take place from time to time, to assess the appropriateness of both expectations and obligations, and to add others that have become significant.

Potential

This activity helps to broaden students' understanding of the concept of health through exploring its dimensions in the context of a very real setting — the classroom. It also makes the crucial link between expectations and obligations in relation to health, thereby encouraging a sense of personal and collective responsibility.

The activity seeks to illustrate the profound interconnections between experiences and achievements in school, and the conducting of personal and family life. The health of the classroom is influenced by the personal well-being of all its members. Such links can be referred to whenever students' achievement in, or enjoyment of, school seems to be in decline.

Variation

Older students could brainstorm their own sets of expectations, rather than using the cards given.

Extension

Students who are having problems or difficulties in the class could be encouraged to draw up and follow a **'Personal Health Contract,'** based on the information contained in the Charter. The contract would focus particularly on problem areas in individual students' lives. For example, students who had few friendships would express their expectations in this regard, then write out some personal obligations to be met over the weeks to come. The Contract would be reviewed from time to time with the class teacher.

Health Rights Continuum

Purpose	Clarifying views regarding complex health-related issues
Grade level	7-12
Time needed	20 minutes
Resources	A clear space, so that participants can form a line from one end of the room to the other

Procedure

Students are asked to take up positions along a single line, stretching from one end of the room to the other, according to whether they agree or disagree with certain **Suggested Rights** which are to be read out by the facilitator (see page 143 for examples). One end of the room should be clearly indicated for those who 'strongly agree,' and the other end for those who 'strongly disagree.' Participants are at liberty to take up any position along the continuum.

When they have found an initial position, students are encouraged to talk to their immediate neighbors and to alter their positions, if necessary, in the light of those discussions.

The facilitator should allow a few minutes' discussion before asking participants to consider the next right.

Potential

A short, active exercise which asks participants to clarify their own views and positions with regard to complex ethical and moral issues relating to health. It is likely that a wide spread of opinions will be apparent from positions taken up, and care should be taken to ensure that certain participants in 'minority' positions are not embarrassed or victimized.

Discussion of this exercise could focus on the spread of views revealed. 'Why is this so?' 'Why are some rights more controversial than others?' 'What is the relationship between moral and legal rights in the context of these issues?' and 'Who should decide what is, and what is not, acceptable behavior?'

Variations

When students are well spaced out along the continuum (so that a good spread of opinions exists), the facilitator can promote further disussion in two possible ways:

1. By breaking the line at its mid-point and asking those in the 'lower' half to slide along towards the 'upper' half (see diagram below). Discussion then takes place between two participants (or small groups) who hold relatively different opinions.

A   BC   D   becomes   A   B
                                   C   D

2. By breaking the line at its mid-point and asking participants at the two opposite ends to 'swing around' so that they face each other (see diagram below). The effect of this will be to promote discussion between opposing viewpoints at one end of the continuum (though students in the middle will discuss with similarly-minded colleagues).

A   BC   D   becomes   A   B
                                   D   C

Extension

It could be pointed out that various individuals and groups help form our positions on health rights. These individuals and groups include: parents, friends, TV and the other media, religious groups, politicians and special interest groups. Working individually or in pairs, students could research the viewpoint of one of these on some of the health rights discussed in this activity. They share the results of their research in an oral or written report.

Figure 1

Suggested Rights

1. Human beings have the right to experiment on other animals to find cures for fatal diseases.

2. Anybody has the right to take his own life.

3. Anybody has the right to assist in the 'mercy killing' of someone who is suffering from an incurable disease.

4. Only a mother has the right to decide the fate of her unborn child.

5. Baby milk (or tobacco) companies have the right to sell their products wherever they can find a market.

6. I have the right to use toxic substances, such as chemical fertilizers, pesticides and cleaning agents.

7. I have the right not to wear a cycle helmet (or seat belt).

8. I have the right to engage in unprotected sexual intercourse.

9. I have the right to be kept alive at all costs, if it is medically possible to do so.

10. I have the right to consume addictive drugs, including alcohol, caffeine, marijuana and tobacco.

World Health Diamond Ranking

Purpose	Becoming familiar with differing perspectives on health issues
Grade level	9-12
Time needed	40 minutes
Resources	9 **World Health Statements** representing a range of opinions on health issues (Copiable Handout 4 ❑) for each pair of students, cut up into separate slips

Procedure

Pairs are given the nine statements and are asked to rank them in diamond formation, as below:

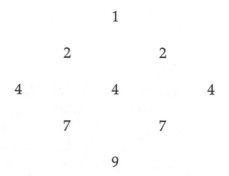

A fairly loose criterion for ranking is given, such as 'convincing,' 'important' or 'thought provoking,' the teacher resisting any requests for her to be more specific about the criterion. The most 'convincing,' 'important' or 'thought provoking' statement is placed at the top of the diamond. The next two are placed in second equal position. The three across the center are fourth equal. The next two are seventh equal. The statement placed at the foot of the diamond is the one considered by the pair to be the least 'convincing,' 'important' or 'thought provoking.'

When pairs have completed their task, they form into sixes. Each pair explains and seeks to justify its ranking to the other two pairs. The six then try to negotiate a consensus ranking for the group as a whole.

Plenary reporting back and discussion follow.

Potential

This activity offers a means of familiarizing students with some significant perspectives and arguments on health issues. It also helps them clarify their own thoughts and feelings about issues while alerting them to the opinions and perspectives of their classmates.

Underpinning the activity is the unspoken assumption that everybody has something relevant and useful to bring to the discussion. The imprecise criterion is itself likely to give rise to debate. What meaning did the pairs and sixes invest in the terms 'convincing,' 'important' and 'thought provoking?' Did it become necessary to try to pin down what it meant more precisely?

WORLD HEALTH STATEMENTS

1. Poverty

Poverty is the real cause of ill health. When people are poor, they cannot afford to eat well, to live in clean conditions and to buy necessary medicine. These are key factors in the spread of disease.

2. Resources

If people have access to proper medical help, they can avoid disease. With better trained medical staff and more clinics and hospitals, the general health of a society will improve.

3. Education

Education is the key to better health. The more people know and understand about disease and how to prevent it, the more likely they are to look after themselves.

4. Environment

People are as healthy or as sick as their environment. Better personal health will only come with a reduction in pollution and the sustainable use of the planet's natural resources.

5. A State of Mind

Health is a state of mind. A positive view of oneself and of one's ability to overcome disease is more valuable than reliance on drugs and medical care.

6. Population

Sickness affects people more in developing countries, where populations are huge and growing fast. To become healthier, all societies have to control their population growth.

7. Natural Selection

Disease is nature's way of sorting out the weak from the strong in all species. It is a natural process which maintains a healthy balance between all populations and their environment. An obsession with curing disease has upset the balance.

8. Traditional Medicine

In many countries, folk remedies and traditional beliefs about illness do more harm than good. People should learn from the advances in health care made by medical science.

9. Big Business

Medical care is big business. Treatment (using medical products) is better for profit-making than prevention (not getting sick). This emphasis is wrong and perpetuates ill health.

Skills used in this activity include discussion, negotiation, accommodation to other perspectives, and consensus seeking. In the plenary debriefing, a group reporting their inability to agree upon a ranking order is as important a focus for discussion as a group reporting that they have achieved consensus.

Potential

Students could research some of the statements, using resources such as United Nations publications. They present the results of their research in formats such as the following: bulletin board display, role play, political speech, position paper or letter to an editor.

Source
Based on an idea in Richardson, E., Flood, M. & S. Fisher. *Debate and Decision: World Studies Project*, 1980.

Decision Wheel

Purpose	Examining potential implications of health-related decisions
Grade level	7-12
Time needed	45 minutes
Resources	A sheet of chart paper and 2 markers (of different colors) for each group of 4 or 5 students.

Procedure

Working in small groups, students write on the center of the chart paper a decision relating to their personal and social lives that has implications for their health. (For example, taking up smoking, taking drugs, engaging in sexual activity, going on a diet, or drinking alcohol.)

A structured process of exploring the multiple consequences of that decision is then undertaken by the group. Several possible consequences (both positive and negative) are written on the paper in circles attached to the central box by one line (see example, Figure 2).

The first-order consequences are then considered, and second-order consequences are recorded (attached by two lines).

Third-, fourth- and even fifth-order consequences are similarly written up, the number of lines increasing by one for each round.

If, during any round, a duplicate consequence is recorded, that particular line of thinking is stopped (indicated on the chart by a straight line), and an additional ring is drawn around the original circle (see example, Figure 3).

Finally, students examine all the recorded consequences and note any contradictions or opposing arguments. These are acknowledged by connecting the relevant circles with lines, using the second color of marker.

Completed **Decision Wheels** are shared with the rest of the class, and discussion follows.

Figure 2

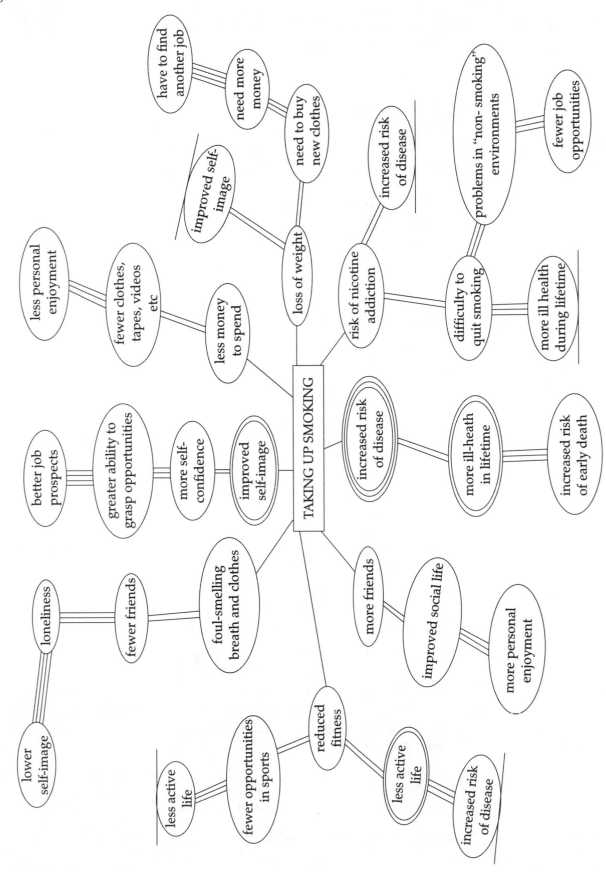

Potential

This activity is designed to help students examine, in a rational and comprehensive manner, the potential implications of any personal decision, so that the decision can be made — or reviewed — in the light of a broad understanding of its likely consequences.

Student groups should be organized so as to represent a wide range of views on the issue under consideration, and members are to be encouraged to record a variety of possible consequences, without necessarily agreeing on their validity. In their reports to the rest of the class, groups can focus on those consequences that were circled more than once (these can be considered the 'most likely') and on any contradictions or inconsistencies that have appeared.

Whole class discussion might include consideration of alternative, less health-threatening ways of achieving the desirable goals listed on the chart.

Source
From an idea in Fitch, R.M. & C.M. Svengalis. *Futures Unlimited*. Washington, DC: National Council for the Social Studies, 1979.

Catching On

Purpose	Introducing issues around the systemic spread of contagious diseases such as tuberculosis, ebola and AIDS
Grade level	9-12
Time needed	20 minutes
Resources	Copiable Handout 1 ☐ for each student (page 135), one handout having the letter V marked on the back. An open space at the front of the classroom.

Procedure

Students engage in the Healthy People Search activity as described on page 134.

At an appropriate point in the debriefing, the facilitator reveals the existence of the letter **V** on the back of one handout and asks the student having that handout to come to the front of the classroom.

The student is told that she has unfortunately been stricken by a new virus for which there is no known cure or treatment. This new virus is effectively passed on through face-to-face oral communication. Therefore any students with whom the affected student has spoken in the course of the activity should also come forward, as they may be similarly affected.

Any remaining students who have talked with anyone now standing at the front should also come forward. (By this time most — if not all — students will be at the front of the classroom.)

General discussion follows.

Potential

This activitiy provides a thought-provoking example of the systemic spread of highly contagious disease. It can be used as an effective introduction to issues relating to specific diseases such as tuberculosis, typhoid, and AIDS.

The activity might also lead students to contemplate the implications for the human population of the rapid spread of a deadly virus such as Ebola or Lassa fever, or of a newly emergent one about which little is yet known.

From a historical perspective, the activity can illustrate the spread of deadly diseases such as the bubonic plague (which killed nearly half of Europe's populations between 1347 and 1350) or virulent strains of influenza (one of which accounted for 22 million deaths in 1917-1918).

Profile 2

Health Issues

by Karen Grose

Empowering children and encouraging them to believe that their opinions, actions and attitudes will shape their futures is an exciting and challenging task.

One day, a conversation revolving around the question of shaping the future arose during our Community Circle Dialoguing, and led to a discussion about the significance of health for our present and future lives. At first, some of the students in my class of 11 and 12 year olds addressed health as something they already had and did not need to think about. After a few of the children shared stories of family members who had health difficulties, however, the class began to see 'good health' not as a given right, but as a complex issue worthy of further understanding. One of the students said that, without reflecting upon the role of health and its importance to our survival, there was no point in discussing preferable futures at all because, without good health, our probable future would be very unsightly.

To develop this line of thinking, I asked the children to sit in groups and to record on chart paper some of the types of health issues that they: 1. were familiar with, 2. wanted to know more about, and 3. were concerned about. I found out that my class was well aware of the different food groups and the importance of maintaining a balanced diet. They understood the effect of exercise and smoking on longevity, and could list the functions of some parts of the human body. However, the class wanted to know more about such topics as their body systems, what they called 'crazy people,' why hospitals are so scary, how to deal with someone who has a disease like cancer or AIDS, and why the starving people they see on TV have 'big full tummies.'

They were concerned about pesticides in fruit, contracting AIDS, having to deal with a dying parent one day, why sometimes they felt fine physically but sad inside (for no apparent reason), and why, as a global community, we aren't reducing pollution to stop the ozone deterioration, even though many people are dying of skin cancer. For the three months following, we explored the questions put forth by the class.

To begin our understanding of health and the interconnections within our own bodies, I broke the class of 32 members into small groups, and had each group research and prepare a short presentation focused on one of the body systems.

After all the groups had presented their findings (through discussion, pictures, diagrams and dramatic presentations), we sat in a circle and I asked the children to revisit what they had done when they had gotten up that morning. As Aparna began to tell her story of waking up to the alarm and getting out of bed, I stopped her and asked the class what body systems she had relied on to get up. The children representing the muscular, skeletal and respiratory systems immediately put up their hands and explained their functions in this process. I held the end of a large ball of yarn, and tossed the ball over to the group representing the respiratory system. They held the string and passed the ball to the group representing the skeletal system. As Aparna's story unfolded, an intricate web of connections formed between the groups of children representing the various body systems. By the time Aparna had reached the point where she sat down for breakfast, the point was well taken. The human body, like any living organism, runs most efficiently as a delicate and interconnected system. To the children, the day-to-day functioning and maintenance of the physical systems of their bodies was no longer taken for granted. 'It's a miracle that I work!' exclaimed Rheama with a big smile.

What happens if one of the body systems becomes jeopardized? This was the next question I posed to the children. With great enthusiasm, they began to brainstorm reasons for this. The children used the example of drinking sour milk to continue to weave their web, and they discovered that the body systems still functioned interdependently to deal with potential problems. Johnny then asked, 'What type of things would cause a permanent breakdown between these connections?' As this question was discussed, the class decided to independently explore interesting issues that could jeopardize body functioning and to present them in a marketplace-style forum nearer to the end of our three-month study, so they could learn from each other's findings.

The issue of mental health, which I term 'wellness,' was another enlightening area of discovery. Not only were the children engaged in a series of self-administered tests (answering such questions as: 'Am I more likely an optimist/pessimist, an introvert/extrovert, a follower/leader, left-brained/right-brained? Do I think in stereotypes? What color is my personality? What body language do I speak?' and 'Am I a critical thinker?') to learn more about themselves. They also reflected both in a journal and in groups about their understanding of the reasons people's attitudes, opinions, beliefs, habits and feelings are different. These reflections were used as vehicles to discuss generational and class differences as well as gender and racial inequities, and this allowed the children to challenge previously conceived assumptions. Commonalities were highlighted, and differences were understood in greater depth.

One of the questions asked at the beginning of the *Health Issues* unit was 'Why are hospitals scary?' As the children in my classroom represent a rich tapestry of cultural diversity, their perceptions of a health facility were varied because their understandings were based on their own practical experiences from many different countries within our global community. Yet common to their beliefs was an element of uncertainty and fear. To address this, I arranged for a community outreach worker from our local health facility, Scarborough General Hospital, in Metropolitan Toronto, Ontario, to visit our classroom to discuss the role of the hospital with the children.

She brought with her many common items and technologies used in the hospital, and talked to the children about their preconceived notions. After her visit, the class visited the hospital on two occasions, and took part in an interactive program where they made finger casts, tried out various types of equipment and toured a number of the units in the facility. One child wrote in her reflective journal: 'The hospital is a happy place. We saw a five hour old newborn baby and the children's playroom. The nurses and doctors are kind, and they showed us all the good things that happen there. Even though people go there when they are in trouble, they are treated well and cared for. Susan's grandmother comes here, and she told us all about her chemotherapy. She says it's a good hospital. People are born in a hospital and sometimes come and die here, too. A hospital is part of our life cycle.'

One concern that arose from our study on health and health facilities was the lack of literature written for young children about hospitals. Following our first visit, a number of children in the class went to the library to search for books about the hospital, and found next to nothing. As a result, the class decided to write story books for children aged six through eight (the same age as their Reading Buddies) about a happy visit to the hospital. The children spent about ten weeks using a Writing Workshop process to create beautiful storybooks which they shared with other classes and then lent to the Scarborough General Hospital for two months, to read to the children staying there.

Connections focused on health beyond ourselves and our community were also established. We discussed and wrote about what health 'looks like' in developing countries and the reasons why (such as economics and technology) health care 'looks' different in developed countries. The concept of what was fair came up continuously, and the children perceived inequities in health care as a growing global concern. They questioned and debated the issue of the imbalance between developed countries' increasing industrialization and quest for power at the expense of human life and our environment.

Health is no longer taken for granted among this group of students. It is a commonality — much like love, dance and food — that we should share with everyone in our 'global village.' By protecting every living being's health, addressing health issues and contributing to social change through peaceful and democratic action, these children have determined that our future could be a lot brighter for everyone.

Karen Grose is Principal of Sir Samuel B. Steele Junior School, Toronto District School Board.

5

Perceptions, perspectives and cross-cultural encounters

Consciousness of perspective is central to global education. A recurring aim across curricula, learning programs and classroom activities is to foster recognition, then understanding, of the multiplicity of perspectives on any issue. The global classroom encourages students to appreciate how perspective is shaped by a variety of factors. Such factors include age, class, creed, culture, ethnicity, gender, ideology, language, nationality, place, race and sexual orientation. The global classroom also helps students recognize that:

- They have their own perspective.
- They interpret reality from within a particular framework of thought and perception, ideas and assumptions.
- There are difficulties and dangers attendant upon using that frame of reference for interpreting the lifestyles, patterns of behavior, values and worldviews of others.

The challenge of diverse perspectives woven into global learning activities can provide a powerful stimulus for reflecting on and reframing personal worldviews. This is a process in which today's students will have to become adept if they are to effectively and creatively confront the seismic shifts and never-ending waves of change likely to characterize the 21st century.

Activities throughout this book explore **perceptions** and **perspectives** on a range of global issues and themes. This chapter, however, focuses particularly upon the nature and validity of perceptions and perspectives as such. The activities ask students to reflect on their **self-perceptions**, on **how others perceive us**, and on **cultural perspectives** on a range of topics (for example, what it means to be a human being, the seasons, sounds, colors, symbols). This chapter's activities thus provide opportunities for consideration of a number of significant themes:

association — how we tend to associate words, images and new information with past experiences that we have already processed (as the saying goes, 'we see what is behind our eyes')

selectivity — how we tend to prioritize and select certain information/arguments/viewpoints, and marginalize or dismiss others, according to our established mindset and predispositions

classification — how we easily fall into classifying and categorizing new data and information into well established pigeonholes of the mind

stereotypes — how we often attribute a range of common (often negative) characteristics to groups of people who are or seem different, hence negating their individuality

objectivity — If people's worldviews are different and if individuals 'see what is behind their eyes,' is objectivity possible or even desirable?

Perspective consciousness is vital in today's increasingly multicultural societies. We need to recognize that our neighbors see things differently. We need to understand those differences, and establish a reciprocity of respect and accommodation. We also need to be aware that **cross-cultural misunderstanding** can happen very easily.

The final activities in this chapter explore issues around **cross-cultural communication**, both **verbal** and **non-verbal**, and the **assumptions** we all too easily carry into cross-cultural situations. The activities also provide a platform for considering, and sharing experiences of, **culture shock.** (This occurs when immersion in a cultural context markedly different from our own jolts us into reassessing our own culture.) As well, the activities provide a platform for exploring **culture clash** (which can easily occur when two or more cultures with radically different values meet and interact).

The interdependent nature of the contemporary world — allowing easy access to different cultural values and practices through mass media, travel or migration of peoples — makes first or second-hand experience of culture clash a common phenomenon in our daily lives. How should the host society respond to those migrant families from sub-Saharan Africa who wish to maintain the traditional practice of female circumcision? Or how should the host schools respond to Muslim parents who object to co-educational physical education or Muslim girls who wish to wear traditional dress to school?

In our objections to child labor, what do we say to those in the Indian sub-continent and South-east Asia who maintain that the transition from childhood to adulthood occurs as early as 12 and that the income earned by young people is vital if the family is to survive? How do we come to terms with radically different definitions of sexual harassment? How do we establish a reciprocity of respect and accommodation in such cases? Are values and standards relative to culture or are there universal standards that should override cultural practices, however long-standing and deep-seated? These issues are considered further in Book 2, in the Equity and Rights and Responsibilities chapters.

PERCEPTIONS

CONCEPTS

	Perceptions	Perspectives	Self-Perceptions	How Others Perceive Us	Cultural Perspectives	Association	Selectivity	Classification	Stereotypes	Objectivity	Cross-Cultural Misunderstanding	Cross-Cultural Communication	Assumptions	Culture Shock	Culture Clash
How I See Myself	*		*	*											
Out of the Bag		*			*										
Moon Calendar		*		*	*	*									
Sounds and Colors	*		*		*	*									
Seeing Symbols	*	*			*	*							*	*	
The Rumor Experiment	*		*	*		*	*	*		*					
Seeing Things Differently	*		*			*									
Alpha Observers		*		*	*						*		*		
Newspapers	*										*	*		*	
Everyday Communication											*	*			
Meetings and Misunderstandings	*										*	*	*		*
Bafa Bafa	*										*	*	*	*	*

CONNECTIONS • A number of activities in this series concern self-perception and others' perceptions of ourselves. See, especially, Tell Me (p.38), You're Like... (p.39), Friends and Enemies (bk 2), Who Am I? (p.39), Likes and Dislikes (p.41). • What's Your Smell? (bk 2), Reading Photographs (bk 2) and Divergent Thinking (p.53) are good introductory activities for work on perspectives. • My View of the World (p.58) asks students to reflect upon their worldview while Selling Mother (p.117) provides a potentially dramatic platform for considering cultural perceptions of land and how language both mirrors and colors perceptions. • Wellness Wheels (p.136) looks at perceptions of health while World Health Diamond Ranking (p.144) explores perspectives on health issues. • Group Pressures (bk 2) examines how dominant perceptions and perspectives can influence individuals. • A number of activities in Book 2 explore stereotypes, assumptions and perceptions around gender and disability. See, especially, Tools Around the Home, Ghost Resort, Take Two, The Disable Label, Gender Expectations and The Real McCoy • How Others See Us (bk 2) focuses on perceptions and stereotypes • A range of activities in Book 2 examine how media influence perceptions, for example, Media Watch, Opposite Messages, Slanted Commentaries, Images in the Media and Deconstructing Television Commercials.

The activities throughout this chapter provide opportunities for students to develop and refine *cross-cultural communication skills* and *skills appropriate to understanding differences in perception and perspective.* In particular, the following skills are addressed:

interpretive skills (**Seeing Symbols; Alpha Observers, Newspapers**)

observation skills (**Rumor Experiment, Seeing Things Differently, Newspapers**)

non-verbal communication skills (**Meetings and Misunderstandings, Bafa Bafa**)

Cross-cultural communication skills are directly addressed in **Everyday Communication, Meetings and Misunderstandings** and **Bafa Bafa.**

Lateral thinking skills are practiced in **Out of the Bag** while *imaging skills* come to the fore in **Sounds and Colors.**

How I See Myself

Purpose	Reflecting on and sharing self-perspectives
Grade level	3-12
Time needed	30 minutes
Resources	Sheet of paper and pen or pencil for each student.

Procedure

The teacher explains to the students that they are going to be asked to see themselves in relation to a series of pairs of words. Each word pair will give rise to a pair of images, and students are to relate the images to the way they see themselves.

Word pairs are then read out in turn. While sufficient time should be allowed for students to note their choices, intervals should be kept to a minimum so that students are responding to first impressions.

How would you describe yourself? Are you more like:
- a cat or a dog?
- solid or liquid?
- Monday or Saturday?
- green or orange?
- wool or nylon?
- a jeep or a luxury car?
- an eagle or a dolphin?
- a boat or an aircraft?
- a bunch of violets or a sunflower?
- a clothesline or a kite string?
- sea or sky?
- a radish or a strawberry?

Students are then asked to think about their choices and to reflect those choices in a sentence beginning: '**One thing I like about myself is....**'

The class divides into groups of three or four to share and discuss their self-perceptions. (One good way of structuring the group work is to have group members speak to their choice from the first word pair, then the second and so on, before, finally, sharing sentences.)

Potential

A light-hearted and non-threatening means of enabling students to reflect on their self-perceptions and share them with others. Discussion is likely to bring out the kaleidoscopic nature of images and perceptions we have of self.

Extension

Group members can be asked to reflect upon whether others would have been able to guess their responses accurately (see **Variation 2** below). This can lead to whole class discussion of the likely accuracy and validity, or otherwise, of our perceptions of other people.

Variations

1. Students can be asked to arrange their word pair choices in a pattern or symbol representing themselves. With their individual consent, the artwork produced can be hung on the classroom walls and reviewed by class members prior to discussion.

2. Students divide their sheets of paper into columns, one column for each group member as well as one for themselves. For each word pair, they make their own choice and also decide what they think other group members will have chosen. They then compose their '**One thing....**' sentence. This variation will raise more directly the question of differences between our perception of self and how others perceive us. This variation should only be attempted with a very well affirmed class.

3. The activity can focus on physical rather than personality self-perception. 'How would you describe your body? Is it more like a... or a...?' **The alternatives chosen by the teacher should always be positive**.

Source
Adapted by Sandy Parker from an idea in: *Taught Not Caught*. UK: Clarity Collective, Learning Development Aids, 1983.

Out Of The Bag

Purpose	Demonstrating how different groups can have different perspectives on what it means to be human
Grade level	1-12
Time needed	45 minutes
Resources	A mystery bag for each group of 3-4 students. Each mystery bag contains: 2 markers (different colors), adhesive tape, piece of string, selection of colored wools, plasticene, 3 paper clips, 2 balloons, glue stick, 2 paper cups, colored paper, scissors. A sheet of newsprint for each group.

Procedure

Each group is given a sheet of newsprint and a mystery bag. The group's task is to use the contents of the bag to depict a **human being**.

It should be emphasized that the depiction can be abstract and/or concrete, and should convey much more than just a physical image of what a human being is.

Each group displays and explains its depiction. The class discusses what is common and what is different in the work of the various groups. (A list of points can be compiled by the teacher as the discussion unfolds.)

Potential

An activity designed to show in a simple and enjoyable way how different groups can have different perspectives on what it means to be human. The task can be made more demanding for students in senior grades by calling for abstract, symbolic or impressionistic depictions only.

Extension

Groups can be asked to consider a range of depictions of human beings from the high art and folk art of different cultures.

Variations

The focus of the activity can be varied. For example, instead of depicting what it means to be human, groups can depict one of the following: our community, our country, Planet Earth, the future.

Source
Adapted by Sandy Parker from an idea in: *Taught Not Caught*. UK: Clarity Collective, Learning Development Aids, 1983.

Moon Calendar

Purpose	Exploring student perspectives on the immediate environment.
	Contrasting those perspectives with the worldview informing the Moon Calendar.
Grade level	5-9
Time needed	60 minutes
Resources	A copy of the Moon Calendar for each student (Copiable Handout 1 ☐). Paper, pencils, markers, large sheets of newsprint.

Procedure

Students are given copies of the Moon Calendar (Copiable Handout 1☐). It is briefly discussed, with the teacher telling students that many of North America's First Nations, or Aboriginal Peoples, developed calendars like this one. The exact content of such calendars depends on the particular First Nation's environment. For example, a calendar might refer to whales if the people lived near the ocean, or to mountain

MOON CALENDAR

Calendar of the Saulteaux (Plains Ojibwa)

January	Half-winter Moon
February	Big Moon
March	Goose Moon
April	Frog Moon
May	Budding Moon
June	Blooming Moon
July	Unripe Berry Moon
August	Ripe Berry Moon
September	Moose Mating Moon
October	Migrating Moon
November	Freezing Up Moon
December	Winter Begins Moon

Source: Pohorecky, Zenon. *Saskatchewan People.*
Saskatoon, Saskatchewan: Saskatchewan
Department of Culture and Youth, 1977, p. 57.

goats if they lived in the mountains. From the content of the Handout, what can students tell about the environment of the people who developed this calendar?

Students can choose to work individually or in pairs. Their task is to devise a similar calendar with appropriate titles for each month of the year. They base their ideas on their own awareness of the environment in which they live. Calendars should be illustrated.

Calendars are displayed and students move around to review each other's work.

Whole-class discussion follows.

Potential

An activity providing students with the opportunity to develop a greater awareness of their own and each other's perspectives on their immediate environment, and to contrast those perspectives with the worldview informing the Moon Calendar.

A critical question for discussion is:
- What would those who go by the Moon Calendar make of our calendars?

Other questions include:
- What do class members/people of different cultures most associate with each month? Do they prioritize environmental, cultural, festival, familial or personal associations?
- Does the passing of the year, and cycle of the seasons, matter as much to everybody?
- Do things we associate with different months make us happier/sadder and affect our attitudes and behaviors?

Note: At an appropriate point, it should be explained that the Moon Calendar depicted in Copiable Handout 1☐ is an approximation. Before contact with European culture, the Western calendar with its 12 months of specific duration was unknown. Also, there were some differences among the Ojibwa peoples as to names given to times of year.

Extension

The class reads stories from Jean Craighead George's *The Thirteen Moons* series. New York: Harper Collins. For instance, they could read *The Moon of the Gray Wolves*, published in 1991. It is the story of a gray wolf and its struggle to survive the month of November in its home on the Alaskan tundra.

Variations

1. The activity can be introduced by a short visualization in which students, relaxed and with eyes closed, explore in their imaginations their experience of their own environment at different times of the year.

2. The activity is attempted in conjunction with sister schools in other parts of the world. Resulting calendars are exchanged by e-mail or

regular mail. A dialogue follows around the worldviews that the different calendars reveal.

3. Students produce an illustrated day calendar for the coming year. They include one page for each month.

Source
Sandy Parker.

Sounds and Colors

Purpose	Becoming aware of the different ways people hear and interpret the same sounds
Grade level	1-12 (For the earlier grades, teachers may wish to use only part of the extract **Tia: Pink or Yellow?** in Copiable Handout 2 ❐.)
Time needed	40 minutes
Resources	A prepared audio cassette of a selection of 10 sounds; for example, birdsong, surf on a beach, traffic noise, thunder, fountain, busy marketplace or mall, stream, various animals. Each sound should be followed by a pause. A copy, or several, of **Tia: Pink or Yellow?** (Copiable Handout 2 ❐.)

Procedure

As an initial focusing and awareness-raising exercise, students are asked to be very still, close their eyes, and listen to all the sounds they can hear outside the classroom.

The class then brainstorms a list of sounds heard and shares their thoughts on the process of listening. What happens when they register a sound? Do they see pictures? Do they immediately make associations with things they know? Are the sounds registered abstractly?

Students are then asked to listen to the audio cassette of ten sounds, and to react to each sound by writing down the **color** the sound brings to mind. Comment and discussion are to be avoided, as is any conscious effort on the students' part to explain their choices to themselves.

Discussion begins with a sharing of colors chosen and an exploration of the wide variety of associations made and their possible reasons. Does any pattern of differing associations emerge that is possibly based on factors such as culture, gender, background and experience? Would people from cultures not represented in the class come up with different color associations?

Finally the extract **Tia: Pink or Yellow?** is read and discussed (Copiable Handout 2 ❐).

Potential

An activity that encourages students to become more aware of the ways in which they hear things, and helps them see that different people register and interpret the same sound differently on account of factors

161

TIA: PINK OR YELLOW?

A walk with (12-year-old) Tia on an island in the Indonesian Archipelago

It was dawn and light was bright and clear on the peak of Gunung Api, the 'fire mountain' at the far end of the island.

We walked together down the beach and a small and mottled heron flew up at our feet, landed ahead on the sand, ruffled, walked, watched us coming on, lengthened its neck in new alarm and flew another few reluctant yards.

Every time it took flight, it uttered a sharp, broken "kew" sound in a descending tone.

"Puchong laut," said Tia and laughed gently. "He sings a green song."

For a moment I simply enjoyed the bird and the poetry of her description, but then it occured to me that only I knew it as a Little Green Heron. In fact it isn't very green at all.

The literal translation of her name for it was something like "longlegs of the sea."

"Why green?" I asked her.

"That is its colour. His voice is like a sharp new leaf or thorn."

"Not brown?"

"No, of course not. Brown is the sound of *katak.*"

Katak was the local toad. The common lumpy one that popped itself up near lights in the village at night and produced a derisory sound that was indeed rather brown.

The idea was beginning to grow on me.

"What makes a black sound?"

"Buffalo. And thunder."

"White?"

"The sea where it touches the sand."

Now I was really hooked.

Tia was giving me these examples without hesitation, as though she was used to hearing sounds in colour.

And what really appealed to me was that the colours were totally appropriate. They were the colours of the objects producing the sound.

I thought of the tawny roar of a lion; the scarlet scream of a macaw; of the deep bronze boom of an important bell, and of how the little ones that tinkled tended to be silver.

"Tia." I said her name clearly. "What colour is that?"

"Pink when *you* say it, like an orchid. Paman Abu makes it yellow."

"And Abu?"

"Sometimes blue, sometimes brown.... It depends."

"On what?"

"The one who says it, and if they feel friendly."

She was clearly getting a little impatient with all this talk about something so obvious, but I couldn't leave it alone.

"All sounds have colours?"

"Astaga! You did not know?"

"No."

"How can you listen to talk or music without colour?" Her eyes were full of pity.

"When the drums talk, they lay a carpet of brown, like soft sand on the ground. A dancer stands on this. Then the gongs call in green and yellow, building forests through which we move and turn. And if we lose our way, there is always the white thread of the flute or the song to guide us home."

She shook her head in sorrow and dismay and, faced with the wisdom of this 12-year-old, I felt like a backward child.

Source: Watson, Lyall. *Gifts of Unknown Things*. London: Hodder & Stoughton, 1976, pp.50-51.

such as background, culture, experience and gender. The **Tia** extract can be used to explore the additional, but related, point that the tone and quality of voice applied to the same word(s) can dramatically influence the impact upon the hearer.

Extension

Students draw images evoked by different pieces of music.

Seeing Symbols

Purpose   Demonstrating different ways people see and interpret the same symbols

Grade level   6-12

Time needed   60-80 minutes, possibly over several class periods

Resources   For **Part A** of the activity, a large card copy or an overhead projection transparency of Copiable Handout 3 ☐, Copiable Handout 4 ☐, Copiable Handout 5 ☐. Note: students should not be given individual copies.

For **Part B** a large card copy or a transparency of Copiable Handout 6 ☐.

For **Part C** a set of 8 small cards (created by photocopying Copiable Handout 7 ☐ and cutting out the cards). Each of the 8 cards is placed in a separate sealed envelope. A large sheet of newsprint and marker for each group of 4.

For the **Variation** a large card copy or a transparency of Copiable Handout 7 ☐.

Procedure, Part A

Copiable Handout 3 ☐ is shown and the class asked 'which straight line is longer?' Responses are noted by show of hands or by having students move and collect in different groups. No discussion is necessary at this stage, but it is important that the teacher draw attention to the fact that different people are seeing the drawings differently.

The process is repeated for Copiable Handout 4 ☐ ('which center circle is larger?') and Copiable Handout 5 ☐ ('can you see the same shape in both drawings?').

Part B

Each drawing in Copiable Handout 6 ☐ is shown in turn. Working individually, students are asked to note, with a word or phrase only, their interpretation and response to each of the drawings.

On the chalkboard the teacher then collates the interpretations and responses to each drawing, encouraging discussion of the different contributions and eliciting possible reasons for them.

Part C

The class divides into groups of four. Each group is given a sealed envelope and is invited to remove the card inside, avoiding communicating its contents to other groups.

Group members are asked to spend a minute or so silently visualizing whatever comes to mind as they think about the object described on the card.

Each group writes the name of the object at the top of its sheet of newsprint and then describes or draws the different interpretations of its four members.

Additionally students are encouraged to list any other interpretations emerging from their discussions.

Group presentations follow.

After all the presentations regarding one of the four objects have been heard, the class discusses the reasons behind the variety (or lack of variety) in the responses.

Potential

An activity demonstrating that people actually do see the same thing differently, and that those differences are intimately connected with how we each view the near-at-hand and wider world.

The debriefing is likely to provoke reflection upon the links between perception, culture and experience. To what extent were the symbols in **Part B** and words in **Part C** interpreted differently because of students' specific life experiences and diverse cultural backgrounds? For instance, how many students saw the first diagram in Copiable Handout 6 ❑ (two crossed lines) as the Chinese figure ten, as a mathematical figure, as a Christian cross, as a crossroads and as a rifle sight? How many saw the diagram in entirely different ways (see Intercultural Communication on page 170 for a discussion of some possibilities)?

At an appropriate stage in the discussion, the following needs to be pointed out: the activity has shown that there is much diversity in perception of simple drawings and objects. Since this is the case, there is probably even more variation (and variance) in our interpretation of sophisticated or abstract concepts such as hope, spirit, peace, rights, freedom and justice.

Variations

1. Other drawings and symbols can be used in **Part B**. Those depicted in Copiable Handout 7 ❑ have proved very effective.

> Other suitable words for **Part C** include: *shoe, ring, egg, candle, lamp, roof, bread, maple leaf, star, sun, moon.*

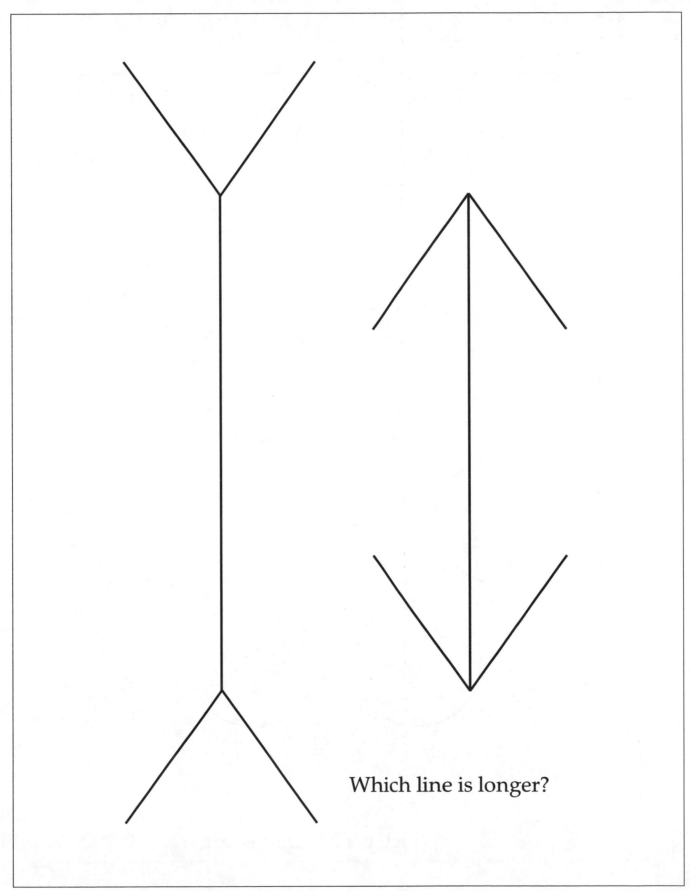

Which line is longer?

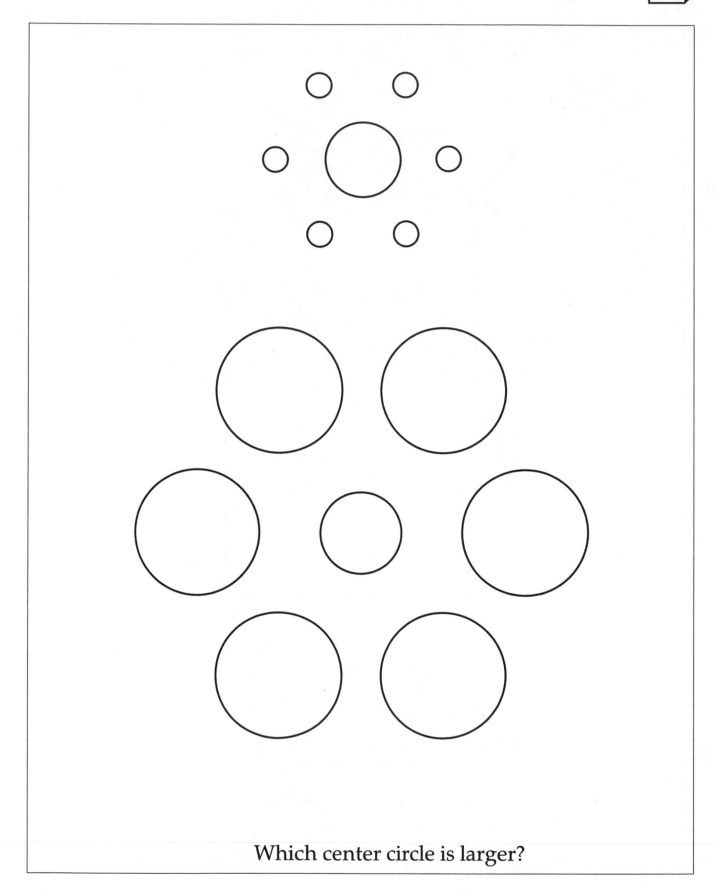

Which center circle is larger?

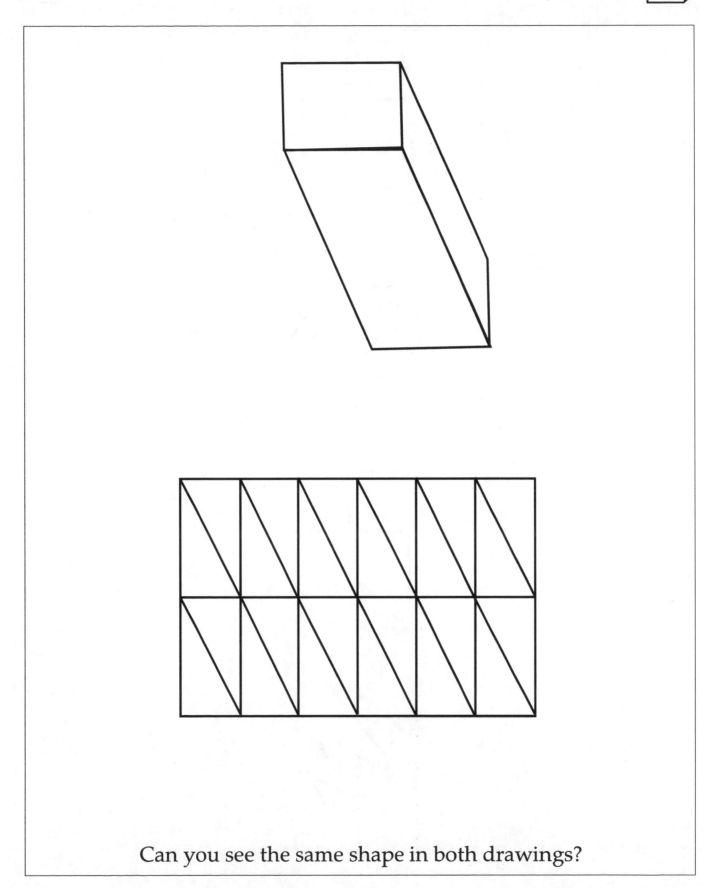

Can you see the same shape in both drawings?

tree	**wolf**
fire	**table**
tree	**wolf**
fire	**table**

2. The impact of the activity can be greatly enhanced by establishing an Internet link with school classes in other parts of the world. Students share, and enter dialogue around activity outcomes.

Extension

Students, consulting with families and friends as appropriate, prepare individual or group presentations on a symbol of significance to their culture or religion. The various presentations are offered to the class over a period of time.

Source
Based on ideas in Singer, Marshall R. *Intercultural Communication: A Perceptual Approach*. Upper Saddle River, New Jersey: Prentice-Hall, 1987, pp. 12-20. See the following excerpt for Singer's experiences with the symbols in Copiable Handout 6 ❏.

Intercultural Communication

The two most common answers I get for the first symbol are "cross" — in the religious sense — and "plus" — in the mathematical sense. Now, since more than half of the participants I get are educated Christians, that is not really a surprising result. Also, since most come from the more developed parts of developing countries, the third most frequent response — "crossroads" — is also not really surprising.

The surprises, for me at least, usually come because of my own perceptual limitations. I am not really surprised by answers like "the letter *T*," "quadrants on a map," " the hands of a compass," "check mark as in *correct* " or "check mark as in *incorrect*," the word *yes*, the word *no*, "Red Cross," and "the sign for Switzerland," although they are not answers I would have thought of myself. The first real surprises came for me when I did this exercise at a United Nations school in Costa Rica with a group of senior Central American civil servants. Virtually every answer I got for that symbol suggested Latin Catholic romantic symbolism: "death and transfiguration," "life after death," "love," "sacrifice," "eternal life," "suffering," "God's son," "redemption," "crucifixion," " resurrection." Not having been raised in a Latin Catholic culture, there was no way I could see those meanings in that symbol.

The second real surprise for me with that symbol came when I did the exercise in Kuala Lumpur, Malaysia, with a group of second-year university students. Virtually every Malaysian of Chinese extraction (about half the students were of Chinese extraction) saw the symbol as the Chinese number ten because — as I discovered that day — that indeed is the way the Chinese write the number ten.

For the second symbol, I have gotten responses that in some ways were even more revealing to me. In one group of participants there was a man from Egypt. When I drew this symbol on the board, he violently threw down his pencil on the desk and in an angry voice said, "I will not draw that symbol! I give my life to oppose it! I will not play games with that symbol!" Whereupon he rolled back one shirt sleeve and asked, "Do you see that scar?" pointing to a long, red scar about three inches (7.5 cm)

---

above his right wrist. "I got that fighting murderous Zionism in Sinai in 1956." Now who am I to argue with his perception of that symbol? Obviously for him it really did mean all of those awful things, and nothing that I was going to say could change that perception. The more I have thought about that Egyptian's reaction to that symbol, and compared it to other reactions I have gotten from different people with different life experiences, the more amazed I am that any communication at all ever takes place.

When I have done this exercise with a group of predominantly Jewish, middle-class, American students from New York City, I have gotten answers like "Manischewitz wine," "Mogen David products," "Jewish star," "star of David," "peace," "chicken soup," " high holy days," and many other meanings that only an American Jew could associate with that symbol. The third symbol, I have always drawn carefully. While there is usually some diversity among the answers, anywhere from 60 to 100 per cent will see it somehow associated with Hitler, fascism or Nazi Germany. The fact is that the symbol is **not** a Nazi swastika. That it is really an ancient Aryan (Indian) symbol in no way changes the depth of one's perception of it as a Nazi swastika.

The fourth symbol is much more ambiguous than the first three, and is open to more interpretation. Still, a great many people see it as a "squiggle" or a "signature" or a "corkscrew." More people from developing countries see it as a "river," a "snake," or a "puff of smoke" than do people from developed countries. I once did this exercise at a graduate school of nursing, and more than 60 per cent of the participants in that group saw it specifically as an "intrauterine device (IUD)" or simply as a "coil" or a "birth-control device." But if you've never seen an IUD, there just is no way you can know what you don't know. **We know what we perceive; we don't know what we don't perceive. Since there is no way that we can know what we don't perceive, we assume that we perceive "correctly" — even if we don't.**

Source
Singer, Marshall R. **Intercultural Communication: A Perceptual Approach**. Upper Saddle River, New Jersey: Prentice-Hall, 1987, pp. 17-20.

The Rumor Experiment

Purpose   Responding to a picture, and considering influences on one's own and others' perceptions and responses

Grade level   All grades (with appropriate simplification for grades 1-8)

Time needed   60 minutes

Resources   Any large picture containing a reasonable amount of detail but not overdetailed. (**Note**: The choice of a picture from a developing country or unfamiliar cultural context can be especially effective in drawing out and raising student awareness of stereotypes.) Masking tape. 6 badges numbered 1 through 6. 6 large pieces of art paper and 6 markers. A checklist for each class member (Copiable Handout 9 ❑). A cassette tape and tape recorder (optional).

THE RUMOR EXPERIMENT						
Item	1	2	3	4	5	6

Procedure, Part A

The teacher asks for six volunteers for an experiment. The class, including the volunteers, are told that the first volunteer will look at a picture for one-and-a-half minutes while the others are out of the room. Then the picture will be put away and the second volunteer invited into the room. The first will describe the picture to the second in as much detail as possible. After the first volunteer has finished her description, she will sit down and draw the picture as she remembers it. Meanwhile, the third person will come in and listen to the description by the second person, the process continuing until the sixth person has heard the description and drawn his version of the picture. The teacher emphasizes that no questions are to be asked and that the class is to remain quiet throughout. The volunteers are given the opportunity to reconsider their participation (and new volunteers are identified if necessary).

Each volunteer puts on a badge designating number 1, 2, 3, 4, 5 or 6. The volunteers stay out of the classroom during the next step of the procedure. Perhaps they can spend the time in the library, the gymnasium or another classroom.

With the volunteers absent, other class members look at the picture and spend a few minutes agreeing upon a list of items in it. They write these in the lefthand column of their own copy of the checklist. It is explained that, as each volunteer describes the picture, class members are to enter a tick (✓) if an item is accurately recalled, a minus (-) if an item is lost, a plus (+) if an item is added to or embellished, and an X if an item is changed. A few spaces are left at the bottom of the lefthand column for continued recording of entirely new items.

Volunteer 1 is then invited in to peruse the picture for one-and-a-half minutes while the other five volunteers are out of the room.

Then the picture is put away and Volunteer 2 is invited into the room. Volunteer 1 describes the picture to Volunteer 2 in as much detail as possible. As this is occurring, listening students fill in column 1 of their checklists. (With the agreement of the volunteers, the process can be tape recorded. This provides backup evidence should there be disagreement in the debriefing as to when an item was added or disappeared, or regarding what was actually said.)

After Volunteer 1 has finished her description, she sits down and draws the picture as she remembers it. Meanwhile Volunteer 3 comes in and listens to the description by Volunteer 2. As this is occurring, listening students fill in column 2 of their checklists.

The process of having volunteers come in and hearing the description by the previous volunteer continues until Volunteer 6 has heard the description and drawn his version of the picture. The teacher emphasizes that no questions are to be asked and that the class is to remain quiet throughout — filling in the appropriate columns of their checklists.

At the end of the process, the original picture and the six pictures drawn by the volunteers are displayed, in sequence, on the classroom wall.

Procedure, Part B

Students should first be encouraged to share their accounts of what actually happened, to identify significant events and moments in the experiment, and to offer some initial explanation of what took place. Within the sharing the volunteers should be offered ample opportunity to speak about their feelings and reactions.

The debriefing should finally veer around to examining the relevance and implications of the experiment for everyday life. Students could discuss what the experiment has to say, for instance, about:

a. the nature of real-life rumors
b. the reliability of courtroom testimony, historical documents, history books, newspaper accounts
c. the relative merits of trial by a single judge or trial by judge and jury
d. scientific or academic objectivity
e. dangers inherent in stereotyping
f. causes of interpersonal, intergroup and international conflict (different people, groups and nations perceiving the same situation differently)

Potential

This engrossing experiment helps students understand why there are often many different interpretations of the same scene or event. They explore factors that may influence people's interpretations. They also consider implications of the experiment for everyday life.

Out of the sharing, a number of key areas for further discussion may emerge:

selection and classification
a. Why did the first volunteer select and/or prioritize certain picture content and disregard and/or relegate other content?
b. Did subsequent volunteers follow a similar selection and valuing process in responding to the description they heard? If so, why?
c. What determined the **amount** of description for different things in the picture? Could some items be conveyed in one word while others required elaborate description?
d. To what extent were items classified or categorized to facilitate the processing and conveying of information?
e. To what extent were **stereotypes** employed?

association
a. When volunteers 2-6 heard a particular word, was there an automatic association with some past experience? Did the association color the new image/description?
b. Does the series of drawn pictures move closer and closer in appearance to some known place or environment? If so, what does this suggest?
c. When we listen to someone tell a story, how much does our mind add associations of our own rather than concentrating purely on what is being said?

emotions and personality
a. To what extent is the adage that 'we see what is behind our eyes' true?
b. Does what we see (value) in a picture or real life scene, or what we hear (value) in a description, reflect our individuality or personality?
c. To what degree was learning or personality style evident in the performance of each volunteer? (Some may have given a concrete factual description, and others a virtually verbatim repetition of what they heard. Others may have invested the description with atmosphere and mood, while others may have tried to imagine the relationship between any people depicted.)
d. How did the last few volunteers react, perhaps faced with greater distortion and illogicality and a description increasingly bereft of detail? Did they inject new information? If so, why? Of what type? On what basis?
e. Does the new information in some way reflect their personalities? How did they react to information that made no sense? Was one prepared to describe what she couldn't understand while another left it out? Why should that be?
f. Is our response to what is hard to grasp a reflection of personality difference?
g. Did volunteers' emotional reactions to the experiment, positive and negative, influence what they remembered and described?

The potential of the activity can be considerably enhanced by arranging with classes in sister schools in different countries to conduct the experiment using the same picture and then to exchange drawings and an experiment report.

Variations

1. Students form groups of six. One member from each group moves to an empty section of the room and, avoiding discussion or comment, looks at the picture. The group representatives who have seen the picture then take a seat within the empty area and out of earshot of each other. The second member of each group comes forward, has the picture described to him and so on. The process of describing and drawing follows that outlined under **Procedure, Part A.**

2. Students form groups of six or eight and sub-divide into pairs. One partner is nominated 'A,' the other 'B.' 'A' students are given one-and-a-half minutes to look at the picture. They then describe the content of the picture to 'B' students out of earshot of any other pair. 'B' students then draw their versions of the picture.

Both variations are more involving of everyone in the class. The second variation produces more experience and data for comparison. Both variations can be undertaken using the same picture for all groups, or a different picture for each group.

Extensions

1. Repeating the experiment, a real-life scene is substituted for a picture. A volunteer goes out into the school corridor or grounds and observes what is happening for a few minutes. Returning to class, she recounts what she has seen to the second volunteer, and so on. This works best if the second to fifth volunteers are not told by the teacher or first volunteer where the described actions took place.

2. At an appropriate moment, another teacher enters the room and engages in a (pre-arranged) conversation with the class teacher. This may be an excited interchange about an event that has just occurred or will soon occur, an argument of mounting vehemence, or some other type of conversation. On the departure of the visitor, the class teacher asks students to write their own records of what took place. In the debriefing that follows, versions from the student witnesses are compared and contrasted, and lessons drawn.

3. The class decides upon a rumor (or several rumors of different types) they wish to spread through the school and/or community. The rumor(s) should be of the innocuous variety. A careful plan is devised for studying and documenting the process of beginning and spreading the rumor(s) and for identifying changes, additions and subtractions as the rumor(s) are repeated.

4. Students study an important international historical event using primary source materials (in effect, appropriate newspapers, speeches, diaries and the like) and secondary source materials (for example, historical accounts, school textbooks). Materials can be exchanged with sister schools in the appropriate countries through telecommunications linkups. The results of study of the same materials by classes in the sister schools can also be exchanged, and compared and contrasted.

Source
Adapted from Wolsk, D. **An Experience-Centered Curriculum: Exercises in Perception, Communication and Action.** Paris: UNESCO Educational Studies and Documents, No. 17, 1975, pp. 30-35.

Seeing Things Differently

Purpose   Becoming sensitized to how people's perspectives influence the significance they place on various phenomena. Becoming alert to the dangers of allowing any group to dictate opinions.

Grade level   5-12 (**Part A**); 10-12 (**Parts B, C** and **D**)

Time needed   60 minutes

Resources   A set of 10 pictures (of, for example, works of art, clothing fashions, sports, townscapes, farmscapes, wilderness, a pop concert, a classical orchestra, a folk music group, a coffee bar). Pictures are displayed around the classroom walls. Each picture should be identified by a letter or number. Paper, pens or pencils for individual work. Newsprint and markers for group work.

Procedure, Part A

Students are given a few minutes to study the pictures without discussing them with anyone.

They are then asked to rank them in order of preference, again without consultation.

When the class reassembles, the teacher asks a number of students to volunteer their first five preferences. These are recorded on the chalkboard.

In the discussion that follows, both the basis and significance of individual decisions are considered:
   a. Were preferences made on the basis of the object/activity/place depicted and/or on the quality of the picture as a picture?
   b. Were other criteria used in making choices?
   c. Is any one criterion 'right' and the others 'wrong?'
   d. Is any ranking of the pictures 'correct' and others, to a greater or lesser extent, 'incorrect?'

Procedure, Part B

In groups of three or four, students brainstorm the consequences that would ensue if society were to judge that certain opinions, viewpoints, tastes or preferences were 'right' and others 'wrong.'

As each group reports back, the teacher records on the chalkboard the ideas put forward.

This is followed by class discussion of conclusions drawn and difficulties raised by the exercise.

Procedure, Part C

In the same groups, students brainstorm the consequences, personal and societal, of being willing to accept differences of opinion, viewpoint, taste or preference.

Once again, groups present, and the teacher records their lists of consequences. The differences between the two sets of lists are thoroughly aired and conclusions are drawn.

Procedure, Part D

Groups reconvene and discuss the following questions:
   a. Are there certain opinions, viewpoints, tastes or preferences that society should not and cannot permit?
   b. What criteria can society reasonably use in deciding whether or not to outlaw those opinions, viewpoints, tastes and preferences?
   c. Who should speak for 'society?'

Reporting back and class discussion follows.

Potential

Part A seeks to sensitize students to the different weight and significance that individuals give to the same object, activity or place, according to their perspective and worldview. **Parts B** and **C** seek to alert students to the dangers attendant upon allowing any group or institution to dictate taste and opinion, and give students the opportunity to identify both the nature and role of the individual and society as a whole in maintaining choice.

Part D counterbalances the liberal thrust of **Parts B** and **C** by having students consider whether, even in a free democratic country, society has the right to curtail conduct and expressions of opinion and taste in particular areas. Issues around racist, sexist and homophobic opinions and behaviors may well emerge in discussion as may topics such as child pornography, incest and pedophilia.

Central to the discussion is the question of how society strikes a balance between promoting freedom and ensuring conformity to certain standards of acceptability.

Source

Adapted from an activity devised by Eileen Porter, Curriculum Development Centre, Dewsbury, West Yorkshire, England, and described in her University of York Diploma in Global and Multicultural Education report, *Medicine and Health Care Around the World,* 1986.

Alpha Observers

Purpose	Raising awareness of cross-cultural misunderstandings
Grade level	6-9
Time needed	60-70 minutes
Resources	A collection of photographs (1 for each 3 students) depicting scenes in their own country and globally. The photographs should include people and embrace images of social and global problems (for example, conflict, environmental degradation, human rights denials) as well as images of everyday life (for example, a busy shopping mall, a hockey game, a street scene). A mission assignment sheet for each student (Copiable Handout 9 ☐).

Procedure

Students form groups of three. Mission assignment sheets are distributed and read. Students are encouraged to try to look at life through Alpha eyes.

When each group is ready, it receives one of the photographs. Each group has ten minutes to brainstorm its (Alpha) impressions of Earth, based on the photograph it received, and write a report.

In the ensuing plenary session, each group delivers its report (in role) and takes questions.

Once all the reports have been heard, each group combines with one or two other groups to write a revised joint report based on the information now available to everybody.

Combined reports are next presented to the whole class, which can, time allowing, negotiate a brief final report summarizing what has been said.

During the first or second plenary session, the teacher can read out the parable of the elephant (Copiable Handout 10 ☐), which points up the dangers of drawing conclusions from limited evidence.

Potential

A role play activity that encourages students to look at the Earth and its inhabitants from a different perspective. The first round of reporting and discussion is designed to raise awareness of cross-cultural misunderstandings and of the difficulties and inadequacies of drawing conclusions from limited information. The work in combined groups asks students to synthesize loosely connected or even conflicting information.

ALPHA TRAVELERS

Your Mission

You have been selected to be part of a team of pioneer explorers and researchers from Planet Alpha. You will be flying in a fleet of specially designed hyperspacecraft to learn about a planet in a distant galaxy. It is called Earth, and very little is known about it. Your mission is to fly as low as possible in order to catch a glimpse of life and report back on how Earth beings live. You will have little time to do this, as Alphas cannot sustain long periods in the area of a yellow sun. Each craft will catch only one brief glimpse of life on Earth, and will not be able to land.

Your Identity

At this moment let us remind you of your identity. As you of course know full well, you are among the group of Alphas who possess the ability to fly. You have two legs, a rudder and wings. You do not talk, but communicate through telepathy. Beings on Alpha have developed a peaceful and harmonious society. Everyone and everything on the planet is loved and respected.

Alpha is a beautiful planet full of clean yellow rivers, deep red seas and marvellous purple growth. Alphas have built houses underground so as to not harm anything on the planet. Alphas keep their world clean and beautiful. The Alpha world has four-legged non-flying Alphas, and various other types of Alphas of all shapes, sizes and colors. We all live happily together. We enjoy the great variety among ourselves as Alphas. We rejoice in our differences.

Your Task

Once your team has flown over Earth's surface and taken a photograph using super electron magnification, please analyze it. Sit down together as a team to decipher what it shows about life on Earth. How do the inhabitants live? Does Earth look like a happy place? How do the inhabitants treat each other? Is Earth like Alpha or not?

When you have analyzed your photograph, put together your report to the beings of Alpha.

REMEMBER!
YOU ARE AN ALPHA AND KNOW VERY LITTLE ABOUT LIFE ON EARTH. EVERYTHING YOU SEE IS NEW. IT MAY EVEN SHOCK YOU. WE AT MISSION CONTROL ARE COUNTING ON YOU TO REVEAL THE MYSTERIES OF THIS FAR-OFF PLANET. KNOW THAT YOU WILL BE REWARDED FOR YOUR COURAGE AND BRAVERY IN TAKING ON THIS MISSION.

THE ELEPHANT

There were six blind people. They heard that the king was visiting the next village, riding on an elephant. None of them had ever seen an elephant. 'An elephant!' they said. 'I wonder what an elephant is like.'

They went to find out. Each of them went alone. The first held the elephant's trunk. The second held a tusk. The third held an ear. The fourth held a leg. The fifth held the stomach. The sixth held the tail. Then they went home, all sure that they now knew exactly what the elephant looked like.

They began to tell each other. 'Oh it's a fantastic elephant,' said the first, 'so slow and soft, long and strong.' 'No,' said the one who had felt the tusk. 'It's quite short, and very sharp.' 'You're both of you wrong,' said the third, who had felt the ear. 'The elephant is flat and thin like a big leaf.' 'Oh, no,' said the fourth, who had felt the leg, 'It's like a tree.'

And the other two joined in, too. 'It's like a wall.' 'It's like a rope.' They argued and argued, and their argument grew very bitter. They began to fight.

Then someone came up who could see. 'You are all right,' said this person who could see. 'All the parts together are the elephant.'

Source: Richardson, R. **Learning for Change in World Society: Reflections, Activities, Resources.** London: World Studies Project, 1979, p.60.

The activity also provides the opportunity to discuss current global problems and hopes for the future by contrasting Alpha and human society. Would students like to live in a society like the former?

Variation

Groups are given photographs depicting people of different cultures within their own country or globally. Their mission is 'to report on our country's society' or 'to report on human society.' The former variation leads nicely into the question 'What does it mean to be a citizen of our country?' Both the former and the latter raise questions surrounding cultural commonalties and differences.

Source
After an idea from David Dunetz, Tel Aviv, Israel.

Newspapers

Purpose	Applying observation skills to operating within an unfamiliar culture
Grade level	6-12
Time needed	40 minutes
Resources	A selection of newspapers in languages other than English and French. (These are available at some newsstands and bookstores, or from the internet.) If possible, the newspapers should all be for the same day.

Procedure

Groups of three are each given one newspaper to look through. None of the three should be able to read the featured language, and the group should not be told what that language is. Their task is to find out all they can about the country and/or culture from which the newspaper originates.

Groups then report their various conclusions to the class, explaining how they reached them.

This is followed by whole-class discussion around learnings from the activity.

Potential

An activity that encourages students to apply their observation skills to the problems of operating within an unfamiliar culture. For those who have not had the experience, it also offers a glimpse of what it might be like to arrive in a place where the language and culture are different from their own. What must it be like to find oneself suddenly in an environment where the street signs, advertisements, newspapers and conversation make no sense to you? (Students who have gone through the arrival experience can be encouraged to share their stories.)

Variation

Groups peruse their newspaper and compile a list of the ten questions they would most like to ask someone from the country/culture in question. Representatives of the countries/cultures are invited to class and, in plenary session, respond to each group's questions.

Source
Derived from ideas developed by John Cogan and Walter Enloe, Global Education Center, University of Minnesota, Minneapolis.

Everyday Communication

Purpose	Applying thinking and communications skills to cross-cultural situations
Grade level	6-12
Time needed	60 minutes
Resources	A selection of cards, each card containing an everyday question people might want to ask; for example:

- What time is it?
- I'm lost; where is the train station?
- Where can I buy a good cheap meal?
- Where can I buy some stamps?
- Is there a hospital nearby?
- When does the last bus leave for the town center?
- What is the cost of a room for the night?
- Where do I find a restroom?

Procedure

Each group of three students is given four cards. The group's task is to work out how they would try to communicate **three** of their questions if they were in a city in another country. The residents do not speak their language(s), and students do not know the local language(s). Groups, having been given four questions in all, are to leave aside the question they feel it would be most difficult to communicate.

In the plenary discussion that follows, groups demonstrate and compare their solutions, discussing the particular difficulties they might encounter.

Finally each group reads out the question it chose not to represent, saying why they thought it would be particularly difficult to communicate.

Potential

An activity that encourages students to apply creative and lateral thinking, and non-verbal communication skills, to cross-cultural situations.

Source
Based on an idea developed by John Cogan and Walter Enloe, Global Education Center, University of Minnesota, Minneapolis.

Meetings and Misunderstandings

Purpose — Developing awareness of non-verbal gestures used by people of different cultures and countries

Grade level — 5-11

Time needed — 60 minutes

Resources — A main classroom and 3 separate adjoining areas. 2 large signs saying 'Bulgarian Merchants' and 'Turkish Merchants.' Masking tape. Currency in various denominations for Tourists and Merchants ($30 total for Tourists; $100 total for Merchants). See Copiable Handout 11 ❑. Information cards for Tourists (12), Bulgarian Merchants (6), Turkish Merchants (6) and Assistants/Observers (6). See Copiable Handout 12 ❑. A selection of postcards (could be pictures cut from tourist magazines and pasted on card) and trinkets/souvenirs for each Merchant. Prices should be marked on each item (postcards might be valued at $2, $3 or $4 according to size, and trinkets/souvenirs at $6 or more). Optional: large map of southeast Europe; tourist posters to set the atmosphere.

Procedure, Part A

The class is divided into 4 groups. With a class of 30, the following group sizes are suggested: Tourists 12, Bulgarian merchants 6, Turkish merchants 6, Assistants/Observers 6.

The teacher sets the scene. The tourists are from the students' own country. They are at the end of a package holiday to Bulgaria and Turkey. They are on the Turkish-Bulgarian border, and have one last chance to buy souvenirs from Turkish and Bulgarian merchants. The bus leaves for the airport in 20 minutes. Each group will be given a few minutes to read its information card, and for group members to practice their roles.

The Assistants/Observers stay in the main classroom. The other groups move to their separate adjoining areas.

Information cards are distributed once the groups are alone.

The Assistants/Observers set up the main room (as indicated on their card) and hand out currency to the Tourists.

The Merchants are invited back first. They take up positions at their stalls (it is emphasized that they can call on the Assistants to help but cannot involve them in bargaining).

The Tourists then enter, and are asked to make the best use of their last chance to purchase souvenirs.

When sufficient time has elapsed (15-20 minutes), trading is suspended.

Procedure, Part B

The class is then brought together to relate and discuss their experiences. The following questions are put, first to the Bulgarian merchants, then the Turkish merchants, then the Tourists. (Members of other groups avoiding interjecting.)

  a. Did you make any good bargains? How did you know? What happened?
  b. Did you ever feel cheated? How did you know? What happened?
  c. Did you ever feel misunderstood? What did you do about it?
  d. (Tourists only) What head signals did you come across? What did you make of them?
  e. (Tourists only) Did you find it easier to deal with the first group of merchants you visited or the second? If so, why? Did you find it easier to trade with Bulgarian or Turkish merchants? If so, why?
  f. (Merchants only) Were you able to take advantage of the Tourists in any way? If so, how?

Finally each Assistant/Observer is given the opportunity to comment upon what they saw happening.

The different head movements are then explained by the teacher. The 'nod-shake' system has long been common in most of Europe, and has transferred to other parts of the world as a commonly understood means of signaling 'yes' and 'no.' However, in Greece, Turkey, and parts of Sicily and southern Italy, the 'dip-toss' system is used. In Bulgaria and parts of the former Yugoslavia, the 'roll-toss' system is more common. The teacher demonstrates each system in turn.

Procedure, Part C

Trading is recommenced for a short period.

The class then comes together again for a further debriefing.

CURRENCY SHEET		
$1	$1	$1
$1	$1	$1
$2	$2	$2
$5	$5	$5
$10	$10	$10
$20	$20	$20

INFORMATION CARDS

TOURISTS

You have been visiting Bulgaria and Turkey. You are now on the border between the two countries and have your last chance to buy souvenirs and postcards. You do not speak any Bulgarian or Turkish. You will have to use sign language and nod your head for 'yes' and shake it for 'no.' You want to obtain the best bargain with the money you have left, and want to buy several souvenirs. You know that you will be able to bargain over prices so, before you enter the marketplace, discuss tactics with the other tourists.

TURKISH MERCHANTS

Your job is to sell your souvenirs and postcards to the tourists. Your aim is to earn as much money as you can for your goods and never sell for less than their cost to you (which is half the marked price). Your customers will expect to bargain over prices. They do not speak Turkish and you do not speak English. You will have to use sign language and also the 'dip-toss' system for signaling 'yes' and 'no.' **Practice this now**. 'Yes' is indicated by dipping the nose and chin and then moving them back to their original position. The movement is not repeated. 'No' is indicated by tossing the nose and chin upwards and then returning them to their original position. The movement is not repeated. The Assistants will help you if you request it, but cannot get involved in the bargaining.

BULGARIAN MERCHANTS

Your job is to sell your souvenirs and postcards to the tourists. Your aim is to earn as much money as you can for your goods and never sell for less than their cost to you (which is half the marked price). Your customers will expect to bargain over prices. They do not speak Bulgarian, and you do not speak English. You will have to use sign language and also the 'roll-toss' system for signaling 'yes' and 'no.' **Practice this now**. 'Yes' is indicated by rocking the head from side to side (the ears moving up and down alternately). 'No' is indicated by tossing the nose and chin upwards — but only once. The movement is not repeated. The Assistants will help you if you request it, but cannot get involved in the bargaining.

ASSISTANTS/OBSERVERS

Your first task is to set up the room while the other groups are out. Set up six market stalls for the Bulgarian merchants at one end of the room. Set up six market stalls for the Turkish merchants at the other. Lay out a range of postcards and trinkets, and currency of various values to a total of $100, on each stall. Give each Tourist $30 in currency of various values. Once the trading starts, watch what happens when merchants and tourists trade. Notice how offers are made and how they are accepted or rejected. Observe how misunderstandings happen. Who seems to be getting the better bargain? You are not to speak or take part in the bargaining but you can help the Merchants in other ways if they ask.

Potential

An activity designed to develop students' awareness that people of different cultures and parts of the world employ a range of non-verbal gestures. The activity also encourages a sensitivity to misunderstandings that may arise when cultures interact, since gestures and signs can mean different things to different people.

Extension

Students approach members of different cultural groups in the community to find out the typical non-verbal gestures of each culture. They should ask about use and movement of fingers, hands, arms, lips and head — separately and in combination — to say 'yes' and 'no,' 'hello' and 'goodbye,' 'it's a deal,' and the like. They should also ask what gestures are used to express emotions such as anger, dislike, friendliness, joy, sadness, surprise.

Source
David Elton, St. Paul, Minnesota.

Bafa Bafa

Purpose   Simulating cross-cultural interactions and exploring assumptions and behaviors involved

Grade level   8-12

Time needed   60 to 80 minutes

Resources   2 cleared rooms, separate, but with easy access to each other.

For Alpha Culture: A set of rules on a wall chart or overhead projection transparency (Copiable Handout 13 ▢). 150 white paper tokens, approximately 5 cm (2 inches) square. 15 sticky dots, all the same color. A pen or pencil for each participant.

For Beta Culture: A set of rules on a wall chart or overhead projection transparency (Copiable Handout 14 ▢). 250 card tokens, approximately 6 cm (2.4 inches) square — 50 each of red, green, yellow, brown, blue. 15 sticky dots, all the same color (but different from Alpha Culture). 2 sheets of writing paper. A pen or pencil for each participant.

Optional: A copy of the **First Encounters** sheet for each student (Copiable Handout 15▢).

General Procedure — Both Alpha and Beta Cultures

Two facilitators are chosen, one assigned to each culture.

Students are told the object of this activity is to experience interaction with a cultural group which has different practices and customs from their own.

Students are then divided into two groups, equal in number and of mixed gender. (The Alpha culture should not have more than 50 per cent female participants.)

The two groups begin in separate rooms by studying and practicing the customs and traditions of their culture (Copiable Handouts 13 ❑ and 14 ❑) for 15-20 minutes.

During this time an 'observer' from each culture is appointed or elected. At a time agreed upon by the two facilitators, the observers visit each other's culture (5 minutes). Their task is to find out as much as they can about the culture they are visiting.

Observers then return to their home cultures to describe and attempt to interpret what they have experienced (5-10 minutes).

The succeeding pattern of interaction between the two cultures is decided by the facilitators.

A suggested sequence is for two or three visitors to be exchanged for about 5 minutes, followed by a further period of discussion and reflection on their experiences. Then another exchange of three or four participants and brief discussion take place in home groups before both cultures meet in one room for a final interaction session. One intermediate stage can be left out if time is short, but all participants should eventually have the opportunity to interact with members of the other culture.

Procedure Specific to Alpha Culture

Copiable Handout 13 ❑ is displayed so only Alphas can see it. Using it as a basis, the Alpha facilitator discusses Alpha characteristics and practices with members of the Alpha Culture. The facilitator encourages them to think and feel their way into being Alphas.

After the facilitator has explained the Alpha code of practice, participants elect the Elder. They affix colored dots (the 'badges' of their culture) to themselves.

They then begin to practice the cultural customs as described above. An observer is appointed by the Elder and briefed for the visit to the Beta culture. (See **General Procedure** above.)

Procedure Specific to Beta Culture

Copiable Handout 14 ❑ is displayed so only Betas can see it. Using it as a basis, the Beta facilitator describes the characteristics and practices of members of the Beta culture. The facilitator encourages Betas to think and feel their way into being Betas.

After the facilitator has explained the Beta code of practice, a Banker is appointed. Participants affix colored dots (the 'badges' of their culture) to themselves. They then begin to practice trading as outlined above.

The facilitator should ensure that an observer is appointed and briefed for the visit to the Alpha culture. (See **General Procedure** above.)

Procedure for Debriefing

Before inviting general discussion, some significant points can be introduced through adopting the following sequence of debriefing.

a. Betas explain how they perceive the Alpha culture.
b. Alphas explain how they perceive the Beta culture.
c. Betas describe their thoughts and feelings when visiting the Alpha culture.
d. Alphas describe their thoughts and feelings when visiting the Beta culture.
e. An Alpha explains the Alpha culture.
f. A Beta explains the Beta culture.

Discussion should then be broadened to consider issues to do with **perceptions** and **assumptions**. Students relate the experience of the game to real life contemporary and historical situations. For example:

a. Did the perception of the other culture differ from person to person?
b. How did one's perception shape one's behavior?
c. What assumptions were made about the practices and behavior of the other culture, and why? Were these assumptions helpful or a hindrance in relating to other people?
d. Did participants feel exploited or badly treated either in their own or in the other culture? If so, why and was it intentional on the part of those who gave offence?
e. Did the specific roles given to men and women in the Alpha culture cause any difficulties, either in relations within the culture or in cross-cultural relations?
f. Was there a clash between the competitive values of the Beta culture and the cooperative values of the Alpha culture?
g. When we go to a foreign country, do we perceive the customs and practices of that country's people the same way they do?
h. Why do we sometimes think new arrivals and visitors to our country 'behave oddly?'
i. How important is language to effective communication between people?

Potential

This is an adaptation of the classic cross-cultural simulation game. Through considerable laughter and enjoyment, it raises some important issues concerning assumptions and behaviors when interacting with members of an unfamiliar culture.

Extension

Each student is given a copy of the **First Encounters** sheet (Copiable Handout 15 ☐). How do the extracts on the sheet tie in with the

ALPHA CULTURE

Alpha people are friendly and relaxed. They enjoy social interaction and conversation, particularly in small groups of three or four people. Respect is gained through cooperative, sociable behavior. Alphas are proud of their culture. They often invent and practice new songs and dances which praise or reflect Alpha values and traditions. Friendship is shown through physical contact. Alphas are wary of people who keep their distance. Older members are respected for the important contributions they have made over centuries in promoting cooperation and friendship as central Alpha characteristics.

The guiding spirit of the Alpha culture is the Elder. This is one of the older (though not necessarily the oldest) female members, elected by the group. Although sociable and friendly, Alphas are anxious about the possible harmful effects of outside influences on their culture. They therefore stick to a rigid code of practice which governs all interaction between members. The code is as follows.

1. It is disrespectful for men to approach women without first seeking permission from the Elder. Women may approach other women and men without permission.

2. Any meeting between two or more individuals should begin and end with handshakes, hugs or other displays of friendship among all concerned.

3. Each member must carry a stock of 'personal worth' cards. These are used to check levels of individual and group cooperation. At the end of each interaction, all individuals involved write down, on each other's card(s), a number between 1 (low) and 10 (high). This number indicates the worth or enjoyment of that interaction to them personally. The cards should be signed, collected and given to the Elder. The Elder may wish to make enquiries into low scores.

4. Visitors are to be treated with respect and friendship. But on no account should the rules and practices of Alpha culture be explained to them. All visitors are given a set of 'personal worth' cards by the Elder.

5. When visiting another culture, Alphas are expected to stick to their cultural rules.

6. All questions and complaints about matters concerning the Alpha culture should be directed to the Elder. The Elder may make additional rulings where necessary. She should appoint a deputy when going on a visit.

7. The above rules should not be on display when visitors are present.

BETA CULTURE

Beta people are sincere and hard-working. Their enviable reputation as business people has been built up over centuries of trading. This has brought them considerable wealth. Respect is gained through success in trading and a healthy bank account. Betas are proud of their cultural traditions. They work hard as traders to ensure their future prosperity. They enjoy doing business with visitors from other cultures. They are, however, cautious about giving away the secrets of their success. Betas have developed a trading language, called *Animalese,* and a special code of practice which must be adhered to by all members. The code is as follows.

1. Trading takes place through exchanging and collecting tokens. Individual tokens have no value. Tokens must be kept absolutely hidden while trading. Their values are as follows.
   a. 3 tokens of the same color — 10 points
   b. 4 tokens of the same color — 20 points
   c. 5 tokens of the same color — 50 points

2. Trading takes place between two people and can **only** be done in *Animalese.* Make the animal noise standing for the token(s) you want according to the following code.
   a. red token — cow
   b. green token — dog
   c. yellow token — cat
   d. brown token — sheep
   e. blue token — chicken

3. To show the number of tokens you want, scratch yourself on the head, arms or shoulders the appropriate number of times. For example, 3 scratches followed by a 'moo' equals 3 red tokens.

4. An exchange of tokens takes place only if the request from each trader can be met. Any number of tokens can be exchanged for any other number.

5. It is customary for both traders to blink the eyes 3 times at each other before bargaining. This indicates that each will try to drive a hard but fair bargain. If the blinks are not returned, the other person may be considered 'fair game.'

6. Sets of tokens can be taken to the Banker at any time and your account credited with the appropriate number of points. The Banker will give you back the same number of tokens, of different colors, as you cash in. The Banker does not trade.

7. Physical contact is not allowed at all during trading or when meeting visitors. Experienced traders stand a respectful distance away from their partners.

8. Visitors are to be treated with respect as potential trading partners. But **on no account** should the rules and practices of the Beta culture be explained to them or changed to suit them. Visitors can obtain a set of tokens from the Banker, to be returned on their departure. Visitors' bank accounts can be arranged with the Banker (through *Animalese* and sign language).

9. When visiting another culture, Betas are expected to stick to their cultural rules. **Only** *Animalese* is to be spoken on visits, or when visitors are present.

10. The above rules should not be on display when visitors are present.

FIRST ENCOUNTERS

1. Native Americans

The land itself...was, for the European, a commodity: to be acquired, bought, sold, deeded and handed down, to be owned, used, developed, mined and plowed, deforested and drained, depleted, abandoned. The land that Native Americans viewed as an integral part of themselves, no more to be bought and sold than people, was to Europeans the source of the colonists' wealth, a resource they respected for itself no more than they respected their slaves.

They believed...that land not actually built upon was unused and therefore unowned...and so available....This was a total misperception of the careful and well worked out patterns of Indian land use, but not even the most sympathetic English colonist...understood.

Source: Lisa Aug. 'Paradise Lost,' in **Turtle quarterly**, Spring-Summer 1992, p. 12.

The Portuguese admiral Cabral...sighted the Brazilian coast in 1500....At this time medieval Portugal was a country of many inequalities. Most of its population was very poor, and diseases were commonplace. The Catholic Church was very powerful and influenced what people did and how they thought about the world. The Portuguese were amazed by what they saw of the Amerindian way of life. One of them recorded in a letter to the King of Portugal: 'Their bodies are so clean and so plump and so beautiful that they could not be more so.' Another wrote: 'In every house they all live together in harmony....They are so friendly that what belongs to one belongs to all.' They were astonished that the people were so healthy, lived so long and were not embarrassed without any clothes.

The reports that began to reach Europe in the 16th century excited the imaginations of those who read them, and laws were made banning the printing and sale of books about South America without a special licence. The reports described an alternative to life in Europe which was far more attractive. Fearing a revolution, the rich and powerful wanted to keep this information to themselves.

Source: Anna Lewington. *Rainforest Amerindians*. Brighton, UK: Wayland, 1992, pp. 29- 30.

2. The Marsh Arabs

We are, by Arab standards, a very insanitary people. The idea of using lavatory paper is disgusting to them — nothing can cleanse except water, or, in the case of desert Arabs, sand....Because it is the left hand that performs these and other unclean tasks, it becomes a thing unclean in itself; and is never, as is the right hand, ornamented with a ring....It should not, however scrupulously it has been washed, touch the face or head,...or be put to any one of the numberless and often aimless uses...which pass unnoticed among Europeans.

Source: Gavin Maxwell. *A Reed Shaken by the Wind*. Harmondsworth, UK: Penguin, 1983, pp. 23-24.

activity? In what ways does Bafa Bafa point up the difficulties and misunderstandings that occurred in the period of European expansion, when Europeans and peoples of other cultures first encountered each other? Why were the encounters often not on a 'level playing field' as they are in Bafa Bafa? (Sometimes larger numbers of Europeans were involved, for example. Europeans were more technologically advanced with respect to ships, weapons and the like.) In what ways did unequal power relationships affect such encounters?

Source
Adapted from 'Bafa Bafa' in Hicks, D. *Minorities*. London: Heinemann Educational, 1981, pp. 82-85.

Profile 3

Perspectives Education: Curriculum of the Ears and Heart

by Karen Grose

Listening to, understanding and accepting others' perspectives is part of the foundation of building a warm and inclusive community within the classroom. By encouraging students to share their stories, express their opinions and listen to alternative viewpoints, we are not only empowering them but also helping them make meaning of their world and connect and empathize with each other. Without hearing the stories of others around us, we have no way of engaging in the process of examining our own beliefs and their origins, challenging our previously held assumptions and arriving at new understandings.

I had the honor of teaching a wonderful class of 12- and 13-year-olds at Lord Roberts Junior Public School in Scarborough, Ontario. The curriculum was primarily student-led and revolved around issues meaningful to the children themselves. Through the topics of study which the children suggested and developed (children's rights, human rights, health issues, the place of media in their lives, their place in the future), they were constantly examining their classmate's perspectives and points of view and, thus, broadening their understanding of their own and others' place in the world. There was little curriculum I could offer this group more powerful than the personal experiences they shared with each other. Stories of fleeing war-torn countries to come to Canada, family difficulties such as death and divorce, fitting into new peer groups, and dealing with difficult gender and cultural issues made our curriculum real, and created an environment where empathy and respect for other people and cultures naturally developed. In order to promote perspectives education, it is helpful to incorporate the following elements into learning programs.

1. **Daily Newspapers** These provide a rich resource of local and global issues and the children can either discuss as a group or respond by writing in their reflective journal. By examining more than one type of

daily newspaper, children can compare and contrast not only the types of information presented but also what is considered newsworthy or not in each paper. Comparing articles encourages awareness of perspective and critical and divergent thinking skills. (See the activity **Newspapers,** p. 183 in this chapter and **Media Watch** in Book 2.)

2. **Continuum** This activity can be used with a variety of topics, in a variety of situations. It begins by asking the children to take a stand on a particular issue and, by first avoiding discussion, to think about why they feel/think this way. For example, if the statement 'It is OK to break the law to ensure the future health of our planet' is posed, the children would ask themselves how they feel about this assertion. They would then stand along an imaginary continuum according to whether they strongly agree, agree, are not sure, disagree or strongly disagree with the statement. The children are asked to listen to each other's point of view for one minute each. Following this the statement is posed again and each child chooses whether to move to a new point or remain at the same point on the continuum. (See, for instance, **Health Rights Continuum,** Chapter 4, p. 141.)

3. **Literature and Art from around the World** Whether books are picked up from the school or local library, or brought by the students from home, literature from around the world provides children with a range of perspectives. Fairy tales from various cultures and countries, descriptions or videos of cultural celebrations and traditions, pictures or artifacts, and compact discs or tapes of music from around the world demonstrate to children that, although there is a wide variety of art and literature within our global community, we all share the same love of writing, reading, storying, song and dance.

4. **The Children's Voices** The actual stories the children share in our classrooms every day are the richest and most powerful tools we can use to promote perspectives, interconnections and deeper mutual understanding. In sharing our stories, we not only learn from one another but we learn to honor and value each other as well. Children's receptivity to and respect for varying perspectives and opinions grow exponentially by listening to and sharing with their peers. This is not surprising. Children are our most valuable resource.

Karen Grose is Principal of Sir Samuel B. Steele Junior School, Toronto District School Board.

6

Technology

Technology has been defined as 'the science and the art of getting things done through the application of knowledge.'[1] Multiple impacts of technology emanate from every field of human endeavor and shape our daily lives. At the simplest level, technology can be represented as the **tools** we employ at home, at school and in the workplace to facilitate the tasks we undertake. Without these tools many common tasks would be impossible to complete, or would take longer, or would endanger our lives. The **benefits** of technology are readily discernible. Also readily discernible is the vast potential of technology for **problem-solving** in order to improve the quality of life of people, other living things and environments.

The towering technological achievements of our time — airplanes, computers, life-support machines, space satellites, for example — are testaments to the immensity and ever-quickening pace of **technological change** over the last century, an extremely brief period in human history. This pace of change, coupled with the potential for future technological developments that it feeds, now demands that we seek satisfactory answers to some urgent questions about the role of technology in our lives. Fundamental to such questioning is the place of personal and social **values** in the development and use of technology. Critical questions include:

Who makes decisions about technological developments, and in whose interests?

Who controls the research, design, development and marketing processes on which technology depends? Who benefits from these?

What are the short-, mid- and long-term **consequences** of present technological trends for humans, other living organisms and the planet?

Are the long-term personal, social and environmental **costs** of technological development sufficiently understood? Can these be justified in terms of the potential benefits?

Does technological advancement promote greater **equity** through being equally accessible and beneficial to people of different cultures, genders, faiths and socioeconomic strata?

In the light of technological innovations that are capable of considerable harm, including mass destruction, what **safeguards** can and should societies enforce to protect their citizens and environments?

What level of technological use is ultimately sustainable?

Appropriate technology offers an alternative technological vision to that which powers the engines of global economic and industrial activity. Its guiding principles are 'low-tech' rather than 'high-tech.' Technology should be environmentally friendly and sustainable. It should be owned and maintained by the community it serves. Furthermore it should suit the needs, lifestyles and development aspirations of its users. Such precepts render appropriate technology a highly suitable — and effective — approach to problem-solving in the poorer and more isolated parts of the developing world. This is particularly the case where conventional technological projects have had little, or even disastrous, impacts.

The wisdom of appropriate technology can also be applied to industrial societies. Solutions to social and environmental problems can be evaluated in terms of their overall 'appropriateness,' for all people and for the planet, rather than on narrower grounds such as economic gain or scientific progress.

Technological visions are at the heart of humans' aspirations for and beliefs about the **future**. For some, **technocentrism** — a belief in the power of technology to solve all problems — creates a vision of the universe in which technology defines human progress, and technological development is limitless. For others, technology is the tool by which humankind engineers its own destruction. In the global classroom, consideration of the questions raised above is vital in terms of affording students **choices** for their future. It is vital in developing the skills and insights that will enable students to make informed and far-sighted decisions.

SKILLS INVENTORY

Most activities in this chapter involve students in the practice and refinement of *cooperation and communication skills.*

Research skills can be developed in **A Day in My Life**, **Technology Scrapbook** and **Technology Timeline**.

Many activities address *values clarification skills* around the uses of technology; see especially **Technologi-Can, Use of Technology, Techno-Choice, Ballooning Technology** and **Assessing New Technologies**.

Creative thinking skills are required in **A Low-Tech Day, Tools for the Future, Technologi-Can** and **Assessing New Technologies**.

Prediction and Forecasting skills are employed in **Technology Timeline, Techno-Future Timeline** and **Assessing New Technologies**.

Tools for the Future provides opportunities for honing *problem-solving skills.*

Techno-Choice and **Ballooning Technology** demand the use of *decision-making skills.*

TECHNOLOGY

CONCEPTS

ACTIVITIES	Tools	Benefits	Problem-solving	Technological Change	Values	Consequences	Costs	Equity	Safeguards	Appropriate Technology	Future	Technocentrism	Choices
A Day in My Life	*	*											
A Low-Tech Day	*	*	*		*					*			
Technology Scrapbook	*	*											
Technology Timeline	*	*	*	*		*	*				*		
Tools for the Future	*	*									*		
Techno-Future Timelines	*	*	*		*	*	*				*	*	*
Technologi-Can	*	*		*	*	*	*	*	*				*
Use of Technology	*	*			*	*	*	*	*				*
Techno-Choice	*	*	*		*	*	*			*			*
Ballooning Technology	*	*			*	*	*	*	*				*
Assessing New Technologies	*	*	*		*	*	*	*		*			

Connections • The following activities can aid students' understanding of the role of technology in our lives: **Made in Canada** (p.75), **Carrying the Can** (p.103) and **World Health Diamond Ranking** (p.144). (The latter two activities also consider appropriate technology.) • Issues of equity in the development and use of technology are addressed in **Development Cartoons** (bk 2), **The Trading Game** (bk 2), **Peaceful Negotiations** (bk 2) and **Tools Around the Home** (bk 2). • Changes brought about by technological innovation can be explored in **The Real McCoy** (bk 2) and **Mass Media Time Line-up** (bk 2). • **What Do I Value?** (bk 2) and **Needs and Wants** (bk 2) can be used to analyze the relationship between technology and personal values.

Graphic skills can be practiced in **Technology Scrapbook** and **Tools for the Future**.

Several activities can be springboards to developing *action skills* around the use of technology, especially **A Low-Tech Day** and **Techno-Future Timeline**.

A Day in My Life

Purpose	Considering technology as a 'tool' in everyday life
Grade level	4-6
Time needed	40 minutes
Resources	A sheet of paper and a pen/pencil for each pair of students. Additional sheets of paper for small groups. Encyclopedias and/or books about technological inventions.

Procedure, Part A

Students are introduced to the idea of technology as a 'tool' — an object that helps us achieve something we want to do, usually with more ease and/or safety.

'Tools' on hand in the classroom can be identified; for example, pen/pencil, chalk, ruler, scissors, telephone, television, computer.

Working in pairs, students draw up lists of common events on an ordinary day in their lives and what 'tools' are normally used; for example:

Event	Tools
wash and get dressed	toothbrush, mirror, hairbrush
eat breakfast	spoon, knife, toaster, cup, plate, microwave
go to school	car, seatbelt, traffic lights
etc.	etc.

Small group or class discussion follows. Topics for discussion could include the age of the tools listed (for example, Would your parents/grandparents have been able to use these tools?), reasons for their invention or development, and any changes in design over time. Students could use encyclopedias and/or books on technological inventions to help answer questions arising out of the discussion.

Procedure, Part B

Working in small groups, students discuss and then place all the tools itemized on their respective lists under one of three headings, according to how important they think the tool is to the successful conclusion of the event or task specified:

Essential	Useful	Not Necessary
toothbrush	mirror	microwave
cup, spoon	toaster	
traffic lights		
etc.		

Discussion can follow on the general importance of technology in our everyday lives, including how the tools we use determine or shape what we do every day.

Potential

This activity is designed to introduce students to the concept of technology as 'tools' and to illustrate how dependent we have become on such tools in everyday life. Students are then asked to consider how **necessary** they think these tools are in their lives.

Disagreement is likely, particularly between Useful and Not Necessary. Students should be encouraged to reach consensus but if not, items can be put under two headings, or between headings.

The reasons for placing items in the Essential column can be explored, to give students an understanding of technology's role in creating a cleaner, safer and more hygienic society.

Extension

The topics explored in **Procedure, Part A** would make good research questions for homework. Students could ask family members and use information sources such as encyclopedias, photograph albums, museums and the Internet.

A Low-Tech Day

Purpose   Examining how important technology is to everyday life, and thinking of low-tech alternatives

Grade level   4-6

Time needed   40 minutes

Resources   Paper. Pen/pencil for each group of students.

Procedure

Using the lists drawn up in **A Day in My Life,** students brainstorm creative ways in which everyday tasks and functions can be carried out using as little technology as possible. For example, perhaps students could walk to school rather than riding in a car or bus. Clothes could be dried on a line rather than in a dryer. Perhaps students could read in sunlight rather than by electric light.

Students work in groups. Each group constructs a story of 'a low-tech day,' giving details of how various tasks were undertaken.

At the end of the story, a list is compiled of the basic tools that had to be used in order to get through the day.

When the stories are read out to the rest of the class, other students can challenge the writers if they feel that the 'low-tech' alternatives are not viable.

Potential

Students are challenged to examine how essential technology is to the undertaking of common tasks. Through creatively thinking of 'low-tech' alternatives, students begin to understand the central role that technology plays in their lives.

Extension

A 'low-tech' day experiment could be undertaken in school, with students and teachers using as few tools as possible. Towards the end of the day, a discussion can be held on the role of technology in learning.

Technology Scrapbook

Purpose	Understanding the role technology has played in the course of students' lives to date
Grade level	4-6
Time needed	Several hours. May be spread over a number of class periods.
Resources	A scrapbook for each student. Pens/pencils. Crayons. Glue sticks.

Procedure

Students are asked to think about ways they have personally benefited from technology during their lives.

They are encouraged to think as broadly as possible. They include aspects such as their health and development (for example, technology used in hospitals, and medical and dental clinics), their interests and leisure pursuits (for example, technology used in sports and hobbies, television and computer games), their travel and holiday experiences, and their everyday life at home and at school.

Initial ideas are written down on rough paper.

Further thinking and research takes place at home, where parents can be asked about technologies used, particularly in the student's early childhood.

Having compiled a list of technologies, any relevant pictures and photographs are collected. These could include photographs from family albums and/or pictures cut out of magazines, flyers and store catalogs.

Finally the scrapbook is assembled. Each technology used is described, perhaps with a personal story or reminiscence. Each is illustrated with a photograph, picture or drawing.

Potential

An activity that helps students understand the role that technology has already played in all aspects of their lives. The scrapbook format is intended to show the links between technology and personal lives.

Technology Timeline

Purpose	Appreciating past technological developments and making predictions about the future
Grade level	4-8
Time needed	40 minutes
Resources	A cut-up set of pictures (Copiable Handout 1☐) for each group of 5-6 students. Blank slips of paper and pens/pencils for each group. Encyclopedias and/or books about inventions.

Procedure

A set of pictures, depicting technologies used at different periods in human history to carry out various tasks, is given to each group of five to six students.

Through discussion and negotiation, students decide upon the various categories of technology. Students group the pictures according to the categories.

Students then try to determine an order in which to place the pictures so as to accurately represent the historical development of these technologies. Encyclopedias and/or books about inventions may be used as reference.

Groups then compare their respective picture sets and try to achieve consensus as a class, with teacher input and/or book research, if necessary. Finally each group is given some blank slips of paper on which

cooking pot on open fire	stove	microwave
salted food	canned food	freezer
horse and cart	cars	airplane
messenger with letter	mail delivery	fax machine
board game	TV	video game
herbal remedies	vaccination	laser surgery

they are asked to depict what the technologies under consideration might look like in 50 or 100 years' time.

Potential

This activity helps students to appreciate developments in technology over time and then asks them to use that understanding in making predictions about future technological advances. Follow-up discussion should focus on what has been gained through such developments (speed? efficiency? health and safety?) and also what has been lost (personal contact? a cleaner environment? traditional skills?)

Students could also undertake individual or group research on developments in a particular technology (for example, transport, food preservation, medicine), culminating in displays or presentations to the rest of the class.

Extension

Students choose a particular technology that can be found at home (for example, appliance, vehicle, computer) and interview parents, grandparents and neighbors to find out how this technology has changed over time. The information gathered is entered on a time line, with appropriate illustrations/descriptions posted at relevant points on the line. Where available, information on technological developments in other countries can also be included on the time line.

Variation

To practice a wide range of communication skills, students can be asked not to show their pictures to each other, but to describe them and then negotiate an agreed sequence before the pictures are placed on the table and seen by all group members.

Tools for the Future

Purpose	Using lateral and creative thinking to discover technological solutions to problems	
Grade level	6-9	
Time needed	40 minutes	
Resources	Paper. Pens/pencils for each small group.	

Procedure

As a class, students brainstorm some present or future scenarios or problems that could be helped through the creative use of technology. The emphasis should be on everyday or relatively simple scenarios relevant to the students, rather than on complex situations. Some examples can be given:

a. a locking device to secure a cycle helmet to a bicycle
b. a means of fastening a tube or bottle of sunscreen lotion to a swimsuit
c. ways of reducing the negative environmental impact of home delivery pizzas (transport and packaging)
d. a clothes hanger that does not allow clothes to slide off
e. a means of peeling an orange without having the juice spatter your clothes
f. a device for holding a plastic cup containing a hot drink
g. a means of keeping a paperback book open without damaging the spine

Students then work in groups on one of the scenarios, developing ideas on how technology might be used. Verbal or written reports, with drawings where appropriate, are presented to the rest of the class.

Potential

Students are required in this activity to use lateral and creative thinking skills in order to see how technology might solve some relatively minor problems. Groups should be encouraged to think of several solutions and designs before deciding upon those they think most suitable.

Extension

Where practicable, mockups of some ideas could be constructed, using craft materials and other easily available materials. Mockups could be displayed in the classroom.

Techno-Future Timelines

Purpose	Projecting forward to probable and preferable futures
Grade level	6-9
Time needed	40 minutes
Resources	A sheet of chart paper and two markers, of different colors, for each pair of students.

Procedure

Working in pairs, students reflect upon key events in their lives so far in which technology has played a significant role. Events might include those associated with home and family (for example, the first bicycle, holiday travel, a medical operation, television viewing to learn about world issues, etc.). They might include those associated with school (for example, learning to use a computer) or with national/global incidents students can recall as having left a lasting impression.

Events identified by the students are marked on a sheet of paper, on the line between B and N (B standing for Birth and N for Now):

Figure 1

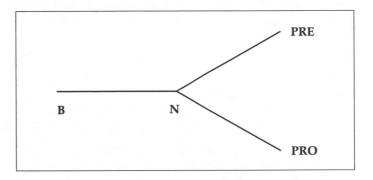

Students then focus on the PRO (probable technological future) and PRE (preferable technological future) lines. Still working in pairs, they briefly note on their charts events and trends that they think will probably happen, and that they would like to have happen. These may include a blend of personal, societal, national and global future scenarios.

When the pairs have completed their charts, two or three pairs join together to compare them. These charts are then used as the basis for classroom discussion and individual writing about the possible roles that technology might play in the future.

Potential

This activity provides the framework for students to assess major technological developments that have taken place in their lives before they are asked to project forward. In so doing, students are exploring and sharing some of their own perspectives on, and assumptions about, technology and its significance in the contemporary world.

The 'probable futures' projection will elicit their views on the role of technology in determining the future, while the focus on 'preferred futures' offers scope for values clarification. The gap between 'preferred' and 'probable' futures highlights the nature and scale of the efforts necessary to achieve technological preferences. In discussion, students might consider what actions they could take right now in their own lives to help realize their preferred futures.

Extension

Some ideas presented on the PRE lines can be used as the springboard for local action and research projects. For example, if 'an end to cancer' appears on the line, students could research what cures are being currently investigated and what they might personally do to help prevent cancer in their own lives.

Technologi-Can

Purpose   Evaluating benefits of technologies as they relate to economic, social and cultural groups

Grade level   6-9

Time needed   40 minutes

Resources   Chart (Copiable Handout 2 ▢) for each student. Pens/pencils.

Procedure

Students brainstorm a list of technological objects that enable people to accomplish things they would not otherwise be able to carry out. Objects might include: wheelchair, artificial limb, elevator, camera, eyeglasses, telescope, telephone, X-ray machine, communications satellite, printing press.

Working in pairs, students then complete a chart (Handout 2 ▢), writing down who benefits from each technology (everybody? certain groups of people?) and identifying some of the benefits.

Three pairs then meet together to share their charts. At this stage disagreements about the beneficiaries and benefits can be discussed. Class discussion follows around such questions as:

   a. For each technology, are there people who rely on it, as distinct from just benefiting from it? (The distinction between needs and wants could be introduced here.)
   b. Is each technology equally available or accessible to all who need it, irrespective of status, wealth, culture or geographical location?
   c. Are there also disadvantages or personal/social costs associated with the use of these technologies?
   d. Are there other costs, such as environmental or health risks?
   e. What might be the consequences of these technologies suddenly becoming unavailable (for example, through component materials running out)?

Potential

This activity focuses students' attention on the benefits of particular technologies and then asks them to evaluate these benefits as they relate to certain economic, social and cultural groups. Underpinning the activity is the idea that technology is not value-free. There are costs as well as benefits, the benefits are not necessarily accessible to all those who need them, and decisions about technological developments are founded upon prevalent personal and societal values. Students are also introduced to the concept that technology requires resources, some of which may be in short supply.

Technology	Who Benefits?	Benefits
1.		
2.		
3.		

Use of Technology

Purpose   Considering controversial technological developments
Grade level   6-12
Time needed   40 minutes
Resources   A cut-up set of cards for each pair of students (see Copiable Handout 3 ☐ — 2 sets of cards are provided).

Procedure

A set of cards is given to each pair of students.

Through questions and discussion, the teacher should check that students understand the nature of the objects listed, and some situations in which they are used.

Each pair then discusses the use of these objects and decides into which of three piles the cards should be placed, according to the following criteria.
   Pile A: There should be no restriction on the use of these objects.
   Pile B: Some restrictions should be placed on the use of these objects.
   Pile C: These objects should not be used at all.

Having sorted their cards, three pairs join together to compare their categorizations and, through negotiation, to try to reach consensus. Class discussion follows on the responsibility of individuals and governments in controlling the use of technologies.

Potential

This activity asks students to consider some of the more controversial technological developments and whether controls should be placed on their use. It reaffirms the link between the control of technology and personal and social values. A good example is the difference in Canadian and American law governing the ownership of handguns.

Debriefing

Follow-up discussion and writing could focus on those objects placed in Pile B. What conditions or restrictions would you want imposed on the use of these objects, and why? Are there situations — or future scenarios — in which you could envisage these being moved to Pile A or Pile C?

USE OF TECHNOLOGY CARDS

computer	oil drilling rig
car	nuclear bomb
chainsaw	bicycle
handgun	surveillance camera
lie detector	radar speed detector
life-support machine	electric chair
television	chemical fertilizer
telephone	land mine
X-ray machine	space satellite
heart pacemaker	antibiotics

Techno-Choice

Purpose	Understanding that individuals have choices in their use of technologies
Grade level	6-9
Time needed	40 minutes
Resources	Copiable Handout 4⬜ for each student

Procedure

A copy of Handout 4⬜ is given to each student.

Working individually, students are asked to choose which of the technologies given they would generally prefer to use, and why.

After comparing their choices in small groups, students list as many advantages and disadvantages of both technologies as they can think of. Their attention should be drawn to the fact that there may be costs and benefits not only to themselves but also to other people, other species and the environment. For example:

a. High concentrations of automobile exhaust have been linked to acid rain and acid fog, which harm certain trees and other plants.
b. The generation of electricity — depending on the method employed — may use up natural resources, harm wildlife habitats or pose nuclear threats.
c. Chemical fertilizers can contribute to environmental pollution.
d. Motorboats can contribute to noise pollution.

Students should be encouraged to think about the short-term, mid-term and long-term implications.

Finally, students are asked to reassess their choices of technology in the light of group discussion. Where appropriate, they may want to stipulate some conditions or limitations on the choices they make.

Potential

This activity suggests that individuals have choices in their use of technologies and that each choice made has ramifications, not only for themselves but for others and for the environment. The choices featured in this activity relate to the role of technology in increasing the ease and efficiency with which students can undertake a task. Through looking at both advantages and disadvantages of alternative technologies, a more informed choice can be made.

Activity	Choice of Technology	Reason
1. Going to school	a. car b. bus	
2. Writing an assignment	a. pen and paper b. word processor	
3. Making a salad	a. food processor b. knife and chopping board	
4. Brushing your teeth	a. electric toothbrush b. manual toothbrush	
5. Lighting your home	a. candles b. electric lights	
6. Mending clothes	a. electric sewing machine b. needle and thread	
7. Greening a lawn	a. organic compost b. chemical fertilizer	
8. Crossing a lake	a. motorboat b. rowboat	
9. Washing a car	a. bucket and sponge b. automatic car wash	
10. Reaching the third floor	a. stairs b. elevator	
11. Communicating with a friend	a. telephone b. letter	
12. Checking spelling	a. dictionary b. computer spell check	

Ballooning Technology

Purpose	Considering the 'neutrality' of new technologies and scientific inventions, and the possible intentions of those who offer them to us
Grade level	7-12
Time needed	10 minutes
Resources	6 hoops of paper 30 cm (12 inches) in diameter, masking tape, 90 round balloons, 3 needles.

Procedure

Students form groups of five. Each group is asked to stand by one of the paper hoops (previously fixed at various points to the classroom wall) and is given fifteen balloons and some masking tape.

The groups are told that the object of the activity is to stick as many fully inflated balloons as possible within the hoop in the three minutes allotted.

After a minute or so, the facilitator secretly approaches a single member of three of the groups, offers her a needle and advises that the needle can be used in any way that seems appropriate. In the excitement generated by the activity, the needle is generally used to burst other groups' balloons.

Class discussion follows.

Potential

This activity raises questions surrounding the 'neutrality' of technology and scientific inventions, and the intentions of those who offer us new technologies. Was the needle a value-free instrument? Or did the needle itself significantly shape subsequent events? Did the facilitator have a clear but unstated agenda in offering needles to students? What were the values implicit in the way(s) in which the needles were used? Did the students have a real choice in deciding what to do? In what ways does the activity mirror the impact new forms of military and civil technology can have upon the future?

Assessing New Technologies

Purpose	Evaluating and forecasting the introduction of new technologies
Grade level	7-12
Time needed	An hour
Resources	Markers. For each 3 or 4 students, an advertisement for a new technology, culled from a newspaper or magazine, or obtained directly from a firm's publicity department. The advertisement should be placed in the center of two pieces of newsprint that have been taped together. The 6 sections should be penned in around the advertisement.

1. Values/Assumptions	2. Purposes	3. Who Benefits? Who Loses?
	ADVERTISEMENT	
6. Reasons Against		4. Consequences
	5. Reasons For	

Procedure

Groups are asked to work clockwise around the six sections:

1. They analyze the images and text presented in the advertisement in terms of values and assumptions:
   a. What values are the promoters of the new technology espousing?
   b. What assumptions are they making about preferable lifestyles, quality of life and social trends and developments?
   c. Is the advertisement directed at everybody or do the promoters have specific groups in mind? Why?

2. Students brainstorm and list the purposes to which they think the new technology will be put.

3. They list possible answers to the following questions.
   a. For whose benefit is the technology being introduced?
   b. Who are some people and other life forms likely to lose from its introduction?

4. Students consider the consequences — economic, environmental, political and social — likely to stem from the technology's widespread uptake.

5. and 6. Students list reasons for and against the technology being widely applied.

Having completed their task, groups join with one or two other groups (who have been — preferably but not necessarily — working on different advertisements) to share their work.

Plenary discussion follows.

Potential

This activity gives students the opportunity to practice assessing and forecasting the introduction of new technologies. The class as a group might wish to reflect upon whether new technology is 'neutral,' an outcome of 'value free' science, or the product of ongoing social and economic processes that are, perhaps, controlled by particular interest groups.

Debriefing

Students could be asked to discuss or write essays, position papers or articles on questions such as the following.
   a. To what degree did groups come to similar conclusions about values, assumptions, purposes, 'winners and losers,' even though they were considering different technologies? Why?
   b. To what extent are inventions that are billed as 'good' for the future serving the present interests of particular people? Should we accept their values and assumptions about the future in an uncritical fashion?
   c. Are there ways we could, as 'ordinary citizens,' exert more influence over technological and scientific trends? Should such influence be exerted?

Students can share their writing through various means such as posting it on a bulletin board or wall, reading it aloud to the class, or submitting it to a school or community newspaper for possible publication.

Extension

It can be a useful values clarification exercise to ask groups to re-form and address the question of what criteria they employed in determining reasons for and against the introduction of the technology in question. They can also be asked to design or identify amended or new technologies of a more 'appropriate' kind, given their responses to the six sections.

Reference
1. Smillie, Ian. *Mastering the Machine.* London: Intermediate Technology, 1991.

7

Futures

The term **alternative futures** is used to signify the wide range of futures — at all levels, personal to global — open to us at any point in time. As has been noted in the Introduction, alternative futures are commonly classified as **possible, probable** and **preferred. Possible futures** include all future scenarios that **might conceivably come about**. The broadest category of all, they include:

- futures in the short, medium and long term
- scenarios emanating from multiple and diverse perspectives
- scenarios that are not hidebound by dominant paradigms and seemingly inexorable contemporary trends

In educational terms, the category of possible futures offers the greatest scope for developing and honing lateral and divergent thinking skills. It also offers the greatest scope for the creative use of the imagination.

Probable futures encompass all future scenarios that are **likely to come about**. They are the firmest category. This is because they, for the most part, involve the short-term projection and interplay of current cultural, economic, political and social trends.

Preferred futures are futures **we would like to see come about,** given our values and priorities. Exploration of preferred futures offers excellent scope for values clarification work in the classroom.

The interplay of the three categories within the educational process is important (Figure 1). Our choice of preferred futures is likely to be based upon a narrow range of options unless study programs encourage exploration of the wealth of possible futures. In the final analysis, there can be no freedom of choice unless 'one understands the full range of options available **and** the possible consequences of each option.' [1] Likewise, our exploration of probable futures is likely to lead us into embracing a 'business as usual' view of the future unless we are actively encouraged to think about how we might translate the possible and preferred into the probable.

Possible and probable future scenarios can embrace both the **optimistic** and **pessimistic**. Preferred futures are mostly optimistic but may involve 'better of two evils' choices among those with a pessimistic view

Figure 1

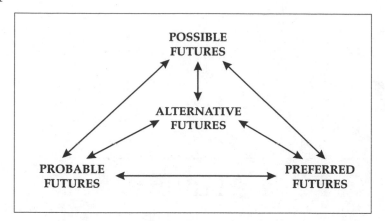

of the future. Other useful ways of exploring alternative futures is to consider them from the point of view of **desirability** and **plausibility**.

Futures-oriented education is only in a limited sense about **prediction** of what is going to happen. It is rather about the future as a '**zone of potentiality**.' It is about knowledge of what is possible rather than knowledge of certainties.[2] It is also about helping students recognize that human choices and actions (including their own choices and actions) flow into, and help shape, the future. Recognizing the increasing **pace of change** helps students gauge their future needs and make informed and far-sighted choices.

Within futures thinking, newly prominent concepts that relate directly to the values of global education are those of **intergenerational justice** and **sustainability**. The former suggests that people alive today have a responsibility to subsequent generations as much as to their own. As the African saying goes, 'Treat the Earth well. It was not given to you by your parents. It was lent to you by your children.' The concept of **intergenerational rights**, and its implications for our present-day behaviors and decisions, provides a powerful focus for the global classroom. (See the activity **Our Inheritance, Their Inheritance**.) **Sustainability** likewise asks that we review, and radically readjust, our expectations out of respect for the Earth and so as to ensure a future for humans, other species and the environment.

The global classroom is, by definition, futures-oriented. Global educators seek to promote cooperation, equity, social justice and respect for all living things as a means of creating a better tomorrow. They advocate an educational process predicated upon those values. This process has as a principal outcome the emergence of 'practical visionaries.' In effect, these are people with a clear vision of a preferred future as well as the commitment, confidence and practical skills to go about realizing that vision.

The global classroom provides a springboard for practicing being 'practical visionaries.' Having identified their individually and collectively preferred futures, students can be encouraged to take steps to realize those futures through school-based social, political and environmental **action** projects. This is what futurist Alvin Toffler has called the process of 'anticipatory democracy.'

FUTURES

FUTURES	Future Timelines	Drawing upon the Future	Questions about the Future	Future Circle	Time Chairs	Acronym	Our Inheritance, Their Inheritance	Inventing the Future Backwards	Futures Bag	Futures Wheel	Futurescapes	My World, My Future	New Year Resolutions
Possible Futures		*	*					*	*	*	*	*	*
Probable Futures	*	*			*	*			*	*	*	*	*
Preferred Futures	*	*	*	*	*			*	*	*	*	*	
Prediction	*		*							*			*
Zone of Potentiality		*	*		*	*	*	*	*		*	*	
Pace of Change					*								*
Intergenerational Justice							*	*					*
Sustainability							*	*			*		*
Action	*			*							*		*

CONNECTIONS • The concept of sustainability is also explored in Chapter 3; see, especially, **Water Watch** (p.100), **Carrying the Can** (p.103), **Fruits of the Forest** (p.116), **Selling Mother** (p.117) and **Frightening Forecasts** (p.121). • Students' understanding of intergenerational rights and justice can be enhanced in **Canadian Capsule** (Bk 2), and **Tackling a Statement** (Bk 2). • Technological change over time, and the benefits and impacts of future technological development, are featured in Chapter 6; see **Technology Timeline** (p.203), **Tools for the Future** (p.205), **Techno-Future Timeline** (p.206) and **Assessing New Technologies** (p.214). • **My View of the World** (p.58) and **My Place** (p.60) look at the impact of change over time at both local and global levels; **Likes and Dislikes** (p.41) points out that personal preferences change, too. • The short- and long-term ramifications of personal and family decisions can be mapped out by students in **Made in Canada** (p.75) and **Decision Wheel** (p.146).

Most activities in this chapter offer opportunities to practice *imaging, envisioning* and *prediction skills* as well as to experience processes of *values clarification.*

Creative, lateral and divergent thinking skills are particularly to the fore in **Future Timelines, Drawing upon the Future, Acronym, Inventing the Future Backwards, Futures Bag, Futures Wheel** and **New Year's Resolutions**.

Creative writing skills can be developed through **Inventing the Future (Backwards)** and **My World, My Future**.

Practice in employing *research* and *information retrieval skills* is offered by **Questions About the Future** and **Inventing the Future Backwards**.

Inventing the Future (Backwards) and **Futures Wheel** provide practice in utilizing *planning skills*.

Interviewing skills are central to **Time Chairs**.

Consensus-building and *negotiation skills* can be practiced through **Acronym.**

Future Timelines

Figure 2

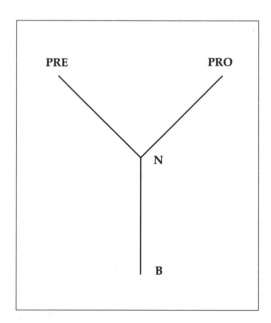

Purpose	Focusing on probable and preferred futures, first in general and then specifically with respect to humane treatment of animals. Considering ways to work towards preferred futures.
Grade level	3-12
Time needed	30 minutes
Resources	Required for each part of the activity: a large sheet of chart paper and 4 markers of different colors for each pair of students.

Procedure, Part A

Working in pairs, students prepare time lines (see Figure 2). Between point B (birth) and N (now), they fill in key events that have happened so far during their lives which they think will influence the future. It is up to pairs to decide whether they focus upon personal, local, national or global events, or whether they operate at more than one level.

From N to PRO (probable futures), they fill in events they consider **are likely to happen** in their lifetimes.

From N to PRE (preferred futures), they fill in events they **would like to see happen** during their lifetimes.

It is for pairs to decide how far apart the PRO and PRE stems should be. If what they consider probable is also their preference, then the two stems can merge into one. If their visions of the probable and preferred are far apart, then that can be represented by two highly divergent lines. Different colored markers can be used to indicate events particular to an individual and/or a failure to achieve consensus around probable and preferred futures.

Pairs join together to share their work prior to plenary debriefing.

Procedure, Part B

Working in pairs, students prepare time lines specifically on humane treatment of animals. Between B and N, they log events, developments and trends during their lifetimes that mark either a more or a less humane treatment of animals.

From N to PRO, they record developments and trends likely to occur in the future.

From N to PRE, they fill in events they would prefer to see happen.

Pairs come together to share and discuss their probable and preferred future scenarios.

Potential

The activity provides a framework for reviewing significant events, developments and trends during students' lifetimes before they are asked to project forward. The focus on preferred futures offers scope for values clarification, while the likely gap between preferred and probable futures highlights the nature and scale of efforts required for students to achieve their preferred vision.

Extension

During the debriefing of the activity, students can be asked to brainstorm things they could do to help towards the realization of some commonly chosen elements of a preferred future. This might, in turn, lead to the establishment of school- or community-based action projects. For example, students might make posters promoting kindness to animals — feeding pets regularly, not teasing dogs, relocating wild animals that become urban pests (such as raccoons and skunks) to more appropriate natural settings.

Source
After an exercise described by Holden, Cathie in *World Studies Journal,* vol. 6, no. 1.

Drawing Upon the Future

Purpose   Envisioning the future and identifying the values and perspectives underlying future visions

Grade level   3-12

Time needed   20 minutes

Resources   An open classroom space. A half-sheet of plain paper for each student. A selection of markers, crayons, pens and pencils.

Procedure

Students, working individually, are asked to think about and then draw their visions or images of the future. No further clarification of the task is given. Students are required to interpret the task in their own ways and to decide for themselves how to represent their visions or images on paper. Graphic representation is encouraged, but additional explanatory writing can be used. It should be understood that quality artwork is not as important as the portrayal of ideas about the future.

After completing their pictures, students move around the room, forming pairs or small groups to explain their drawings and hear about the future visions of others.

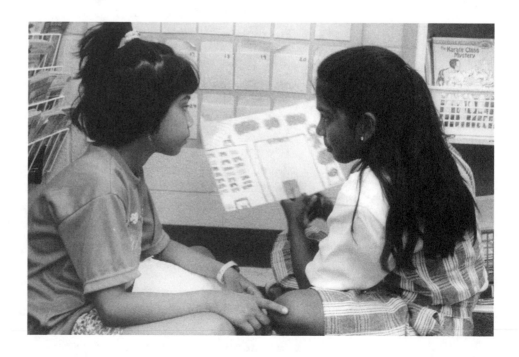

Plenary discussion follows. Questions might include:

    a. What aspects were common to all or most of the drawings you saw?

    b. Were the future visions, in general terms, optimistic or pessimistic?

    c. Were they **probable, possible** or **preferred futures**?

    d. Did they focus primarily on personal and local futures, or on national and global developments?

    e. Where do our visions and images of the future originate, and what do they tell us about ourselves?

    f. What could be our personal roles in helping to promote the future we desire and/or preventing negative future scenarios from being realized?

Potential

A simple activity, but one that can be profoundly revealing. The indeterminate nature of the task encourages students to represent their own values, beliefs and perspectives about the future, while the sharing of drawings is likely to bring students face to face with a variety of visions and images.

Questions About the Future

Purpose	Brainstorming questions about the future, and exploring the **zone of potentiality** with regard to a specific question
Grade level	3-12
Time needed	Several lessons
Resources	Access to information sources about the future; for example, books, magazines, internet sites, experts who might be interviewed

Procedure

Working in small groups, students brainstorm things they would like to know about the future, at any level from personal to global.

A list of 'top ten' items is then selected by each group and formulated into 'The ten questions about the future that we would most like answered.'

Following group presentations of 'top tens,' the class as a whole decides on ten priority questions.

This is followed by a brainstorming session, to which the teacher can contribute, on possible sources of information and opinions that might help in framing a response to each question. The sources can be divided into the following two categories:

    a. primary ('expert' opinion, unpublished information, personal observation and reflection, etc.)

    b. secondary (published information and opinion, computer databases, media programs, etc.)

Students, again working in small groups, begin a research phase by selecting one question and following up as many sources as they can, including, if possible, letters to and/or interviews with key people. The aim is to seek out a range of perspectives and viewpoints, rather than a single "right" answer.

Finally groups present their responses to the whole class and give their own considered opinions.

Questions About the Future

Will I still be laughing when I'm 50?
Will we find out about Pluto?
Will our friends be the same?
What will our mums and dads look like?
Will there be a war soon?
How many more animals will be extinct?
Will the jungles be destroyed?
Will cars still have leaded petrol?
Will pollution stop divers going under the sea?
Will people still use pencils?
Will they invent irons to run off solar heat?

Questions from grade 3 students at an elementary school in southwest England.

Source: Hicks, David. 'Preparing for the Millennium,' in *Futures*, July/August 1991, pp. 623-636.

Potential

An activity that builds upon students' innate curiosity about the future and then encourages them to explore the **zone of potentiality** with respect to a particular question. The initial brainstorming and prioritization stages require students to think creatively and then decide what is really important for them to know about the future.

Many research skills are practiced as they follow up sources of information and opinion, some of which may present contradictory or conflicting views. It should be stressed that multiple viewpoints are to be included in the final presentation, though students also have the right to express informed opinions of their own.

Older students might want to categorize the various scenarios presented in terms of 'possible' or 'probable' futures. They might also wish to speculate upon the consequences of each scenario for people in diverse social, economic and geographical contexts.

Future Circle

Purpose	Identifying characteristics that lend themselves to realizing preferred futures
Grade level	4-12
Time needed	20 minutes
Resources	None except for an open space

Procedure

Students form a circle. They turn so each is facing a neighbor (the facilitator should join in, if necessary, so that everybody is paired).

Students are then asked to reflect for a while on the one human quality they would most like to take into the future, so that the future is a better place to be. For example, such qualities might include love, compassion, flexibility, hope, curiosity.

At a signal from the facilitator, they share the quality with the person they are facing, avoiding explanation or discussion.

As they pass each other, they take on the other person's chosen quality as their own, and offer it to the next person they face.

The process continues until they again face their original partner.

Potential

A brisk and lively way of focusing upon those human characteristics that appear to most lend themselves to realizing preferred futures. The activity's simplicity is deceptive: careful and repeated explanation of the procedure is required for it to work effectively.

The activity can be used without debriefing as a good closing energizer to a session on futures. For debriefing suggestions, see the **Extension** section that follows.

Extension

During debriefing students can be asked to reflect upon the degree of commonality/overlap in the qualities chosen.

    a. To what extent are they the most prized qualities in today's society?
    b. What would happen if individuals, groups and institutions sought to adjust their attitudes, behaviors and relationships to accord more closely with the cluster of qualities pooled?

The qualities can be written up in chart form and subsequently used as a focus for reflection on whether the class, individually and collectively, is 'walking the talk.'

Time Chairs

Purpose	Considering the interlocking nature of past, present and future
Grade level	6-12
Time needed	50 minutes
Resources	An open classroom space. 3 chairs for each pair of students. A tape recorder or compact disc player with a recording of electronic or New Age music. A chart or overhead projector transparency of the sets of questions (see samples, Copiable Handout 1 ☐).

Procedure, Part A

The class forms pairs. Each pair sets up its three chairs in a line facing the same direction.

One partner sits in the center chair.

The standing partner is told she has the role of interviewer.

The seated partner chooses the set of questions upon which he wishes to be interviewed, and the interview begins (follow-up questions are permitted). Some five minutes are allowed for interviews to run their course.

Seated students are then told that, when the music begins, they will move from the center (present) chair ten years back in time to the rear (past) chair. As they move back, they should try to express physically how they looked, and moved, ten years ago.

Note: the number of years into the past and future should, of course, be reduced for younger students. The activity can, indeed, be attempted using a span of a few months rather than ten years.

When the music stops, the interviewer is to repeat the interview (same set of questions) and the questions are to be answered as if in the past.

After five minutes the music moves the interviewee past the present chair and ten years into the future (the front chair). As before she should try to express how she thinks she will look, and move, in ten years' time.

The same interview is repeated.

Time is given for a short feedback session (so that impressions are secured as part of the collective memory).

Procedure, Part B

The interviewer and interviewee change roles and the entire procedure is repeated. The new interviewee has the right to opt for the set of questions of his choice.

When the second round of interviews is concluded, a thorough class debriefing follows.

Personal

1. How old are you?

2. What kind of home do you have?

3. Tell me about an ordinary day in your life.

4. What is the most important thing you have learned over the last ten years?

5. What is your greatest personal wish?

Global

1. How old are you?

2. What three things please you about the state of the planet Earth?

3. What three things concern you about the state of the planet Earth?

4. What do you think has been the greatest tragedy for the world's people in the last ten years?

5. What good changes for the world's people have you seen over the last ten years?

Potential

An activity in which students are likely to become absorbed in freshly recalled memories and future imaginings; so much so that it may prove impossible to restrict interviews to five minutes. The activity promotes an understanding of the interlocking nature of past, present and future.

Debriefing/Extensions

The debriefing can usefully begin with a sharing of feelings engendered. The sharing can lead directly into discussion of a number of interesting areas; for example:

a. Was it more difficult to be interviewed about past, present or future? Why?
b. Which set of questions proved to be most challenging, especially during the 'past' and 'future' interviews? Why?
c. Did interviewees find it easy or difficult to recall their past attitudes and hopes?
d. Were they thinking about similar issues ten (or chosen number of) years back to those of today?
e. Were their views of the future optimistic or pessimistic?
f. Did students feel they could affect the future?
g. What thoughts has the interview experience raised about the speed and effects of change at all levels personal to global?
h. In what ways has it pointed up the interlocking nature of past, present and future?

Another stimulating follow-up activity is to ask students to design sets of questions for other groups.

Variation

The three chairs can be set facing forward in a triangle. The rear chair represents the present. The two front chairs represent the probable and preferred future respectively. Seated students are interviewed on their chosen set of questions. They answer in the present and from the vantage point of their envisaged probable and preferred futures.

Source
Michal Pasternak, International School of Geneva.

Acronym

Purpose   Reflecting on and sharing values. Exercising lateral thinking, consensus-seeking and negotiation.

Grade level   6-12

Time needed   40 minutes

Resources   Sheet of paper and marker for each student. A selection of markers of different colors. 7 half sheets of chart paper.

Procedure

The term *acronym* is explained and illustrated with examples such as the following.

  a. NATO (**N**orth **A**tlantic **T**reaty **O**rganization)

  b. UNESCO (**U**nited **N**ations **E**ducational, **S**cientific and **C**ultural **O**rganization)

  c. MADD (**M**others **A**gainst **D**runk **D**riving)

  d. U-BOP (**U**nidentified **B**ird **o**f **P**rey)

Class members are also asked to volunteer any acronyms with which they are familiar.

Working individually, students are then set the task of devising a snappy, attractive-sounding acronym of four to ten letters reflecting their favored vision of the world of the future. Examples: ROBE (Respecting Our Beautiful Earth), WOMB (Women Overturn Macho Behavior), PRIDE (People Respecting Individual Differences Everywhere), CAKE (Caring And Kindness Everywhere), HUMANE (Hopeful, Understanding, Multiracial, Aware, Nonviolent, Ecological). The acronym should reflect the sense of what it stands for if at all possible.

Sufficient time having been allowed for the task, students form groups of four or five. One by one, they read their acronyms to each other and explain the thinking behind their choice.

The group's next task is to devise a new acronym reflecting the shared aspects of their vision of the world of the future. The acronym is written with markers on the chart paper provided. Appropriate decoration may be added. Other possibilities at this stage include:

  a. the design and drawing of logos or symbols reflecting the acronym

  b. badge production

  c. the preparation and presentation of short dramatic sketches pointing up the message of the acronym

Groups present their work and share their thinking with the rest of the class.

Discussion follows.

Potential

An activity that encourages students to reflect upon and share their values, and that is likely to involve some challenge to those values. A useful activity for exercising lateral thinking, consensus-seeking and negotiation skills.

Debriefing

Debriefing questions that could be explored include:
   a. How easy was it for individuals to express their favored vision of the world of the future, given the constraints of the acronym?
   b. To what extent did their difficulty mirror the problem of living according to one's values in the real world?
   c. Were acronyms broad-focused, covering a range of issues, or narrow-focused? If they were the latter, what issues in particular were focused upon and why?
   d. Did acronyms concentrate on personal, local, national or global futures?
   e. When groups formed, what degree of overlap was there between the acronyms?
   f. How easy was it to achieve a consensus view of a preferred future and an acronym sufficiently reflecting that view?
   g. Was the final acronym a bold visionary statement or a watered-down, compromised version of individual acronyms?

Our Inheritance, Their Inheritance

Purpose	Considering intergenerational justice
Grade level	6-12
Time needed	60 minutes
Resources	2 copies of the **Inheritance** chart (Copiable Handout 2 ❑) and a blank sheet of paper for each group of 3 to 4 students.

Procedure, Part A

A few examples are given of how life today has been beneficially and adversely affected by the actions of past generations. Among examples that could be cited are:
   a. Beneficial — To help people in need, a number of charitable organizations have been started in the past and continue to this day. (It is important to give examples with which students are familiar.)
   b. Beneficial — Museums have been built to preserve important objects from the past such as dinosaur bones, paintings, tools, pottery and old books.
   c. Adverse — Wars were fought, resulting in death, devastation and physical and psychological damage.
   d. Adverse — Passenger pigeons were once plentiful in North America but, because of over-hunting, there are none left now. Other wildlife species have also become extinct because of over-hunting or other human actions.

Through consideration of such examples, students are introduced to the idea that what one generation does can in some respects improve the quality of life for future generations. In other respects it can lead to a deterioration in quality of life for subsequent generations.

On the first copy of the **Inheritance** chart (Handout 2 ❏), groups make their own lists of positive and negative inheritances from previous generations.

Lists are shared and discussed as a class.

Procedure, Part B

Using the second copy of the **Inheritance** chart (Handout 2 ❏), groups imagine themselves as young people in two generations' time. They list ways the previous two generations have:

    a. enhanced their quality of life
    b. undermined their quality of life

Groups then compose a 'To Whom It May Concern' letter to someone living in the 1990s. They point out what was and was not being done then to ensure that future generations enjoyed equal life benefits and opportunities.

Lists are shared and letters read out.

> The Iroquois tribal council began each meeting with this invocation. 'Let us remember in our deliberations the effect our decisions may have on the next seven generations.' Any vote taken was not only for those present, but also for those who would live two hundred years in the future.
>
> Kathryn Sheehan and Mary Waidner [3]

Potential

A simple but effective way of helping students understand the concept of intergenerational justice.

Extension

A comparison of the two sets of lists can be very instructive. Are we storing up a more negative inheritance for future generations than our predecessors left us? What are the main problems we are leaving people in the future? Are they problems that could easily be overcome, or are they difficult or impossible to solve?

INHERITANCE	
Positive	Negative

Inventing the Future (Backwards)

Purpose   Writing history backwards to explore alternative and preferred futures

Grade level   6-12

Time needed   Best attempted in stages over a period of several weeks

Resources   6 large sheets of paper for each group of students. Markers, as well as pens and pencils for each group. Information sources such as newspapers, reference books, the Internet, vertical files, experts in various fields.

Procedure, Part A

Students form groups of four.

Each group is asked to decide upon a major breakthrough towards the realization of a better world. The breakthrough is one they think could happen in the mid-term future (2020-2070) or more distant future (2070 or after). Example: the end of famine worldwide, the discovery of a cure for diabetes or asthma, the dismantling of all weapons of mass destruction, a marked decline in inter-racial tension.

Groups then prepare a front page newspaper story and headline covering the breakthrough in question.

Procedure, Part B

Having written their front page story and headline, students go on to write *five previous* front page stories and headlines covering important landmarks in the chain of events leading up to their breakthrough. To do this, students will need to think about how the situation might have evolved — from where we are now — to the breakthrough they see occurring.

Each front page is to be dated and is to show clearly the linkages, negative and/or positive, between one landmark and the next. In writing each front page story, groups are asked to take into account the possible ecological, economic, political, social and technological impacts and implications of the particular development they are describing. They might also speculate on results that might then arise, which would in turn affect the rate and direction of future change.

As they work on their front page stories, groups may wish to consult a variety of information sources. For example, they could explore library or project collections on their chosen topic and/or consult people in the community with a special knowledge or interest in the topic.

In writing and formating their front pages, groups can decide to follow the style of a particular newspaper or, alternatively, try to reflect the changing face of newspapers through future years as they imagine they might develop.

The task is complete when a group has prepared six front pages that, taken together, present a comprehensive picture of how the envisaged breakthrough towards a better world actually came about.

Potential

This is a powerful and multi-faceted approach to exploring alternative and preferred futures. It allows free rein to the imagination, while requiring that students think through the implications of their future projections. It also gives students the opportunity to examine and, if necessary, adjust their values as they speculate about future possibilities and the impact of those possibilities on various stakeholders in society.

The process of writing history backwards draws upon and helps refine divergent, convergent and reflective thinking skills, creative writing skills, research and information retrieval skills and forecasting skills. The activity promotes group consensus-seeking, planning and problem solving.

Extension

The activity can be debriefed in plenary discussion, with each group presenting its work and responding to questions. Alternatively the **Circus** procedure can be adopted. Each group posts its six front pages on the classroom wall, leaving one group member beside the pages as a 'guide.' Other members go to examine the work of other groups, asking the guides for any necessary explanation or clarification. Group members take turns as guide, thus giving everybody a chance to circulate. Plenary discussion follows the **Circus**.

Variations

1. An alternative — resources allowing — is to ask groups to prepare a tape/slide or video presentation based around their future scenario. This could be done by drawing from existing slide collections, by collecting pictures that can be made into slides, or by taking new photographs. The students write and tape an accompanying narrative. If desired, they could add appropriate background music.

2. The students can be given the option of choosing positive or negative future scenarios. If a group chooses a somewhat negative future, a crucial part of the debriefing will be to challenge the group in particular and the class in general to confront the question of what they, and others, could do towards averting such a future.

3. **Short activity**. A breakthrough at a fixed date is chosen. Groups prepare only one front page newspaper story and headline, presenting the breakthrough and a summary of events leading up to it.

Futures Bag

Purpose	Using metaphors as a means of reflecting on the future
Grade level	6-12
Time needed	20 minutes
Resources	A bag of common objects (one per class member) from home or school. Examples: rubber band, ball of yarn, Plasticine, unused exercise book, dice, piece of model railway track, toy ship, tennis ball, pack of cards, ruler, calculator, Christmas cracker, whistle, paper dart, bagatelle game, balsa wood, kaleidoscope, binoculars.

Procedure

Several examples such as the following are written on the chalkboard.

    a. The future is a highway leading over the horizon.
    b. The future is a ladder to the stars.
    c. The future is a snowy hillside unmarked by footprints.
    d. The future is a lottery.

By means of such examples, students are reminded that *a metaphor is a comparison between two unlike objects having one point in common.* The future, for example, is quite unlike a highway except that both lead forward.

Students are also reminded that, though similes use *like* or *as,* metaphors do not. Examples:

Simile: The future is like a beckoning hand.
Metaphor: The future is a beckoning hand.

Each student picks an object from the bag (no rummaging!) and thinks about it as a metaphor for the future.

At a signal from the teacher, class members circulate and share and discuss metaphors.

Potential

A lively, interesting, and often humorous way of promoting reflection on the relationship between present and future, and on human control over the process and direction of change.

    Some of the more outstanding metaphors could be the basis for songs or poems written by the students. These could be performed for the class with suitable musical accompaniment.

Extensions

In discussion students could consider questions such as the following.

    a. Did the metaphors prompted by the objects suggest that the future is predetermined, open to human influence, or more like a lottery in which anything could happen?
    b. Was the future seen as predominantly positive or negative?

c. Did students find that others were able to suggest alternative metaphors for the object they had picked from the bag? How did they respond to the suggestions offered?
d. To what extent does their chosen metaphor actually reflect their view of the future and of the degree of human control over the future?
e. (For older students) Is it possible to create a typology of views of the future from the metaphors shared?
f. Which metaphors are students unwilling to embrace? Why?

Source

After an idea suggested by Eleanora Ralph, Frontenac Secondary School, Kingston, Ontario, and Lois Kuebler, Moira Secondary School, Belleville, Ontario.

Futures Wheel

Purpose   Considering possible consequences of an event, idea or trend and exploring the interplay between consequences

Grade level   8-12

Time needed   45 minutes

Resources   Large sheet of paper and marker for each group of 3 or 4 students

Procedure

Students form groups of three or four. Each group receives a large sheet of paper and a marker.

An event, idea or trend likely to have far-reaching repercussions is briefly noted and circled in the center of each group's sheet of paper. Examples:
a. Event: Banning of smoking in many public places.
b. Idea: Women should be in the workplace rather than at home taking care of children.
c. Trend: The continued development of faster and more powerful computers.

Groups are then asked to consider possible consequences of that event, idea or trend. Single lines are drawn outwards and the consequences written in and circled.

Groups go on to consider the range of possible results from the first set of consequences (or *first-order consequences*). This time they draw double lines outwards, writing in and circling second-order consequences.

The process is continued for third-, fourth- and, possibly, fifth-order consequences. (See example on page 238.)

Groups are given the opportunity to carefully examine each other's work.

Extension

Discussion can usefully focus upon:

a. differences in group presentations
b. the problematic nature of forecasting given the unknowns and variables involved
c. possible interrelationships between the various second-, third-, fourth- and fifth-order consequences

Potential

Future wheels offer a linear model of causality. It is important also to consider relationships between items not directly linked together on the wheel. An additional exercise can be for students to discuss and draw in links between such items. They might reflect on whether and how any of the outward-moving causal links might thus be modified or reversed.

Variation

A newspaper article describing a current event, idea or trend can be used for the center of the wheel. Students proceed to examine consequences as above.

Note: **Decision Wheel**, p. 146, offers a variation on **Futures Wheel**.

Source
From an idea in Fitch, R.M. & C.M. Svengalis. *Futures Unlimited*. Washington, DC: National Council for the Social Studies, 1979.

Futurescapes

Purpose	Confronting a range of perspectives and value positions on global issues
Grade level	8-12
Time needed	50 minutes
Resources	A **Futurescapes** chart (see Copiable Handout 3 ▢) and 2 pens of different colors for each student. A sheet of chart paper and marker for each group of 6.

Procedure, Part A

Working individually, students complete the **Futurescapes** chart, indicating whether each of the future scenarios described is, in their view, **possible** (**might just** come about), **probable** (**likely** to come about), **improbable** (**not likely** to come about) or **impossible** (could **never happen**). To indicate their choices, they circle the appropriate word after each scenario.

Students also decide whether each scenario is **desired** or **undesired** (a future they would or would not like to have happen). Again they indicate their choices by circling the appropriate word after each scenario.

Students then form pairs to share, explain and discuss their individual decisions.

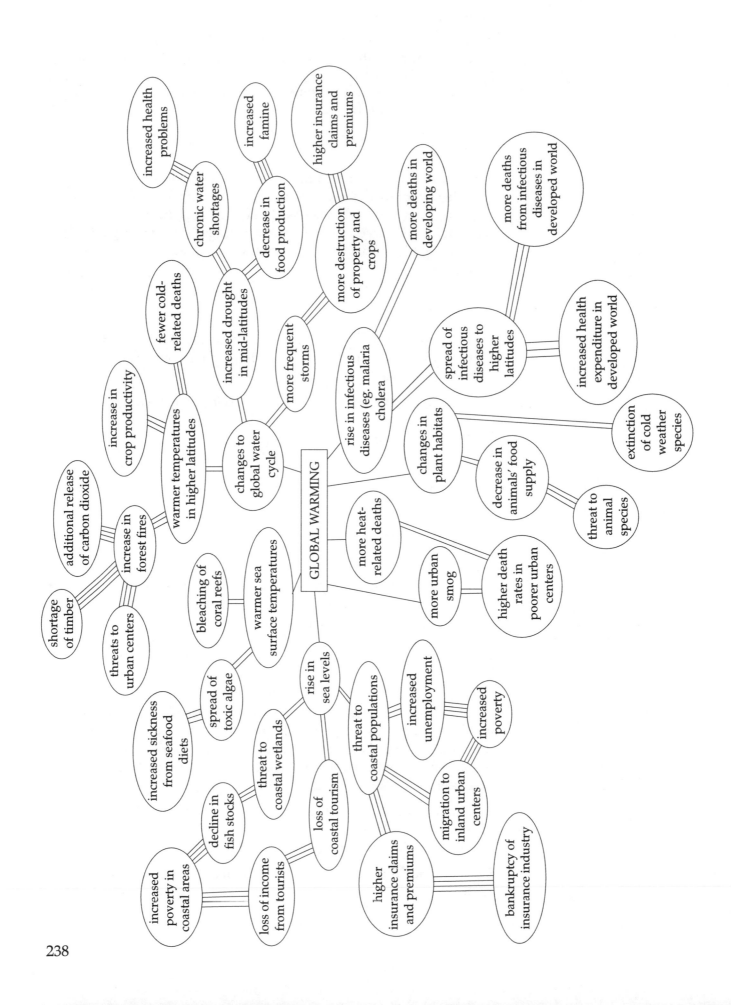

As a result of the interchange, there may be a change of mind on the part of a pair or individual regarding the circling of a word. This should be indicated by crossing out the circled word with a different colored marker and drawing an arrow to the newly circled word now preferred.

Procedure, Part B

Pairs next form groups of six and repeat the process of sharing, explaining, reviewing and amending their decisions. In addition, groups choose one scenario which all group members have identified as a desired future. Using the chart paper provided, they brainstorm ideas as to what they could do individually and collectively to help realize that future. Should there be no common desired scenario, the group can break into two to brainstorm ideas around two different scenarios.

Plenary discussion follows.

Potential

An activity requiring students to confront a range of perspectives and value positions on local and global issues; also to explore in some detail the social, economic and ethical implications of different future scenarios. The final brainstorming section provides students with an opportunity to consider and evaluate strategies for change.

Extension

The debriefing can begin by asking one group to report their discussions around a scenario that provoked controversy and disagreement. The issues raised can then be thrown open to the whole class. At appropriate moments other groups can be asked to share responses to other scenarios as a stimulus to further class discussion.

Consideration of action plans is perhaps best left until responses to all the scenarios have been aired.

Extension

The activity is undertaken simultaneously in different schools (preferably in different locations — inner city and rural — or different countries). The results (and a report on the plenary discussion) are shared by regular mail or e-mail. Comments on respective results and reports are subsequently exchanged, and the dialogue continued until it has run its course.

Variations

Students are given a skeleton chart and asked to write in one scenario each, prior to forming pairs. Each student writes in her partner's scenario, circling the words best reflecting their reactions to that scenario.

Pair discussion follows. Groups of six or eight are then formed. Scenarios are written in and words circled prior to discussion.

The teacher can also replace some or all of the scenarios. With due simplification, **Futurescapes** can be attempted with younger students. For example, the scenarios can feature changes that might take place in school, in the community or in students' personal lives over the next few weeks or months.

My World, My Future

Purpose	Considering the extent to which perceptions of the future are universally shared or culturally conditioned
Grade level	8-12
Time needed	2 hours, or a few lessons
Resources	Writing paper and copies of **My World in the Year 2000** (Copiable Handout 4 ❏)

Procedure, Part A

Each student is asked to write, anonymously, a short essay (about 500 words) entitled 'My world in twenty-one years' time.'

On completion the essays are collected and randomly redistributed around the class so that no student has his own essay.

Students are then asked to analyze the essays according to the following criteria:
  a. To what extent is the writer's vision of the future optimistic and/or pessimistic?
  b. To what extent is the writer's future vision realistic and/or unrealistic?
  c. To what extent is the writer's future vision personally oriented and/or globally oriented?

Working in groups of six, students share their analyses of the six essays and compile a group report representing their collective analysis. The aim of the report-writing is to establish the range of visions that exist and to encourage students to reflect upon the origins of those visions.

A plenary reporting and discussion stage follows.

Procedure, Part B

The facilitator then hands out copies of **My World in the Year 2000,** and explains that these essays or extracts were written in 1979.

Returning to their groups, students discuss the readings in terms of the criteria used previously. Class discussion follows.

Finally, in light of the ideas generated throughout the activity, students write a brief commentary on the essays they originally analyzed and hand them back to the authors.

FUTURESCAPES

1. Up to half the world's energy will be created through wind and water power. Huge power stations will be built around coastlines, and many people will have windmills in their backyards.

DURING MY LIFETIME: POSSIBLE PROBABLE IMPROBABLE IMPOSSIBLE DESIRED UNDESIRED

2. There will be a major breakthrough in genetic engineering so that we will have farm animals, looking quite different from those we now know, which will produce a higher yield of meat for less food intake in a shorter space of time.

DURING MY LIFETIME: POSSIBLE PROBABLE IMPROBABLE IMPOSSIBLE DESIRED UNDESIRED

3. A rare and endangered plant in the Amazon rainforest will be found to contain a chemical substance that can cure many types of cancer.

DURING MY LIFETIME: POSSIBLE PROBABLE IMPROBABLE IMPOSSIBLE DESIRED UNDESIRED

4. To achieve peace in the Middle East, Arab and Jewish leaders will decide to divide their disputed territories into zones in which only their own people can live and from which all others are banned.

DURING MY LIFETIME: POSSIBLE PROBABLE IMPROBABLE IMPOSSIBLE DESIRED UNDESIRED

5. In a worldwide attempt to end famine in Africa, all surplus food grown on other continents will be shipped to various African ports and then taken by UN trucks to the towns and villages where the food is needed.

DURING MY LIFETIME: POSSIBLE PROBABLE IMPROBABLE IMPOSSIBLE DESIRED UNDESIRED

6. To solve the problem of the growing number of children in the developing world whose parents are unable to care for them, families in countries such as Canada will be encouraged to adopt these children and treat them as their own.

DURING MY LIFETIME: POSSIBLE PROBABLE IMPROBABLE IMPOSSIBLE DESIRED UNDESIRED

7. A binding international agreement will be reached to protect all remaining wilderness areas from exploitation by humans. These areas will include the remaining rainforests, Antarctica, and the Canadian North.

DURING MY LIFETIME: POSSIBLE PROBABLE IMPROBABLE IMPOSSIBLE DESIRED UNDESIRED

8. For health reasons and to avoid cruelty to animals, vegetarianism (eating no meat) and veganism (eating no meat or animal products) will become so widespread that meat eaters are reduced to a small minority.

DURING MY LIFETIME: POSSIBLE PROBABLE IMPROBABLE IMPOSSIBLE DESIRED UNDESIRED

9. The United Nations will pass a resolution encouraging governments to pay billions of dollars in compensation to all Aboriginal and Native peoples whose land was taken by colonizing groups.

DURING MY LIFETIME: POSSIBLE PROBABLE IMPROBABLE IMPOSSIBLE DESIRED UNDESIRED

10. The cost of a new car will be four times higher than today because laws will require manufacturers to pay for the environmental damage caused by making cars.

DURING MY LIFETIME: POSSIBLE PROBABLE IMPROBABLE IMPOSSIBLE DESIRED UNDESIRED

Potential

This is a thought-provoking activity designed to raise students' awareness of their perceptions of the future and the extent to which these are universally shared or culturally conditioned.

Debriefing

Key questions for consideration and discussion are:
  a. How does an individual's future vision develop? To what extent does it direct or influence present practice?
  b. Do factors such as gender and social class have any significant bearing on future perspectives?
  c. Can there be future visions that are universally shared?
  d. To what extent are optimism and pessimism regarding the future derived from an optimistic or pessimistic view of oneself and one's contribution to society?
  e. How can individuals help turn their preferred future into reality?

New Year's Resolutions

Purpose	Gaining perspective on the impact human beings have had on the planet in recent times
Grade level	10-12
Time needed	50 minutes
Resources	A metronome. A sheet of chart paper and marker for each pair of students.

Procedure

With the metronome ticking, the teacher reads **Story of a Year** aloud.

At the close of the reading, students are asked to form pairs. Pairs are given five minutes to decide what the next two sentences in the story might be.

Sentences are shared with the class.

Pairs are then asked to agree upon ten New Year's resolutions. The resolutions are written, in prioritized order, on chart paper.

Pairs then form sixes to share and discuss their lists.

Reporting back and class discussion follow.

Potential

A provocative fable, designed to put into perspective the enormous impact of human beings on the planet in very recent times, **Story of a Year** can elicit strong reactions.

MY WORLD IN THE YEAR 2000
(Essays and Extracts Written by Students in 1979)

It would be nice to have something that wouldn't change

The year 2000 is too much a radical change for me to think about. But it's one of the reasons that I want to move out of this country. I'm kind of getting future shock here. It scares me that so much is happening at once, like moving house a lot, losing old friends, and new friends being rushed on me too fast. It would be nice if I could have something to latch onto that wouldn't change or run away from me.

I'll try to think about a day in Year 2000 for the normal person. He'll get up in the morning and turn on the tri-tube (three-dimensional television) and quickly get all the news that is happening today — the wars, how many people are getting killed in Lebanon and so on — for about 10 minutes. Then he goes down the bounce tube which is like an elevator except it works by anti-gravity. He gets into his air-pressured car and shoots to work at 150 miles an hour (240 km/h), watching some more of the tri-tube. He presses a few buttons and does paperwork and then goes home to his wife and kids.

In the evening he won't be able to go out because it's not safe and there is a curfew at 8:00. Every night he hears about 20 screams and 10 gunshots. So in the evening he plays computer games and watches the tri-tube. Television phones will be very popular then. Houses will be about the same as now. I think they are still going to have rugs, transparent nylon shiny rugs where you can see the floor underneath like the ones you see in commercials for floor wax.

On the weekend the man goes out to a pleasure farm where they have real trees (not the plastic kind) and water that you can swim in without wearing protective suits. He can't do this too often because there is a constant line of people who want his job so he has to be pretty good at it or he is out.

It would not be like that for me. I am getting out. I am going to be a vet. Not the kind that takes care of French poodles. I am going to Africa. They need vets there.

I want my wife to work with me. It would be more income into the house. I don't want to be poor but I don't want to be super-snobbish rich either.

When the kids are really young, my wife's probably going to take a few years off. I'd like to take off just as much time as she to take care of the kids because that is what a father should do.

I might want to marry either a widow or a divorcee who already has a kid, because I don't relish the thought of raising a little child for two or three years. I want to have a child about the age where I can make an impression on him. He will learn my ideas and appreciate them and maybe think them over and use them.

I'd have very high ambitions for my kids. I want my kids to be professional people — medicine or law — I don't want them to be plumbers or laborers or anything like that. I kind of want them to be better than me. My father was a Rhodes Scholar and went to school on scholarships. My mother won lots of scholarships, too. That kind of upsets me, because I am never going to be like that.

John Paden, 14, Illinois, USA

I am a Bangladeshi to every cell of my body

In the Year 2000 I would be 38. There is every possibility that I may not be still alive. But if I am, I will be an architect. I want to build buildings which will not only beautify the world but bring happiness. People who live in my buildings cannot help but smile and be happy.

I will live in Bangladesh because I am a Bangladeshi to every cell of my body. So I have spiritual relations with the soil, the water and the soul of every other Bangladeshi. And for this reason I intend to live in Bangladesh as long as I live.

Bangladesh wants many things from me. The responsibility to develop this country will be our responsibility.

Most of the people of our country are cultivators. They work hard, heart and soul. But the tools for cultivation are poor. In the Year 2000 there will be better tools and, with hard work, there will be more food. The poor people will not die from famine and our country will be developed like America, Japan, Russia and China. Then we will all live happily.

The houses by then will not be made of mud. They will be stone and will not fall down easily. Bridges will be made over the rivers and good roads will run from town to town. Everything will be changed except for our favorite rice and fish.

There will be machines. But the machines should not take the vitality out of you and take out the happiness evident in small things. There should be pitch-forks for pitching hay, for example, but I would like a machine to wake me up and give me tea in the morning.

Population growth threatens the nation. By 2000 AD the population will be nearly doubled and it will be impossible to live in Bangladesh. If all of us only have two children then it will be possible to live in this land. I will only have two children. I know that if I marry I will never be able to shine in my life, but even then I dream of having children.

When my own parents are old, I will of course want them to stay with me. Then I will be able to make sure that they are happy and comfortable and it will be my chance to love them though I can never give back the love they have given me all their lives.

Finally I aspire that in the Year 2000 AD there will be one nation, and that is human beings; that there is one race and that is the human race; and that there is one religion and that is humanity; and that there is one country and that is the Earth; and lastly that the entire mankind may lead a harmonious life of peaceful existence and tolerance.

Anawara Khan, 15, Dacca, Bangladesh

The endless rows of trees will be gone and there will be barbed wire instead. Really, I don't think there'll be anything after the Year 2000. I just think it will stop then.

Bjorn Kellman, 15, Sweden

In 2000 AD I will be a farmer. I will have a dip and fences for my cattle. I will have crop rotation and fertilizers. I hope to do a lot for the country so everyone will have a lot of food.

Tom Odhiambo, 14, Kenya

I don't ever want to go broke. The husband I have would have to be in pretty good shape moneywise because of the lifestyle I've grown up with. I want the same level of living because it's hard to drop down.

Tracy Cernan, 15, USA

I don't want to be rich. People just envy you. Why should you have more than you need? Once you've got a home, family, friends and a job, you should be satisfied.

Desmond Thomas, 14, Jamaica

My feather alarm tickles my feet. I get up and my robot, Gaston, serves breakfast. Electronic life is OK but boring. I take my helicopter to work and check that the orders I gave yesterday are obeyed.

Valerie Bouget, 14, France

The houses will be made of stone. They will cost $250 and will last a long time. The roads will be made of tar. There will not be any beggars and poor people. Everyone will have jobs and food.

Asanatu Koroma, 13, Sierra Leone

I picture myself coming home at, say, six o'clock. I've been away acting in a play on Broadway. I kiss my wife — maybe she won't be my wife. We have a middle-class house with rounded corners.

David Wall, 12, Canada

In the Year 2000 I want there to be peace and I want all parents to be like mine, to understand their children and not beat them. Some parents beat them on the head with wire which can damage their eyes.

Maribel Olaya, 11, Peru

When we are adults the United Nations will be even stronger. Then it will order all countries to get rid of weapons which can extinguish life on earth. Most countries have not yet realized the importance of the UN.

Kariuki Kihiko, 15, Kenya

We will stop industry, which keeps going deeper and deeper into nature, and save from extinction all rare species and help animals to live in the wilderness.

Danuta Adamczyk, 14, Poland

Source: ***New Internationalist,*** No. 76, June 1979.

Some students are likely to identify easily with its thrust. Others are likely to object to the heavy responsibility it places on the 'rich North' for the present state of the planet. Some students may respond to the story's challenge with positive and innovative ideas for personal and social change. Some may be daunted by the range and scale of the problems we face.

Extension

The differences aired and particular points of contention identified can provide a stimulus for subsequent individual and group research.

Extension

The resolutions can be discussed in terms of their relevance for our present global condition. Students can consider whether they are realistic and acceptable, and what their impact is likely to be should they be embraced. Resolutions most commonly occurring should be identified and the reason(s) for their prevalence discussed. Would groups of students in other countries, cultures or sections of society have come up with similar reactions to the story and similar lists and prioritizations? At some point the teacher should remind the class that most New Year's resolutions are broken within a few days. What is likely to happen if we fail to make, or adhere to, our resolutions for the future?

Story of a Year

And then, as the bells chimed the beginning of the new year, the people had the world to themselves. For many months, so far as we know, they were very quiet. From 1 January until the end of September, they just wandered around in small groups — hunting animals with spears and arrows; sheltering in caves; dressing themselves in animal skins. On about 1 October they began to learn about seeds and manure and so on, and about how to herd and milk animals. By about 23 October some of them were living in biggish cities. This was mainly in Egypt and North India, and in the countries between.

Moses came and went on about 11 November. Buddha in India, Socrates in Greece, Confucius in China — all came and went together, though they didn't know each other, on about 3 December. Christ appeared on 8 December, as also, give or take a few hours, did the Great Wall of China and Julius Caesar. Mohammed was on 15 December.

On about 23 December there began to be biggish cities in northern Europe. On about 27 December and into the next day, people went out from these cities and they began stealing from the rest of the world. They stole the Americas, both North and South. They stole India and, during the last hour of 29 December, they stole Africa. Just before midday on 30 December, they had a big war among themselves, and then had another big war late in the afternoon.

In the last 30 hours of the year, the people from Europe were pushed back out of India and Africa. They were also pushed back out of many other countries, though not out of North America and parts of Oceania, where they had become very settled indeed. Also, as the closing hours of the year fled away, the people originating in Europe invented nuclear weapons and landed on the moon. Their beguiling materialist culture caused more oil and more metal to be used up than had been used in the previous 364 days put together. It was also responsible for the building of huge, sprawling cities; an unprecedented rate of destruction of natural and wilderness environments; and a phenomenal escalation in land, sea and air pollution.

The bells were chiming again. It was the start of a new year....

Source
The story is based upon (but much changed from) 'History of a Day' in Richardson, R. *Learning for Change in World Society: Reflections, Activities and Resources.* World Studies Project, 1979, p. 59.

References
1. Kauffman, D.L. *Futurism and Future Studies.* National Education Association of the United States, p. 11.
2. *Ibid.*
3. Sheehan, K. & M. Waidner. *Earthchild: Games, Stories, Activities,Experiments & Ideas About Living Lightly on Planet Earth.* Tulsa: Council Oak Books, p. 5.

Select Annotated Bibliography

Anderson, C., S. Nicklas & A. Crawford. *Global understandings: a framework for teaching and learning.* Alexandria, VA: Association for Supervision and Curriculum Development, 1994. Offers a framework of four 'messages' ('You are a human being,' 'Your home is Planet Earth,' 'You are a citizen of a multicultural society,' 'You live in an interrelated world') as a vehicle for integrating global education into school programs. Includes sample integrated programs. Useful section on performance assessment in global education.

Biggs, D. *In our own backyard: a teaching guide for the rights of the child.* UNICEF Canada, 1995. Innovative and interactive ways for helping grade 1 to 8 students explore the 1989 United Nations Convention on the Rights of the Child.

Borba, M. *Esteem builders: a K-8 self esteem curriculum for improving student achievement, behavior and school climate.* Torrance, CA: Jalmar, 1989. Identifies the components of self esteem, describes how to build an affirmative classroom environment, and offers a wide range of classroom activities.

Caduto, M.J. & J. Bruchac. *Keepers of the Earth: Native American stories and environmental activities for children.* Golden, CO: Fulcrum, 1988. Outstanding compilation of Native American stories, and classroom and outdoor environmental activities for all grades.

Chasty, J., T. Palmer & D. Spencer. *The green school.* Toronto: Secondary School Teachers' Federation, 1991. A rich source of environmentally related activities and ideas for use across the secondary school curriculum.

Choldin, E., T. Franks, M. Jarvey, L. Martenet & B. Sargent. *Children of the world: a primary unit.* Edmonton: Global Education Project, 1990. An activity-based unit for the primary grades, organized around the ten rights of the 1959 UN Declaration of the Rights of the Child.

Fountain, S., *Education for development: a teacher's resource for global learning.* London: Hodder & Stoughton, 1995. A UNICEF compendium of K to 12 activities organized in five sections: interdependence, images and perceptions, social justice, conflict and conflict resolution, and change and the future.

Hicks, D.W. *Educating for the future: a practical classroom guide.* Godalming, Surrey, UK: World Wide Fund for Nature UK, 1994. Offers a good range of activities for teachers wishing to give their classrooms a more explicit futures orientation.

Hill, R., G. Pike & D. Selby. *Perspectives on childhood: a resource book for teachers.* London: Cassell, 1998. Twenty-two activities exploring the meaning of childhood, identity formation in childhood and the rights of the child.

Johnson, J., J. Benegar & L.R. Singleton. *Global issues in the middle school: grades 5-8 (third edition).* Boulder/Denver, CO: Social Science Education Consortium/Center for Teaching International Relations, 1994. Activities for the middle school exploring the interrelated themes of human values, global systems, global issues and global history. See also the Massachusetts Global Education Project, *Global issues in the elementary classroom.* Boulder/Denver, CO: Social Science Education Consortium/Center for Teaching International Relations, 1993.

McDaniel, R. and J. Petrie. *A two-way approach to understanding: issues in global education (second edition).* Fredericton: YM-YWCA/Global Education Centre, 1992. Fifty-seven activities for grades 6-12 on themes related to world development. Includes an appendix on games from many countries.

Maheu, B., D. Hein & J. Osborne. *Global interconnections: a resource handbook for high school social studies teachers.* Edmonton: Global Education Project, 1995. An extensive collection of readings and activities on the themes of development, disparity, diversity, interdependence and quality of life.

Ministry of Education, Ontario. *Media literacy: intermediate and senior divisions.* Toronto, 1989. Excellent resource and activity guide for promoting media awareness and media literacy skills.

Pike, G., & D. Selby. *Global teacher, global learner.* London: Hodder & Stoughton, 1988. Describes a four-dimensional model for global education, examines appropriate teaching and learning approaches, and offers a wide range of K-12 activities.

Pike, G. & D. Selby. *Human rights: an activity file.* Toronto: Bacon & Hughes, 1997. Twenty-eight group discussion, experiential, simulation and role play activities designed to help students (grades 7 to 12) explore human rights issues.

Pike, G. & D. Selby. *Reconnecting: from national to global curriculum.* Godalming, Surrey, UK: World Wide Fund for Nature UK, 1995. Activities for infusing global education across the grade 7 to 12 curriculum.

Sawyer, D. & H. Green. *The NESA activities handbook for Native and multicultural classrooms.* Vancouver: Tillacum/Native Education Services Associates, 1984. Excellent compendium of twenty-five K to grade 13 activities. Equally worth exploring are: Sawyer, D. & A. Napoleon. *The NESA activities handbook, volume 2.* Tillacum/NESA, 1991. Sawyer, D. & W. Lundeberg. *The NESA activities handbook, volume 3.* Tillacum/NESA, 1993.

Selby, D. *Earthkind: a teachers' handbook on humane education.* Stoke-on-Trent, UK: Trentham, 1995. Explores the theory and practice of humane education and the relationship of the field to other 'educations' falling under the global education umbrella. Some 170 activities.

Sheehan, K. & M. Waidner. *Earthchild: games, stories, activities, experiments and ideas about living lightly on Planet Earth.* Tulsa, OK: Council Oak Books, 1991. Excellent collection of environmental and animal-related elementary level activities. A goldmine of resource suggestions.

Steiner, M. *Learning from experience: co-operative learning and global education: a world studies sourcebook.* Stoke-on-Trent, UK: Trentham, 1993. Demonstrates how global education can offer a relevant, active learning approach to mainstream curriculum subjects. Good range of activities.

UNICEF Canada Education for Development Committee. *Windows on the world: an education for development activity guide.* UNICEF Canada, 1994. Activities for grades 1 to 10 on development themes, based on case studies of three countries: Bolivia (education); Mali (water/environment); the Philippines (urban working children).

Wade, R.C. *Joining hands: from personal to planetary friendship in the primary classroom.* Tucson, AR: Zephyr Press, 1991. Activity ideas for developing a caring classroom community.

Walters, J.L., & L. Hamilton. *Integrating environmental education into the curriculum painlessly.* Bloomington, IN: National Educational Service, 1992. Integrated and subject-specific projects on environmental themes.

Activities Index

Permissions

Every effort has been made to identify, to acknowledge and to credit properly all sources of copyrighted material. However both the publisher and the authors would welcome being informed of any inadvertent omissions, which they will be happy to correct.

The publishers would like to thank the following for permission to reproduce copyrighted material:

The David Suzuki Foundation, Suite 219, 2211 West 4th Avenue, Vancouver, B.C. V6K 4S2, tel: (604) 732-4228, for excerpts from the Foundation's Declaration of Interdependence

Reproduced from Rainforest Amerindians by Anna Lewington with the kind permission of Wayland Publishers Limited, 61 Western Road, Hove, East Sussex BN3 1JD, England

New International Magazine for excerpts from an article on children's perceptions of the future (N.I., no. 76, June 1979) and from The Man Who Grew Happiness by Simon Lewis (N.I., no. 184, June 1988)

From Marshall R. Singer, Intercultural Communication: A Perceptual Approach. ©1987. All rights reserved For an activity from J. Canfield and H.C. Wells, 100 Ways to Enhance Self-concept in the Classroom. ©1976. Reprinted by permission of Allyn & Bacon. All rights reserved.

Excerpted from Make a World of Difference, Office on Global Education/Church World Service, Baltimore, MD, 1989

An activity from: Connecting Rainbows by Bob Stanish, 1982 ©Good Apple; A division of Frank Schaffer Publications, 23740 Hawthorne Boulevard, Torrance, CA 90505

Activities from J.S. Greenberg's Health Education: Learner-centered Instructional Strategies, ©1989, Dubuque, Iowa, Wm. C. Brown, reproduced with the permission of The McGraw-Hill Companies

Green Teacher for extracts from 'Our Ecological Footprint' by Mathis Wackernagal and William Rees (G.T., no. 45, December 1995 — January 1996)

UNICEF/HQ97-0710/Robert Grossman for the photograph in "Splitting Images"

Eland, London, for permission to reprint an extract from A Reed Shaken by the Wind by Gavin Maxwell, © Gavin Maxwell Enterprises Ltd 1957.

Pollution Probe for permission to reprint an extract titled Household Water Use in Canada, from Water, copyright © Pollution Probe.

David Higham Associates Limited and Hodder Headline PLC for an extract from Gifts of Unknown Things by Lyall Watson, published by Hodder & Stoughton.